THE FATHERS
OF THE CHURCH

A NEW TRANSLATION

VOLUME 145

THE FATHERS OF THE CHURCH

A NEW TRANSLATION

EDITORIAL BOARD

David G. Hunter
Boston College
Editorial Director

Paul M. Blowers
Emmanuel Christian Seminary

William E. Klingshirn
The Catholic University of America

Aaron Butts
The Catholic University of America

Andrew Cain
University of Colorado

Joseph T. Lienhard, S.J.
Fordham University

Mark DelCogliano
University of St. Thomas

Rebecca Lyman
Church Divinity School of the Pacific

Robert A. Kitchen
Regina, Saskatchewan

Wendy Mayer
Australian Lutheran College

Trevor Lipscombe
Director, The Catholic University of America Press

FORMER EDITORIAL DIRECTORS

Ludwig Schopp, Roy J. Deferrari, Bernard M. Peebles,
Hermigild Dressler, O.F.M., Thomas P. Halton

Carole Monica C. Burnett, *Staff Editor*

ST. EPHREM THE SYRIAN

SONGS FOR THE FAST AND PASCHA

Translated by
JOSHUA FALCONER, BLAKE HARTUNG,
AND J. EDWARD WALTERS

THE CATHOLIC UNIVERSITY OF AMERICA PRESS
Washington, D.C.

Copyright © 2022
THE CATHOLIC UNIVERSITY OF AMERICA PRESS
All rights reserved
Printed in the United States of America

J. Edward Walters' revised translation of the
Teaching Songs on the Unleavened Bread is printed in this volume
by the kind cooperation of Gorgias Press.

The paper used in this publication meets the minimum
requirements of the American National Standards for Information
Science—Permanence of Paper for Printed Library Materials,
ANSI z39.48–1984.
∞

ISBN 978-0-8132-3573-8

CIP data is available from the Library of Congress.

CONTENTS

Abbreviations	ix
Select Bibliography	xi
INTRODUCTION by Blake Hartung	3

TEACHING SONGS ON THE HOLY FAST
Translated by Joshua Falconer

On the Holy Fast 1	51
On the Holy Fast 2	61
On the Holy Fast 3	65
On the Holy Fast 4	70
On the Holy Fast 5	79
On the Holy Fast 6	87
On the Holy Fast 7	91
On the Holy Fast 8	98
On the Holy Fast 9	102
On the Holy Fast 10	109

TEACHING SONGS ON THE CRUCIFIXION
Translated by Blake Hartung

On the Crucifixion 1	117
On the Crucifixion 2	125
On the Crucifixion 3	130
On the Crucifixion 4	139

On the Crucifixion 5	150
On the Crucifixion 6	161
On the Crucifixion 7	173
On the Crucifixion 8	178
On the Crucifixion 9	184

TEACHING SONGS ON THE RESURRECTION
Translated by Blake Hartung

On the Resurrection 1	189
On the Resurrection 2	195
On the Resurrection 3	200
On the Resurrection 4	209
On the Resurrection 5	218

TEACHING SONGS ON THE UNLEAVENED BREAD
Translated by J. Edward Walters

On the Unleavened Bread 1	223
On the Unleavened Bread 2	228
On the Unleavened Bread 3	232
On the Unleavened Bread 4	236
On the Unleavened Bread 5	241
On the Unleavened Bread 6	246
[On the Unleavened Bread 8?]	249
[On the Unleavened Bread 9?]	253
On the Unleavened Bread 12	258
On the Unleavened Bread 13	261
On the Unleavened Bread 14	268
On the Unleavened Bread 15	273
On the Unleavened Bread 16	279

CONTENTS

On the Unleavened Bread 17	286
On the Unleavened Bread 18	290
On the Unleavened Bread 19	294
On the Unleavened Bread 20	299
On the Unleavened Bread 21	303

INDICES

General Index	311
Index of Holy Scripture	320

ABBREVIATIONS

Ephrem's Madrāšē Cycles

Azym.	*de Azymis (On the Unleavened Bread)*
Cruc.	*de Crucifixione (On the Crucifixion)*
Haer.	*contra Haereses (Against Heresies)*
Eccl.	*de Ecclesia (On the Church)*
Fid.	*de Fide (On Faith)*
Ieiun.	*de Ieiunio (On the Fast)*
Jul.	*contra Julianum (Against Julian)*
Nat.	*de Nativitate (On the Nativity)*
Nis.	*Carmina Nisibena (Nisibene Madrāšē)*
Par.	*de Paradiso (On Paradise)*
Res.	*de Resurrectione (On the Resurrection)*
Virg.	*de Virginitate (On Virginity)*

Other Works Attributed to Ephrem

CD	*Commentary on the Diatessaron*
CG	*Commentary on Genesis*
Dom.	*The Discourse Called "Of Domnus"*
PR	*Prose Refutations*
Pub.	*Letter to Publius*

Other Primary Sources

Dem.	Aphrahat, *Demonstrations*
Euch.	Cyrillona, *Mēmrē on the Institution of the Eucharist*
FM	Mosul Fenqitho
OS	Old Syriac version
P	Peshitta version

ABBREVIATIONS

Grammars and Lexicons

Aray.	Thomas Arayathinal, *Aramaic Grammar*
Nöld.	Theodor Nöldeke, *Compendious Syriac Grammar*
RPS	Robert Payne Smith, *Thesaurus Syriacus*

Languages

CPA	Christian Palestinian Aramaic
JBA	Jewish Babylonian Aramaic
JPA	Jewish Palestinian Aramaic
PTA	Palestinian Targumic Aramaic
Syr	Syriac

Manuscripts

Beck's MS B	BL Add MS 14,627
C	Curetonian Gospels / BL Add MS 14,451
Beck's MS D	BL Add MS 14,571
Beck's MS J	BL Add MS 14,506
Beck's MS P	BL Add MS 14,512
S	Syriac Sinaiticus MS 30

Journals and Series

CSCO	Corpus Scriptorum Christianorum Orientalium
JECS	*Journal of Early Christian Studies*
OCA	Orientalia Christiana Analecta
OCP	*Orientalia Christiana Periodica*
PG	Patrologia Graeca
PO	*Parole de l'Orient*
SC	Sources Chrétiennes
ZAC	*Zeitschrift für Antikes Christentum*

Other Abbreviations

R	ʿonitā (refrain)

SELECT BIBLIOGRAPHY

Texts and Translations

Aphrahat. *Aphraatis Sapientis Persae Demonstrationes*. 2 vols. Edited by J. Parisot. Paris: Firmin-Didot, 1894 (Vol. 1) and 1907 (Vol. 2).

Ephrem of Nisibis. *Des heiligen Ephraem des Syrers Hymnen de Ieiunio*. Edited by Edmund Beck. CSCO 246–47. Syr. 106–7. Leuven: Peeters, 1964.

———. *Des heiligen Ephraem des Syrers Paschahymnen: De azymis, de crucifixione, de resurrectione*. Edited by Edmund Beck. CSCO 248–49. Syr. 108–9. Leuven: Peeters, 1964.

———. *Efrem il Siro. Inni pasquali. Sugli azzimi. Sulla Crocifissione. Sulla resurrezione*. Edited by Ignazio De Francesco. Letture cristiane del primo millennio 31. Milan: Paoline, 2001.

———. *Éphrem. Célébrons la Pâque*. Edited by Dominique Cerbelaud. Les pères dans la foi 58. Paris: Migne, 1995.

———. *Éphrem de Nisibe, Hymnes pascales*. Edited by François Cassingena-Trévedy. SC 502. Paris: Éditions du Cerf, 2006.

———. *Ephrem the Syrian: Hymns on the Nativity, Hymns Against Julian, Hymns on Virginity and on the Symbols of the Lord*. The Classics of Western Spirituality. Translated by Kathleen McVey. New York and Mahwah, NJ: Paulist Press, 1989.

———. *Ephrem the Syrian: Select Poems*. Edited by Sebastian P. Brock and George A. Kiraz. Eastern Christian Texts 2. Provo, UT: Brigham Young University Press, 2007.

———. *Hymns on the Unleavened Bread*. Edited by J. Edward Walters. Texts from Christian Late Antiquity 30. Piscataway, NJ: Gorgias Press, 2011.

———. *S. Ephraim's Prose Refutations of Mani, Marcion, and Bardaisan of which the Greater Part has been Transcribed from the Palimpsest B.M. Add 14623 and is now First Published*. 2 vols. Edited by C. W. Mitchell. Oxford: Williams and Norgate, 1912 (Vol. 1) and 1921 (Vol. 2).

———. *The Hymns on Faith*. Translated by Jeffrey T. Wickes. Fathers of the Church 130. Washington, DC: The Catholic University of America Press, 2015.

Gregory of Nazianzus. *Carmina*. Edited by J.-P. Migne. PG 37–38.

———. *Selected Poems of Gregory of Nazianzus: I.2.17; II.1.10, 19, 32: A Critical Edition with Introduction and Commentary*. Edited by Christos Semilidis. Göttingen: Vandenhoeck and Ruprecht, 2009.

Jacob of Sarug. *Metrical Homily on Holy Mar Ephrem*. Edited by Joseph Amar. PO 47, fasc. 1, N. 209. Turnhout: Brepols, 1995.

Rule for the Qyāmā. In *Syriac and Arabic Documents: Regarding Legislation Relative to Syrian Asceticism.* Edited by Arthur Vööbus. *Papers of the Estonian Theological Society in Exile* 11. Stockholm: Estonian Theological Society in Exile, 1960.

The Syriac Vita *Tradition of Ephrem the Syrian.* Edited and translated by Joseph P. Amar. CSCO 629/630. Leuven: Peeters, 2011.

Secondary Sources

Amar, Joseph P. "Byzantine Ascetic Monachism and Greek Bias in the *Vita* Tradition of Ephrem the Syrian." *OCP* 58 (1992): 123–56.

Baumgarten, Albert I. "Marcel Simon's *Verus Israel* as a Contribution to Jewish History." *Harvard Theological Review* 92, no. 4 (1999): 465–78.

Beck, Edmund. *Ephräm der Syrer. Lobgesang aus der Wüste.* Sophia: Quellen östlicher Theologie 7. Freiburg: Lambertus-Verlag, 1967.

―――. "Ephräm des Syrers Hymnik." In *Liturgie und Dichtung: Ein interdisziplinäres Kompendium: Gualtero Duerig annum vitae septuagesimum feliciter complenti,* edited by Hansjacob Becker and Reiner Kaczynski, vol. 1, 345–79. St. Ottilien: EOS Verlag Erzabtei St. Ottilien, 1983.

―――. "ΤΕΧΝΗ und ΤΕΧΝΙΤΗΣ bei dem Syrer Ephräm." *OCP* 47 (1981): 295–331.

Behr, John. *The Mystery of Christ: Life in Death.* Crestwood, NY: St Vladimir's Seminary Press, 2006.

Benin, Stephen D. "Commandments, Covenants and the Jews in Aphrahat, Ephrem and Jacob of Sarug." In *Approaches to Judaism in Medieval Times,* edited by David R. Blumenthal, 135–56. Chico, CA: Scholars Press, 1984.

Bou Mansour, Tanios. "Étude de la terminologie symbolique chez saint Éphrem." *Parole de l'Orient* 14 (1987): 221–62.

Boyarin, Daniel. *Border Lines: The Partition of Judaeo-Christianity.* Philadelphia: University of Pennsylvania Press, 2004.

Bradshaw, Paul F. *The Search for the Origins of Christian Worship.* 2nd edition. Oxford: Oxford University Press, 2002.

Brock, Sebastian P. "Fire from Heaven: From Abel's Sacrifice to the Eucharist: A Theme in Syriac Christianity." *Studia Patristica* 25 (1993): 229–43. Reprinted in *Fire from Heaven: Studies in Syriac Theology and Liturgy,* edited by Sebastian Brock. Variorum Collected Studies Series. Aldershot, UK, and Burlington, VT: Ashgate, 2006.

―――. *The Luminous Eye: The Spiritual World Vision of Saint Ephrem.* Cistercian Studies. Kalamazoo, MI: Cistercian Publications, 1992.

―――. "The Poetic Artistry of St. Ephrem." *Parole de l'Orient* 6–7 (1975–76): 21–28.

―――. "Poetry and Hymnography (3): Syriac." In *The Oxford Handbook of Early Christian Studies,* edited by Susan Ashbrook Harvey and David G. Hunter, 657–71. Oxford: Oxford University Press, 2008.

―――. "The Robe of Glory: A Biblical Image in the Syriac Tradition." *The Way* 39:3 (1999): 247–59.

―――. "St. Ephrem: A Brief Guide to the Main Editions and Translations." http://syri.ac/brock/ephrem.

———. "Two Syriac Dialogue Poems on Abel and Cain." *Le Muséon* 113 (2000): 333–75.

———. "The Transmission of Ephrem's Madrashe in the Syriac Liturgical Tradition." *Studia Patristica* 33 (Leuven: Peeters, 1997): 490–505.

Brown, Peter. *The Body and Society: Men, Women, and Sexual Renunciation in Early Christianity*. New York: Columbia University Press, 1988.

Cerbelaud, Dominique. "L'antijudaïsme dans les hymnes de Pascha d'Éphrem le Syrien." *Parole de l'Orient* 20 (1995): 201–7.

Daly, SJ, Robert J. *Sacrifice Unveiled: The True Meaning of Christian Sacrifice*. London: T&T Clark, 2009.

Darling, R. A. "The 'Church From the Nations' in the Exegesis of Ephrem." In *IV Symposium Syriacum 1984: Literary Genres in Syriac Literature*, edited by H. J. W. Drijvers, R. Lavenant, C. Molenberg, and G. J. Reinink, 111–22. Orientalia Christiana Analecta. Rome: Pontificium Institutum Studiorum Orientalium, 1987.

den Biesen, Kees. *Simple and Bold: Ephrem's Art of Symbolic Thought*. Piscataway, NJ: Gorgias Press, 2014.

Drijvers, H. J. W. "Jews and Christians at Edessa." *Journal of Jewish Studies* 36, no. 1 (1985): 88–102.

Fiey, Jean-Maurice. "Les évêques de Nisibe au temps de Saint Éphrem." *Parole de l'Orient* 4 (1973): 123–35.

Gribomont, Jean. "Le triomphe de Pâques d'après S. Éphrem." *Parole de l'Orient* 4, no. 1–2 (1973): 147–89.

Griffith, Sidney. "Asceticism in the Church of Syria: The Hermeneutics of Early Syrian Monasticism." In *Asceticism*, edited by V. L. Wimbush and R. Valantasis, 220–48. New York: Oxford University Press, 1995.

———. "Ephraem the Syrian's Hymns 'Against Julian': Meditations on History and Imperial Power." *Vigiliae Christianae* 41, no. 3 (1987): 238–66.

———. "Ephrem, the Deacon of Edessa, and the Church of the Empire." In *Diakonia: Studies in Honor of Robert T. Meyer*, edited by Thomas Halton and Joseph P. Williman, 22–52. Washington, DC: The Catholic University of America Press, 1986.

Halleux, André de. "Une clé pour les hymnes d'Éphrem dans le Ms. Sinaï Syr. 10." *Le Muséon* 85 (1972): 171–99.

Hartung, Blake. "The Authorship and Dating of the Syriac Corpus Attributed to Ephrem of Nisibis: A Reassessment." *ZAC* 22, no. 2 (2018): 296–321.

———. "The Significance of Astronomical and Calendrical Theories for Ephrem's Interpretation of the Three Days of Jesus' Death." In *Syriac Christian Culture: Beginnings to Renaissance*, edited by Aaron Michael Butts and Robin Darling Young, 37–49. Washington, DC: The Catholic University of America Press, 2020.

Harvey, Susan Ashbrook. "Performance As Exegesis: Women's Liturgical Choirs in Syriac Tradition." In *Inquiries Into Eastern Christian Worship: Acts of the Second International Congress of the Society of Oriental Liturgy*, edited by Basilius J. Groen and Steven Hawkes Teeples, 47–64. Leuven: Peeters, 2010.

———. "Revisiting the Daughters of the Covenant: Women's Choirs and Sacred Song in Ancient Syriac Christianity." *Hugoye: Journal of Syriac Studies* 8.2 (2005): 125–49. https://hugoye.bethmardutho.org/article/hv8n2harvey.

Hayman, A. Peter. "The Image of the Jew in the Syriac Anti-Jewish Polemical Literature." In *To See Ourselves As Others See Us: Christians, Jews, "Others" in Late Antiquity*, edited by Jacob Neusner, Ernest S. Frerichs, and Caroline McCracken-Flesher, 423–41. Chico, CA: Scholars Press, 1985.

Heyman, George. *The Power of Sacrifice: Roman and Christian Discourse in Conflict*. Washington, DC: The Catholic University of America Press, 2007.

Kazan, Stanley. "Isaac of Antioch's Homily Against the Jews (Part 3)." *Oriens Christianus* 47, no. 1 (1963): 89–97.

Kiraz, George, ed. *Comparative Edition of the Syriac Gospels: Aligning the Sinaiticus, Curetonianus, Peshitta, and Harklean Versions, Vol. 1: Matthew*. 3rd edition. Piscataway, NJ: Gorgias Press, 2004.

Kronholm, T. *Motifs from Genesis I–II in the Genuine Hymns of Ephrem the Syrian with Particular Reference to the Influence of Jewish Exegetical Tradition*. Coniectanea Biblica Old Testament Series, 11. Lund: Gleerup, 1978.

Krueger, Derek. *Writing and Holiness: The Practice of Authorship in the Early Christian East*. Philadelphia: University of Pennsylvania Press, 2004.

Kuhlmann, Karl H. "The Harp Out of Tune: The Anti-Judaism/Anti-Semitism of St. Ephrem." *The Harp* 17 (2004): 177–83.

Lange, Christian. *The Portrayal of Christ in the Syriac Commentary on the Diatessaron*. CSCO 616. Subsidia 118. Leuven: Peeters, 2005.

Lattke, Michael. "Sind Ephraems Madrāšē Hymnen?" *Oriens Christianus* 73 (1983): 38–43.

Lieu, Judith. *Neither Jew nor Greek?: Constructing Early Christianity*. New York: A&C Black, 2005.

McVey, Kathleen. "The Anti-Judaic Polemic of Ephrem Syrus' Hymns on the Nativity." In *Of Scribes and Scrolls: Studies on the Hebrew Bible, Intertestamental Judaism, and Christian Origins Presented to John Strugnell*, edited by Thomas H. Tobin, John J. Collins, and Harold W. Attridge, 229–40. College Theology Society Resources in Religion. Lanham, MD: University Press of America, 1990.

———. "Were the Earliest Madrâšê Songs or Recitations?" In *After Bardaisan: Studies on Continuity and Change in Syriac Christianity in Honor of Professor Han J. W. Drijvers*, edited by G. J. Reinink and A. C. Klugkist, OCA, 185–99. Leuven: Peeters, 1999.

Monnickendam, Yifat. "How Greek is Ephrem's Syriac?: Ephrem's Commentary on Genesis as a Case Study." *JECS* 23, no. 2 (2015): 213–44.

Murray, Robert. "The Exhortation to Candidates for Ascetical Vows at Baptism in the Ancient Syriac Church." *New Testament Studies* 21 (1974): 59–80.

———. "The Lance Which Re-Opened Paradise: A Mysterious Reading in the Early Syriac Fathers." *Orientalia Christiana Periodica* 39, no. 1 (1973): 224–34.

———. "Some Rhetorical Patterns in Early Syriac Literature." In *A Tribute to Arthur Vööbus: Some Studies in Early Christian Literature and Its Environment, Primarily in the Syrian East*, edited by Robert H. Fischer, 109–31. Chicago: Lutheran School of Theology at Chicago, 1977.

———. *Symbols of Church and Kingdom: A Study in Early Syriac Tradition*. London and New York: T&T Clark International, 2006.
Nedungatt, George. "The Covenanters of the Early Syriac-Speaking Church." *OCP* 39 (1973): 419–44.
Outtier, Bernard. "Saint Éphrem d'après ses biographies et ses œuvres." *Parole de l'Orient* 4:1–2 (1973): 11–33, 12–15.
Palmer, Andrew. "A Single Human Being Divided in Himself: Ephraim the Syrian, Man in the Middle." *Hugoye* 1, no. 2 (1998): 119–63.
Possekel, Ute. *Evidence of Greek Philosophical Concepts in the Writings of Ephrem the Syrian*. CSCO 580, Subsidia 102. Leuven: Peeters, 1999.
Roberts, Michael. *The Jeweled Style: Poetry and Poetics in Late Antiquity*. Ithaca, NY: Cornell University Press, 1989.
Rouwhorst, Gerard. "Jewish Liturgical Traditions in Early Syriac Christianity." *Vigiliae Christianae* 51, no. 1 (1997): 72–93.
———. *Les hymnes pascales d'Éphrem de Nisibe. Analyse théologique et recherche sur l'évolution de la fête pascale chrétienne à Nisibe et à Edesse et dans quelques églises voisines au quatrième siècle*, vol. 1. Supplements to Vigiliae Christianae 7. Leiden: Brill, 1989.
———. "L'évocation du mois de Nisan dans les Hymnes sur la Résurrection d'Éphrem de Nisibe." In *IV Symposium Syriacum, 1984: Literary Genres in Syriac Literature (Groningen-Oosterhesselen 10–12 September)*, edited by H. J. W. Drijvers, René Lavenant, Corrie Molenberg, and Gerrit J. Reinink, 101–10. OCA 229. Rome: Pontificium Institutum Studiorum Orientalium, 1987.
Russell, Paul S. "Nisibis As the Background to the Life of Ephrem the Syrian." *Hugoye: Journal of Syriac Studies* 8.2 (2005): 179–235.
Shepardson, Christine. *Anti-Judaism and Christian Orthodoxy: Ephrem's Hymns in Fourth-Century Syria*. Washington, DC: The Catholic University of America Press, 2008.
———. "Exchanging Reed for Reed: Mapping Contemporary Heretics onto Biblical Jews in Ephrem's *Hymns on Faith*." *Hugoye: Journal of Syriac Studies* 5.1 (2002): 15–33.
———. "Paschal Politics: Deploying the Temple's Destruction against Fourth-Century Judaizers." *Vigiliae Christianae* 62 (2008): 233–60.
Simon, Marcel. *Verus Israel: A Study of the Relations Between Christians and Jews in the Roman Empire, 135–425*. Translated by H. McKeating. Oxford: Oxford University Press, 1986.
Stern, Sacha. *Calendars in Antiquity: Empires, States, and Societies*. Oxford and New York: Oxford University Press, 2012.
Stroumsa, Guy G. "From Anti-Judaism to Antisemitism in Early Christianity?" In *Contra Judaeos: Ancient and Medieval Polemics between Christians and Jews*, edited by Ora Limor and Guy G. Stroumsa, 1–26. Tübingen: Mohr Siebeck, 1995.
Talley, Thomas. *The Origins of the Liturgical Year*. 2nd edition. Collegeville, MN: Liturgical Press, 1991.
Taylor, Miriam S. *Anti-Judaism and Early Christian Identity: A Critique of the Scholarly Consensus*. Leiden: Brill, 1995.
Vergani, Emidio. "Giustizia e grazia di Dio per la città assediata. Le raffigurazi-

oni del nemico negli inni su Nisibi (1–12) di Efrem il Siro." In *I nemici della cristianità*, edited by Giuseppe Ruggieri, 21–58. Testi e ricerche di scienze religiose, nuova serie 19. Bologna: Il Mulino, 1997.

Webb, Ruth. *Ekphrasis, Imagination and Persuasion in Ancient Rhetorical Theory and Practice*. Farnham, UK: Ashgate, 2009.

Wickes, Jeffrey. "Between Liturgy and School: Reassessing the Performative Context of Ephrem's *Madrāšê*." *JECS* 26, no. 1 (2018): 25–51.

Wilken, Robert Louis. *John Chrysostom and the Jews: Rhetoric and Reality in the Late 4th Century*. Berkeley: University of California Press, 1983.

Wright, William. *Catalogue of the Syriac Manuscripts in the British Museum acquired since the year 1838*, Vol. 2. London: British Museum, 1871.

INTRODUCTION

By BLAKE HARTUNG

INTRODUCTION

Among the writers of the Syriac Christian tradition, none is so renowned as St. Ephrem of Nisibis (*ca.* 307–373), known to much of the later Christian world simply as "the Syrian." Evidence for Syriac Christian literature prior to Ephrem is very sparse, leaving scholars with many unanswered questions regarding the education, practices, and structures of early Syriac Christianity. The life of Ephrem is similarly shadowy, with his historical biography obscured by layers of hagiographical revision and embellishment.

Ephrem was a prolific writer whose works were copied, translated, and imitated across the Late Antique Christian world. Among his extant writings are over four hundred *madrāšē* (often translated as "hymns"), dozens of *mēmrē* ("discourses" or "homilies"), and several other prose works, including biblical commentaries on Genesis and Exodus. The vast majority (at least 75%) of this corpus is in the form of poetry (of which the *madrāšē* cycles comprise the largest portion). Among other early Christian writers of the fourth century, Ephrem's corpus stands out because, unlike those of most of his contemporaries and predecessors, the majority of his writings are poetic. Only Gregory of Nazianzus is comparable, though most of his poetic works remain unedited.[1] In Syriac Christian literature, although he likely drew extensively on (unknown) earlier mod-

---

1. The Benedictine edition of Gregory's poems, published by Armand Benjamin Caillau in 1842, was reprinted in two volumes by J.-P. Migne (Gregory of Nazianzus, *Carmina* [PG 37–38]). A new critical edition was initially spearheaded by Martin Sicherl at the University of Münster until his death in 2009. The edition is now being prepared by Christos Simelidis, who has previously published an edition of some selected poems: see Simelidis, *Selected Poems of Gregory of Nazianzus: I.2.17; II.1.10, 19, 32: A Critical Edition with Introduction and Commentary* (Göttingen: Vandenhoeck and Ruprecht, 2009), 11.

els, Ephrem seems to have set the standard for the liturgical and para-liturgical use of metered poetry.[2]

This volume presents English translations of four complete *madrāšē* cycles of Ephrem: *On the Fast*,[3] *On the Unleavened Bread, On the Crucifixion,* and *On the Resurrection*.[4] These four particular cycles appear together in the two extant sixth-century manuscripts.[5] They are among the most liturgically oriented poems in Ephrem's corpus, and, as such, provide a window into the celebration of Lent and Easter in the Syriac-speaking churches of northern Mesopotamia in the fourth century. They are, even more significantly, some of the oldest poems or songs composed for Lent and Easter in the entire Christian tradition. These *madrāšē* reveal a contested religious atmosphere in which Ephrem strove to promote the Christian Pascha and Christian interpretations of Scripture over and against the paschal celebration of Jewish communities. Of these four cycles, only one (*On the Unleavened Bread*) has been published in En-

---

2. Kathleen McVey argues that before Bardaisan the *madrasha* was a literary genre, which Bardaisan himself "transformed ... into song." See McVey, "Were the Earliest Madrâšê Songs or Recitations?" in *After Bardaisan: Studies on Continuity and Change in Syriac Christianity in Honor of Professor Han J. W. Drijvers,* ed. G. J. Reinink and A. C. Klugkist, OCA (Leuven: Peeters, 1999), 186.

3. Edmund Beck, ed., *Des heiligen Ephraem des Syrers Hymnen de Ieiunio,* CSCO 246–247, Syr. 106–7 (Leuven: Peeters, 1964). The cycle *On the Fast* has been translated into German (Beck); French (Dominique Cerbelaud, *Saint Éphrem: Hymnes sur le jeûne,* Spiritualité Orientale 69 [Bégrolles en Mauge, 1997]); and Italian (Emilio Vergani, *Efrem il Siro: La restituzione del debito, Melodie e istruzioni sul Digiuno* [Milan: Centro Ambrosiano, 2011]; I. de Francesco, in I. de Francesco, C. Noce, M. B. Artioli, *Il Digiuno nella Chiesa Antica. Testi Siri, Latini, e Greci* [Milan: Paoline, 2011]).

4. Edmund Beck, ed., *Des heiligen Ephraem des Syrers Paschahymnen: De azymis, de crucifixione, de resurrectione,* CSCO 248–249, Syr. 108–109 (Leuven: Peeters, 1964). Beck's edition is also accompanied by a German translation. These Paschal cycles have been translated into several other modern languages. See G. A. M. Rouwhorst, *Les hymnes pascales d'Éphrem de Nisibe. Analyse théologique et recherche sur l'évolution de la fête pascale chrétienne à Nisibe et à Edesse et dans quelques églises voisines au quatrième siècle,* vol. 1, Supplements to Vigiliae Christianae 7 (Leiden: Brill, 1989); Dominique Cerbelaud, *Ephrem. Célébrons la Pâque,* Les pères dans la foi 58 (Paris: J.-P. Migne, 1995); Ignazio de Francesco, *Efrem il Siro. Inni pasquali. Sugli azzimi. Sulla Crocifissione. Sulla resurrezione,* Letture cristiane del primo millennio 31 (Milan: Paoline, 2001); François Cassingena-Trévedy, *Éphrem de Nisibe, Hymnes pascales,* SC 502 (Paris: Éditions du Cerf, 2006).

5. London, BL Add MS 14571 (Beck's MS D); London, BL Add MS 14627 (Beck's MS B).

glish translation by James E. Walters.⁶ Thanks to the cooperation of the original translator and the permission of Gorgias Press, we are republishing that translation with some revisions.

The Life of Ephrem

The life of Ephrem is difficult to reconstruct reliably, obscured by a lack of early sources and a preponderance of later, anachronistic hagiographical traditions.⁷ Even the traditional date of Ephrem's birth (306 or 307) is little more than an educated guess.⁸ He lived the great majority of his life on the Roman-Persian frontier, in the Roman border town of Nisibis (modern Nusaybin, Turkey). He seems to have been a consecrated celibate, one of the "Sons and Daughters of the Covenant" (*bnay qyāmā*), and to have had some role in the Nisibene church, but he never refers to himself as a "deacon," as later traditions describe him.⁹ According to his own testimony, his life and service in Nisibis corresponded with the tenures of four consecutive bishops: Jacob (*ca.* 308–338), Babu (338–346), Vologeses (346–361), and Abraham (361–363?).¹⁰

---

6. J. Edward Walters, *Hymns on the Unleavened Bread*, Texts from Christian Late Antiquity 30 (Piscataway, NJ: Gorgias Press, 2011).

7. With respect to the historical details of the life of Ephrem, scholars reject the Syriac *Life of Ephrem* and *Testament of Ephrem* as later compositions that convey little accurate data regarding Ephrem's life. For this problem, see *The Syriac Vita Tradition of Ephrem the Syrian*, ed. and trans. Joseph P. Amar, CSCO 629/630 (Leuven: Peeters, 2011); idem, "Byzantine Ascetic Monachism and Greek Bias in the *Vita* Tradition of Ephrem the Syrian," *OCP* 58 (1992): 123–56; Bernard Outtier, "Saint Éphrem d'après ses biographies et ses œuvres," *Parole de l'Orient* 4: 1–2 (1973): 11–33, especially 12–15.

8. See Sebastian P. Brock, *The Luminous Eye: The Spiritual World Vision of Saint Ephrem*, Cistercian Studies (Kalamazoo, MI: Cistercian Publications, 1992), 4; Christian Lange, *The Portrayal of Christ in the Syriac Commentary on the Diatessaron*, CSCO 616, Subsidia 118 (Leuven: Peeters, 2005), 25.

9. On these early Syriac ascetic movements, see Sidney Griffith, "Asceticism in the Church of Syria: The Hermeneutics of Early Syrian Monasticism," in *Asceticism*, ed. V. L. Wimbush and R. Valantasis (New York: Oxford University Press, 1995), 220–48; George Nedungatt, "The Covenanters of the Early Syriac-Speaking Church," *OCP* 39 (1973): 419–44; Robert Murray, "The Exhortation to Candidates for Ascetical Vows at Baptism in the Ancient Syriac Church," *New Testament Studies* 21 (1974): 59–80.

10. See his reflections on these bishops in *Nis.* 13–21. See also Jean-Maurice Fiey, "Les évêques de Nisibe au temps de Saint Éphrem," *Parole de l'Orient* 4 (1973): 123–35.

During the Roman-Persian wars of the mid-fourth century, the city of Nisibis was caught between the dueling ambitions of the two late antique imperial powers. Ephrem and his community became the victims of no less than three sieges at the hands of the Persian emperor Shapur II (in 338, 350, and 359). One of his *madrāšē*, probably written in 350, paints a vivid picture of the chaotic battle scene that unfolded during that siege:

> [*Nis*. 2.18] When the wall was breached,
>   when the elephants broke in,
>   when the arrows rained down,
>   and when men acted boldly,
> That was a sight for the heavenly beings![11]

Crafting a continuity between the suffering of the Nisibenes and biblical accounts of divine judgment, Ephrem perceives the hand of God's judgment against the city, comparing it to Noah's ark[12] and its Persian attackers to "foul Assyria" and Baal worshipers.[13]

In 363, the Roman emperor Julian "the Apostate" pursued a bold campaign aimed at crippling the Persians by striking at the capital city of Seleucia-Ctesiphon, deep within Persian territory. The operation did not go as planned. During a hasty retreat from the Persian capital, the emperor's army was harried by Persian forces, and Julian himself was killed. In the tumultuous aftermath, the new emperor, Jovian, signed a treaty with the Persians, which, among other things, surrendered Nisibis to the Persians. In one of his *madrāšē Against Julian*, Ephrem recounts seeing the corpse of the dead emperor brought through the streets, and the Persian banner raised triumphantly over Nisibis.[14]

---

11. All translations are my own, unless otherwise indicated.

12. *Nis*. 1.5. See Emidio Vergani, "Giustizia e grazia di Dio per la città assediata. Le raffigurazioni del nemico negli inni su Nisibi (1–12) di Efrem il Siro," in *I nemici della cristianità*, ed. Giuseppe Ruggieri, Testi e ricerche di scienze religiose, nuova serie 19 (Bologna: Il Mulino, 1997).

13. See, e.g., *Nis*. 10.13 (Sodom); 11.11–13 (plagues in Egypt); 5.6–8 (Nebuchadnezzar); 1.8 (Jericho).

14. *Jul*. 3.1–7. See Sidney Griffith, "Ephraem the Syrian's Hymns 'Against Julian': Meditations on History and Imperial Power," *Vigiliae Christianae* 41, no. 3 (1987): 238–66, especially 247–50. See also the English translation of these poems in Kathleen McVey, trans., *Ephrem the Syrian: Hymns* (Mahwah, NJ: Paulist Press, 1989), 219–57.

Under the terms of surrender, the Christian community of the now-Persian city of Nisibis (including Ephrem) was exiled. Ephrem eventually settled in Edessa (modern Şanlıurfa, Turkey), a city over one hundred miles to the west. Upon his arrival in Edessa, Ephrem became a leading figure in the pro-Nicene church of that city. We know few details of his role there, however, and can reliably date only a few of his writings to his time there. Nevertheless, Christian tradition has primarily remembered Ephrem in association with Edessa, a characterization that is profoundly misleading.[15] As Paul Russell has argued, we ought to think of Ephrem not as the "deacon of Edessa" but as a Nisibene, only finally uprooted from his birthplace by the vagaries of war.[16]

Apart from this brief sketch of Ephrem's life, we can say little for certain. One of the primary problems with reconstructing a historically accurate biography of Ephrem is the almost-complete silence about himself and his life in his writings. The lack of personal information (for example, in the form of surviving correspondence, an invaluable resource for other early Christian writers) is striking, given the size and scope of Ephrem's extant corpus.

Ephrem's Writings

The poems translated in this volume are syllabic metrical compositions known in Syriac as *madrāšē*. Ephrem composed two forms of metrical composition: *mēmrē* and *madrāšē*. While Ephrem's metrical *mēmrē* are relatively simple isosyllabic couplets, the *madrāšē* display huge metrical variety: in the approximately four hundred

---

15. In his introduction to the critical edition of the *Life of Ephrem*, Amar argues that the *Life* retains very little of the historical biography of the saint, instead reshaping him in the image of the later monastic traditions of the eastern Mediterranean. As Amar notes, the *Life* seems to be "a product of the monastic foundations which took root in and around Edessa in the decades following Ephrem's death" (Amar, *Vita*, CSCO 630, v). As such, it ties Ephrem almost entirely to the city of Edessa, paying very little attention to Ephrem's life in Nisibis. In one recension (Paris Syr 235), Ephrem is as young as 18 when he leaves Nisibis for Edessa (Amar, *Vita*, CSCO 629, 22)!

16. Paul S. Russell, "Nisibis as the Background to the Life of Ephrem the Syrian," *Hugoye* 8 (2005): 179–235.

extant *madrāšē*, we find almost fifty meters,[17] which can range in structure from simple (for example, three isosyllabic lines of 7+7)[18] to extremely complex (for example, eight lines of 4+4, 4+4, 9, 7+7, 7+7, 4+7, 7, 10).[19] They share, however, some common characteristics, notably an *ʿonītā* (refrain) and a prefatory *qālā* (melody).[20]

Ephrem's *madrāšē* were likely sung, though this may not have been the original function of the literary form.[21] Because Ephrem's *madrāšē* are not primarily doxological in nature (and doxology is central to the idea of what constitutes a "hymn" in both ancient and modern usage), there is some dispute over whether the traditional classification of the *madrāšē* as "hymns" is appropriate.[22] Sev-

17. Brock, "Poetry and Hymnography (3): Syriac," in *The Oxford Handbook of Early Christian Studies*, ed. Susan Ashbrook Harvey and David G. Hunter (Oxford: Oxford University Press, 2008), 661.

18. E.g., *Fid.* 1.

19. E.g., *Nis.* 35–42.

20. Scholars typically assume that Ephrem's originals possessed these musical features (although the original melodies and refrains may have been different). We cannot be confident of this fact, however. The earliest manuscripts of the *madrāšē* date to the early sixth century, over a century after Ephrem's death. The earliest, BL Add MS 14571, is dated to 519. Indeed, the refrains found in these manuscripts do not always match the themes of the poems they accompany. See Edmund Beck, "Ephräm Des Syrers Hymnik," in *Liturgie und Dichtung: Ein interdisziplinäres Kompendium: Gualtero Duerig annum vitae septuagesimum feliciter complenti*, ed. Hansjacob Becker and Reiner Kaczynski, vol. 1 (St. Ottilien: EOS Verlag Erzabtei St. Ottilien, 1983), 345–79, especially 348–50.

21. Kathleen McVey has argued (on the basis of *CH* 53.1–5) that the heterodox Christian teacher Bar Dayṣan of Edessa was responsible for transforming *madrāšē* from recitations into sung works. Drawing upon extant hymnic material from the pre-Ephremic Syriac tradition, particularly the two "hymns" of the Acts of Judas Thomas, the so-called "Hymn of the Bride" and the "Hymn of the Pearl," she argues that the "Hymn of the Pearl" reflects an early recitation-form of a *madrāšā*. McVey thus complicates our picture of early Syriac poetic composition, showing two forms of *madrāšē* as well as the presence of non-*madrāšā* hymnody in Syriac tradition (as in the "Hymn of the Bride"). See McVey, "Were the Earliest Madrâsê Songs or Recitations?" We would add that the variety in meter and thematic content in Ephrem's *madrāšē* may reflect a medium in transition of the *madrāšā* into a musical form. In other words, this variety may indicate that there may still have been a considerable degree of flexibility in Ephrem's time as to what constituted a *madrāšā*. By contrast, fifth-century Syriac metrical works attest to considerable standardization in meter and form. See Brock, "Poetry and Hymnography (3): Syriac."

22. Michael Lattke challenges the editor of most of Ephrem's Syriac works, Dom Edmund Beck, who argued for understanding Ephrem's *madrāšē* as "Hymnik." (See

eral scholars have therefore offered alternative English renderings: the most notable of these are Robert Murray's "doctrinal hymn" and Andrew Palmer's "teaching song," both of which seek to convey the sense of the Syriac verbal root *d-r-š*, cognate to that of the Hebrew word *midrash*.[23] In this volume, we have opted to translate the word as "song," or occasionally "poem."

The historical evidence for the performance of the *madrāšē* supports the idea that these songs had a particular teaching function.[24] In his oft-cited *mēmrā* on Ephrem, Jacob of Sarug (ca. 449–521) lauds his great forerunner for instructing choirs of women in the singing of his *madrāšē* in order to teach the people.[25] Indeed, in one of the *madrāšē* translated here, Ephrem obliquely refers to "chaste women" (presumably the ascetic *bnāt qyāmā*, "Daughters of the Covenant")[26] weaving the crown for the Paschal feast through "their *madrāšē*."[27] Thus, as Susan Harvey observes, the performance of *madrāšē* by

---

Beck, "Ephräm Des Syrers Hymnik.") Lattke takes issue with this terminology precisely because most of Ephrem's *madrāšē* do not fit the standard definitions of ὕμνος in antiquity, which tend to emphasize doxology. See Michael Lattke, "Sind Ephraems Madrāšē Hymnen?" *Oriens Christianus* 73 (1983): 38–43, especially 42.

23. Murray, *Symbols of Church and Kingdom: A Study in Early Syriac Tradition* (London and New York: T&T Clark International, 2006), 31; Andrew Palmer, "A Single Human Being Divided in Himself: Ephraim the Syrian, Man in the Middle," *Hugoye* 1, no. 2 (1998): 119–63. Palmer is followed by Kees den Biesen, *Simple and Bold: Ephrem's Art of Symbolic Thought* (Piscataway, NJ: Gorgias Press, 2014), xxii.

24. See Susan Ashbrook Harvey, "Performance As Exegesis: Women's Liturgical Choirs in Syriac Tradition," in *Inquiries Into Eastern Christian Worship: Acts of the Second International Congress of the Society of Oriental Liturgy*, ed. Basilius J. Groen and Steven Hawkes Teeples (Leuven: Peeters, 2010), 54. See also Sidney H. Griffith, "Ephrem, the Deacon of Edessa, and the Church of the Empire," in *Diakonia: Studies in Honor of Robert T. Meyer*, ed. Thomas Halton and Joseph P. Williman, 22–52 (Washington, DC: The Catholic University of America Press, 1986).

25. Jacob of Sarug, Metrical Homily on Holy Mar Ephrem 40–43 (ed. Joseph Amar, PO 47, fasc. 1, N. 209 [Turnhout: Brepols, 1995], 34–35). Decades before Jacob's *mēmrā*, Rabbūlā of Edessa prescribed that the *bnat qyāmā* should learn *madrāšē*. See *Rule for the Qyāmā* §20 (Vööbus, *Syriac and Arabic Documents: Regarding Legislation Relative to Syrian Asceticism, Papers of the Estonian Theological Society in Exile* 11 [Stockholm: Estonian Theological Society in Exile, 1960], 41).

26. On the "Daughters of the Covenant," see Susan Ashbrook Harvey, "Revisiting the Daughters of the Covenant: Women's Choirs and Sacred Song in Ancient Syriac Christianity," *Hugoye: Journal of Syriac Studies* 8.2 (2005): 125–49.

27. *Res.* 2.9: "Let ... the chaste women [plait in it] their songs (*madrāšē*)" (ed. Beck, *Paschahymnen*, 84).

female choirs put a form of liturgical instruction in the mouths of women—an unusual phenomenon in late antiquity, a period when female ecclesiastical offices were increasingly circumscribed.[28]

Despite these pieces of evidence, we know relatively little about the performative context(s) of Ephrem's *madrāšē*. The situation of modern readers of the *madrāšē* is the inverse of that of the original audience: we have only the texts and not the performance, while they had the performance and not the texts. Further, Ephrem's poems rarely offer any insights into their performative contexts.[29] This fact complicates recent scholarly attempts to portray Ephrem as the consummate liturgical poet of ancient Syrian Christianity and a vigorous public defender of Nicene Orthodoxy through the weekly public liturgical performance of his *madrāšē*. In fact, we should be cautious about assuming a public liturgical context for each one of the *madrāšē*. As I have argued, some seem thematically more suited to the schoolroom or the monastic community than to the public liturgy.[30]

Generally speaking, however, the poems included in this volume appear to be among the most liturgically oriented compositions in Ephrem's corpus. In other words, many of them meet the three criteria offered by Jeffrey Wickes to identify a *madrāšā* of Ephrem as "liturgical." Liturgical *madrāšē*, according to Wickes, reference

28. Harvey, "Performance as Exegesis," 55–56.

29. Scholars have imagined Ephrem as a metrical, Syriac equivalent of a pro-Nicene orator like John Chrysostom. See Peter Brown, *The Body and Society: Men, Women, and Sexual Renunciation in Early Christianity* (New York: Columbia University Press, 1988), 329. See also Christine Shepardson, *Anti-Judaism and Christian Orthodoxy: Ephrem's Hymns in Fourth-Century Syria* (Washington, DC: The Catholic University of America Press, 2008), 65. Given the lack of evidence regarding the public performance of Ephrem's writings, such a comparison could easily be overstated. For this critique, see Jeffrey Wickes, "Between Liturgy and School: Reassessing the Performative Context of Ephrem's *Madrāšē*," *JECS* 26, no. 1 (2018): 25–51.

30. It is likely that some *madrāšē* (e.g., *Against Heresies*, *On Paradise*) were performed in an "academic" setting, providing opportunities for a community of students and/or ascetics to meditate upon passages of Scripture or hear poetic refutations of rival religious communities. I made this argument in a conference paper delivered at the 7th North American Syriac Symposium (2015): "The Significance of Astronomical and Calendrical Theories for Ephrem's Interpretation of the Three Days of Jesus' Death." A revised version of this paper is found in *Syriac Christian Culture: Beginnings to Renaissance*, ed. Aaron M. Butts and Robin Darling Young (Washington, DC: The Catholic University of America Press, 2020), 37–49.

feasts or fasts known to have been celebrated in the fourth century. They employ scriptural references or allusions associated with those feasts. Finally, they cite rituals practiced in the context of liturgy.[31] While these criteria should not necessarily be used as hard and fast rules to determine which *madrāšē* were performed in a liturgical context and which were not, they do offer some helpful benchmarks by which we might attempt to identify the original audiences and contexts of the *madrāšē* in the Lenten and Paschal cycles.

The Songs for the Fast and Pascha

Although scholars have attempted to localize these cycles to a particular period in Ephrem's career, they are exceedingly difficult to date.[32] For one, the cycles were likely assembled by later editors based upon common themes, rather than composed as treatises were at a particular period in Ephrem's life.[33] Another problem is the general lack of internal evidence with respect to particular places and events that could assist in dating particular writings of Ephrem. In response to this paucity of information, scholars have made certain conjectures about the cities of Nisibis and Edessa, their Christian communities, and the debates and opponents Ephrem would have confronted in each city. For the most part, these conjectures cannot be proven and should not serve as the basis for an overarching chronology of Ephrem's writings. As I have suggested elsewhere, a more cautious approach would be "to limit the discussion of periodization to individual texts which make clear references to a particular place or event."[34]

As Beck asserted, this sequence of four cycles likely reflects

---

31. Wickes, "Between Liturgy and School," 37–38.
32. Christian Lange and Edmund Beck date both cycles to Ephrem's "Nisibene" period (i.e., prior to 363). See Lange, *The Portrayal of Christ,* 30–31; Edmund Beck, *Ephräm der Syrer. Lobgesang aus der Wüste,* Sophia: Quellen östlicher Theologie 7 (Freiburg, 1967), 15. Sebastian Brock, however, cautions: "In the present state of knowledge very little can be said with any certainty concerning the chronology of Ephrem's works." See Sebastian Brock, "St. Ephrem: A Brief Guide to the Main Editions and Translations" (http://syri.ac/brock/ephrem [accessed 24 April 2018]).
33. For this hypothesis, see Blake Hartung, "The Authorship and Dating of the Syriac Corpus Attributed to Ephrem of Nisibis: A Reassessment," *ZAC* 22, no. 2 (2018): 296–321, especially 306–11.
34. Hartung, "The Authorship and Dating," 312.

the later liturgical sequence of Lent, Holy Week, and Easter.[35] The original liturgical or para-liturgical function of the poems in Ephrem's lifetime is much less clear.[36] The rubric of the earliest dated manuscript (BL Add MS 14,571) identifies the first cycle as "on the forty-day fast," an indication that *madrāšē* in that cycle were used from an early date for the season of Lent. Although early scribes associated the cycle *On the Fast* with Lent, it is possible that Ephrem originally composed some or all of the poems for *other* liturgical fasts or simply as theological reflections on the virtues of fasting. Likewise, as Jean Gribomont argues, the names of the three Paschal cycles (*On the Unleavened Bread*, *On the Crucifixion*, and *On the Resurrection*) suggest a liturgical order corresponding to a chronological progression of the events of Jesus's Passion, death, and Resurrection. Yet this is not how the *madrāšē* in these cycles are organized.[37] Rather, there is considerable thematic overlap in their contents.[38] For example, the nine poems surviving under the heading *On the Crucifixion* are not all about the Crucifixion. In fact, several are more resonant with themes common to many of the poems in the cycle *On the Unleavened Bread* (like the Exodus from Egypt).[39]

Gerard Rouwhorst therefore suggests that the poems within all three cycles were originally composed for the Paschal season, and that their organization into distinct cycles was the result of a subsequent editorial attempt to conform them to a Holy Week-Good Friday-Easter Sunday liturgical calendar.[40] Despite the later edito-

---

35. Beck, *Paschahymnen*, i.
36. Although Beck published the latter three cycles under the title *Paschahymnen* (a convention followed also by French and Italian translators), this designation does not appear in the manuscripts, but is rather a name of Beck's own invention. Nevertheless, we believe that the common descriptor "Paschal" is useful for emphasizing the continuities between the three cycles.
37. Jean Gribomont, "Le triomphe de Pâques d'après S. Ephrem," *Parole de l'Orient* 4, no. 1–2 (1973): 147–89, especially 149.
38. On the general tendency of early Christian texts to "blur" distinctions between the events of the Passion and the Resurrection, especially in art and liturgy, see John Behr, *The Mystery of Christ: Life in Death* (Crestwood, NY: St Vladimir's Seminary Press, 2006), 28.
39. See, e.g., *Cruc.* 2 and 3.
40. G. A. M. Rouwhorst, *Les hymnes pascales d'Éphrem de Nisibe. Analyse théologique et recherche sur l'évolution de la fête pascale chrétienne à Nisibe et à Edesse et dans quelques églises

rial hand in the collection of the cycles, the poems themselves do offer some insight into the nature of the pre-Paschal fast and the Paschal celebration in Ephrem's community, which I will explore in greater detail below.[41]

On the Fast

Portions of the *madrāšē* cycle *On the Fast* survive in five different manuscripts,[42] yet none of these transmit the cycle of ten *madrāšē* in full.[43] Edmund Beck reconstructed that complete cycle in his critical edition. In its full edited form, the cycle is a compilation of three metrical sub-units. The poems of the first group, *Ieiun.* 1–5, bear the melody "This is the Firstborn's Fast" and share a common, albeit very complex, meter.[44] These poems are also thematically coherent. They extol the benefits of fasting through biblical examples and warn against the temptations of the Evil One. Ephrem's reference in *Ieiun.* 3.4 to "our fast" seems to suggest a liturgical or para-liturgical context, but the five *madrāšē* do not provide any clearer indications of their date of composition or per-

---

voisines au quatrième siècle, Vol. 2, Supplements to Vigiliae Christianae 7 (Leiden: Brill, 1989), 191–92. If the Sinai index of Ephrem's *qālē* (Sinai Syr. 10) is to be believed, a different editorial arrangement may also have existed. The index ascribes six *qālē* to the *madrāšē* collection *On the Fast*, while our extant cycle only has three, just one of which ("This is the Firstborn's Fast") appears in the index's record. These poems therefore appear to have been grouped in several different ways. For the Sinai index, see André de Halleux, "Une clé pour les hymnes d'Éphrem dans le Ms. Sinai Syr. 10," *Le Muséon* 85 (1972): 171–99, especially 178.

41. See Rouwhorst, *Hymnes pascales*, Vol. 1, *passim*.

42. BL Add MS 14,571 (MS D), BL Add MS 14,627 (MS B), BL Add MS 14,506 (MS J), BL Add MS 14,512 (MS P), BL Add MS 14,438 (MS C). See Beck, ed., *Hymnen de Ieiunio*, i–iii. In addition to the manuscripts utilized by Beck, portions of *Ieiun.* 3.2–5 also exist in MS Deir al-Surian Fragment 59 (a fragment that joins with Beck's MS B).

43. The complete cycle of ten is attested by the colophon of BL Add MS 14,571, fol. 16v. This manuscript, Beck's MS D, is the earliest manuscript of the cycle (dated to 519), and the most complete, containing *Ieiun.* 5–10 (prior folios are lost). For more on this manuscript, see William Wright, *Catalogue of the Syriac Manuscripts in the British Museum acquired since the year 1838*, Vol. 2 (London: British Museum, 1871), 410–13.

44. For an introduction to the metrical issues, see Sebastian P. Brock and George A. Kiraz, *Ephrem the Syrian: Select Poems*, Eastern Christian Texts 2 (Provo, UT: Brigham Young University Press), 96–97.

formative context.[45] Our most informative clues are stereotyped references to "the fast," or "our fast," as in *Ieiun.* 5.6: "Come, let us recall in the fast what the fools did in their fasts."[46]

Ieiun. 6 has its own meter-melody, perhaps indicating that the editors inserted it between the other two meter-melody cycles for thematic purposes.[47] Much as the poems of the initial and final sections of the cycle do, it praises the fast as a treasury full of gifts and lauds Christ as the healer of human blindness. An exhortation to an undefined audience to "gather in the fast" in the first stanza likely indicates a performative context connected to the liturgical or para-liturgical commemoration of a fast.

The final unit of *madrāšē* shares the meter-melody "God in His Mercy"[48] and the common theme: to offer Daniel and his three friends (*Ieiun.* 7–9) and Moses (*Ieiun.* 10) as examples of righteous fasting. A single exhortation to "meet our blessed fast" in *Ieiun.* 7.1 may indicate that these final *madrāšē* were also performed in a liturgical or para-liturgical setting, but we lack sufficient evidence to say much for certain.

On the Unleavened Bread

According to the colophon in the primary manuscript (BL Add MS 14,627), the *madrāšē* cycle *On the Unleavened Bread* originally contained twenty-one poems.[49] Due, however, to a lacuna in this manuscript, *Azym.* 7–11 are partially lost. Beck recovered the poems he numbered 8 and 9 from another manuscript (although *Azym.* 9 is fragmentary).[50]

When examined as a whole, the extant cycle is a compilation of two metrical sub-units: *Azym.* 1–2 and *Azym.* 3–21. Each of these

---

45. *Ieiun.* 4.7–9 offer a series of exhortations or admonitions to the audience about clothing in the midst of fasting.

46. Cf. *Ieiun.* 1.1: "This is the firstborn's fast"; 3.8: "Let not our fast be a feast day for the Evil One"; 4.1: "See the remedial fast."

47. The melody is "You, Lord, have written it." The meter is five lines per stanza, with a 5+6 + 7+4 + 4+4 + 4+5 + 5+6 syllable count.

48. Eight lines per stanza, with a 9+9+9+9+10+10+6+9 syllable count.

49. On this manuscript, see Wright, *Catalogue*, Vol. 2, 415.

50. Scholars have recently discovered additional manuscript witnesses that were not available to Beck: the first stanza of *Azym.* 20 and the eleventh stanza of *Azym.* 1 appear in MS Deir al-Surian 28. MS Deir al-Surian 38 contains *Azym.* 12 and 14. MS Deir al-Surian 40 contains *Azym.* 6.2.

units has its own meter-melody.[51] Furthermore, *Azym.* 1–2 form a continuous, albeit incomplete, acrostic, suggesting that there may originally have been additional poems in the sequence.[52] The compilers of the cycle probably attached *Azym.* 1–2 to *Azym.* 3–21 because of their common themes: the contrast between the "Paschal lamb" and the "true lamb," and the rejection of Jesus by the Jewish people. The second section, however, *Azym.* 3–21, is more forceful in its anti-Jewish polemic and its warnings against Christian participation in the Jewish Passover.[53]

On the Crucifixion

The nine-poem cycle *On the Crucifixion*, as published in Beck's critical edition, is an artificial construct. A cycle of *madrāšē* entitled "On the Crucifixion" survives in two different manuscripts, but these two cycles share no *madrāšē* in common.[54] When compiling his edition, Beck combined the two into a single unit. The first three *madrāšē*, from Beck's MS B, are each written in different meter-melodies and are thematically distinct from one another.[55] The second part of the cycle, *Cruc.* 4–9, is slightly more cohesive. The initial three *madrāšē* (*Cruc.* 4–6) share the meter-melody "The King's Bride" and offer symbolic exegesis of various events

---

51. *Azym.* 1–2 are written in three-line stanzas of 5+5 syllables, to the melody "He Who is Patient in Spirit." The poems of *Azym.* 3–21 are couplets of 5+4 syllables, set to the melody "Gather Together to Sacrifice in the Month of Nisan."

52. The acrostic form of *Azym.* 1 runs from the letter *ʾālap* to the letter *ṭet*, while *Azym.* 2 runs from *yōd* to *ʿayn*.

53. We will discuss these issues in greater detail below.

54. BL Add MS 14,571 (MS D) and BL Add MS 14,627 (MS B). In Beck's edition, *Cruc.* 1–3 come from MS B, while *Cruc.* 4–9 come from MS D. See Beck's comments in the introduction to his German translation (Beck, *Paschahymnen* [trans.], i–iii). MS Deir al-Surian 38 (not used by Beck) also preserves *Cruc.* 1 and 2 in full.

55. *Cruc.* 1 is written to the melody "God in His Mercy," with an eight-line meter built upon a 9 + 9 + 9 + 9 + 10 + 10 + 6 + 9 syllable pattern. It focuses on the betrayal of the Bridegroom, Jesus, by the Bride, "the daughter of Zion," upon his entry into Jerusalem. *Cruc.* 2 bears the meter-melody "The Infants were Slain," in five lines of 7+7 syllables. It begins with a reflection on the symbols of the Passover lamb, and then transitions to discuss the binding of Isaac and the murder of Abel as other biblical symbols of shepherds and lambs. *Cruc.* 3 is set to the meter-melody "Blessed are You, Ephratha" (eight lines per stanza, with an unclear syllable pattern). It meditates upon Jesus's Last Supper in the upper room.

in the Passion narratives.⁵⁶ *Cruc.* 7 is distinctive, with its own meter-melody, and a subject matter (the month of Nisan) more akin to *Res.* 2–5.⁵⁷ *Cruc.* 8 and 9 (*Cruc.* 9 is fragmentary, ending at stanza 3) are set to a common meter-melody and provide symbolic interpretations of events and figures in the Passion narratives.

Thematically, the *madrāšē* of this cycle are exceptionally diverse. It is therefore unclear what liturgical or para-liturgical functions they may have originally played in the Paschal season. They give the impression of a later editorial attempt to order various Ephremic poems in such a way as to coincide with a liturgical celebration of Holy Week.

On the Resurrection

The cycle *On the Resurrection* is the shortest of those included in this volume, comprising five poems (the last of which is fragmentary). These poems survive in full only in BL Add MS 14,627 (Beck's MS B), although Sebastian Brock discovered lost lines of the first stanza of *Res.* 1 in a nineteenth-century printed liturgical hymnary.⁵⁸ Despite the title *On the Resurrection*, its contents do not especially focus on the narrative of the Resurrection of Christ. These poems are, however, the most "festal" of the three Paschal cycles, reflecting directly upon the liturgical celebration of Pascha. *Res.* 1 is an outlier in the cycle, written in an acrostic format and bearing its own meter-melody (although the melody title is lost).⁵⁹ It is likewise thematically distinct from the remainder of the cycle, focusing not on the Paschal feast, but on the paradox of Christ as divine and human, with reference to events of his life described in the Gospels. *Res.* 2–3 and 4–5, although set to different meter-melodies, are relatively consistent in their thematic focus.⁶⁰ They extol the Paschal

56. Six lines per stanza, with an unclear syllable pattern.

57. *Cruc.* 7 bears the melody title "The Exalted Assembly," and is arranged on a seven-line stanzaic pattern, with a 10 + 10 + 10 + 10 + 8 + 8 + 8 syllable count.

58. Sebastian P. Brock, "The Transmission of Ephrem's Madrashe in the Syriac Liturgical Tradition," in *Studia Patristica* 33 (Leuven: Peeters, 1997), 490–505, especially 504.

59. Five lines per stanza: four of eight syllables and one of four syllables.

60. *Res.* 2–3: "The Infants were Slain" (five lines per stanza, with a 7+7 syllable pattern); *Res.* 4–5: "This is the Fast of the Firstborn" (the meter is unclear, but Beck arranges the poem in stanzas of seven lines each).

feast and the month of Nisan, exploring the symbolic resonance between the natural phenomena of the arrival of spring, the biblical narratives of Jesus's Passion and Resurrection, and the Church's liturgical celebration of Pascha.

Because these collections of poems appear to have been compiled together at a later date, it is difficult to make generalizations about the critical themes and concepts of each cycle in distinction from one another. The cycles *On the Unleavened Bread*, *On the Crucifixion*, and *On the Resurrection* are not topical "treatises," but compilations of individual poems originally composed and performed for distinct audiences. In this sense, each poem stands on its own. They do not all share the same meter and melody, nor were they likely composed to be read in a series.[61] Nevertheless, some common themes emerge.

General Features of the Songs for the Fast and Pascha

Hints of Performance

Generally speaking, the poems in the cycle *On the Fast* are opaque with regard to their setting and performative function. We cannot say for certain whether all the poems were originally composed and performed for a forty-day fast prior to Pascha (Lent), as the manuscript rubrics ("the fast of the forty days") indicate, or whether some originally accompanied other periods of fasting.[62] Regardless, at the time of the compilation of these poems in the extant manuscripts, scribes obviously saw these particular poems as appropriate for a Lenten collection.

Major questions remain unanswered, however, regarding the

---

61. In a recent article, I argued that the sixth-century cycles of Ephrem's *madrāšē* represent (sometimes loosely) thematic compilations by editors, not cohesive volumes composed at a single point in time. I contended that examining the smaller metrical sub-units that share a common meter and melody ("meter-melodies") offers a more productive approach to considering questions of authenticity and dating in regard to the *madrāšē* of Ephrem. See Hartung, "The Authorship and Dating," 318–20.

62. Scholars tend to view the forty-day fast as originally an Egyptian practice, which only became widespread throughout the Christian world by the mid-fourth century. See Paul F. Bradshaw, *The Search for the Origins of Christian Worship*, 2nd ed. (Oxford: Oxford University Press, 2002), 183–85; Thomas Talley, *The Origins of the Liturgical Year*, 2nd ed. (Collegeville, MN: Liturgical Press, 1991), 189–214.

practice of fasting in Ephrem's community. For instance, how long was this fast? It is likely that the fast included the first two days of what we now call the *triduum*, given the many references to the Passion narrative in some of these *madrāšē*, especially *Ieiun.* 5.[63] Also, what does Ephrem mean by "fasting" in this cycle? Note that he refers to a meatless diet (that is, pulses or vegetables) and abstinence from wine in several *madrāšē*.[64] There are also a number of references here to other penitential practices such as vigil, prayer, and wearing sackcloth and ashes.[65] Are these references reflective of the actual practices of fasting in Ephrem's community? How do they compare to what we know about other practices of fasting among Christians in the fourth century? It is also clear that these *madrāšē* were offering lessons about biblical readings that correspond to the liturgical practice of fasting (such as readings on Daniel, Moses on Mount Sinai, Elijah, and Jonah). What is less clear is how these biblical allusions and references shed light on the lectionary of Ephrem's church. The possibilities here are intriguing but inconclusive.

Unlike most of Ephrem's other poems, a number of the poems contained in the Paschal cycles show signs of composition for liturgical or para-liturgical performance during the Paschal season. In other words, they refer openly to the Pascha and the Paschal month of Nisan. The clearest examples are *Res.* 2 and 4. In *Res.* 2, Ephrem imagines the "cheerful feast day" as a garland of flowers offered to Christ by the Christian community. Various parts of the community "plait" their own blossoms into the garland through their roles in the public worship:

> [*Res.* 2.9] Let the bishop plait his interpretations
>   into it as his blossoms,
> the priests their victorious deeds,
>   the deacons their readings,

63. Bradshaw argues that the practice of fasting on the Friday and Saturday prior to Easter was already commonplace by the third century. It is unclear, however, whether this fast would have been joined to a larger forty-day fast, or considered distinct from it; see Bradshaw, *The Search for the Origins,* 180–81, 185.

64. *Ieiun.* 1.3, 7.2–3, 9.12. These descriptions fit well the diet of bread, vegetables, and water mandated for fasting in the *Apostolic Constitutions* 5.18.

65. For sackcloth, see *Ieiun.* 4.8. For the correlation of fasting, prayer, and vigil, see the refrains of *Ieiun.* 1 and 5.

> the youths their praises,
> > the children their psalms,
> > the chaste women their songs,
> > > the leaders their actions,
> > and the common people their customs.
> > > Blessed is he who has multiplied our victories!

The image we gather from this poem is of a communal vigil, lit by "lamps" (stanza 3) and full of song, led by the *madrāšē* of the "chaste women" (stanzas 6 and 8) and perhaps also involving the singing of psalms by children (stanzas 2, 7, 8–10). *Res.* 4 evokes a similar scene, drawing on the same imagery of communal song and springtime thunder. Here, Ephrem presents the Church, like the stormy weather of the month of Nisan, as "wordy" or perhaps "eloquent" (*mellē*) with praise. He goes on to present explicitly the feast of Pascha as a counterpart (or "yokefellow") to the feast of the Nativity (stanzas 3 and 4), framing the two festivals as the poles of the Christian year.

Unfortunately for the modern reader curious to gain more insight into the nature of the liturgies of Nisibis and Edessa in the mid-fourth century, not all of these poems are so descriptive. Some (for example, *Azym.* 5, 8, 12), highlighting the distinction between the Jewish and Christian festivals, employ a contrast between "this feast" and "that feast." For instance, *Azym.* 5.16 calls attention to the two "lambs" of the two feasts, arguing for the superiority of "this feast": "In this feast the blood / of the true lamb / is mixed among the disciples." The implication is that the poem is playing some role in the celebration of the Paschal feast. One other poem (*Azym.* 13) opens with a poetic exhortation referencing the feast and the festal month of Nisan (April): "Come, my brothers and sisters, / let us celebrate in the month of April / the feast of the victories / of the true lamb!" Other than these brief hints, most of the poems in Ephrem's Paschal cycles are characteristically silent about their performative context.

The Month of Nisan

Although scholars know little about the performative context of most of Ephrem's publicly performed writings, the many references to the Paschal feast and the month of Nisan in these cycles (April in the solar Syro-Antiochene calendar) provide some much-needed context to a few of Ephrem's poems.[66] Most notably, Ephrem uses a set of motifs associated with springtime weather (including warmth, melting snow, blossoms, rainstorms, and bees) to inform his depiction of the events of the Passion narratives, the Exodus narrative, and the Church's celebration of the Paschal feast. There are many examples of this in our cycles, but it is most prevalent in *Res.* 2–5.[67] The opening stanza of *Res.* 4 is particularly striking:

> [*Res.* 4.1] Extend to us, blessed Lord,
>   a little of your richness
>   in the all-enriching month:
> in April, your gift
>   has been spread out over all:
>   in it, enriched and adorned are
> mountains with grasses,
>   furrows with seeds,
> seas with goods,
>   dry land with possessions,
> the heights with glimmering lights,
>   and valleys with blossoms.
> April, adornment of the earth,
>   and April's feast,
>   the adornment of the holy church.

In an essay, Gerard Rouwhorst demonstrates that Ephrem shares many of these springtime motifs with roughly contemporaneous fourth-century Greek Christian texts on the Paschal feast.[68] He

---

66. This calendar was the Syrian variant of the Roman solar (Julian) calendar promulgated by Augustus. See Sacha Stern, *Calendars in Antiquity: Empires, States, and Societies* (Oxford and New York: Oxford University Press, 2012), 255–57.

67. Examples outside of the *Res.* cycle include *Azym.* 8 and 9 and *Cruc.* 7.

68. Gerard Rouwhorst, "L'évocation du mois de Nisan dans les Hymnes sur la Résurrection d'Éphrem de Nisibe," in *IV Symposium Syriacum, 1984: Literary Genres in Syriac Literature* (Groningen-Oosterhesselen 10–12 September), ed. H. J. W. Drijvers, René Lavenant, Corrie Molenberg, and Gerrit J. Reinink, OCA 229 (Rome: Pontificium Institutum Studiorum Orientalium, 1987), 101–10. Rouwhorst cites three texts: the sixth homily in a collection attributed to Hippolytus (ed. Pierre Nautin, *Homélies pascales I. Une homélie inspirée du traité sur la Pâque d'Hippolyte,* SC 27 [Paris: Cerf, 1950], 144–47; a portion of Eusebius of Caesarea's treatise *On the Paschal Feast* (PG 24.696–

then argues that Ephrem and the other fourth-century sources drew upon an earlier Hellenistic "canon" of stock images for spring.[69] Ephrem's vivid descriptions of springtime also resemble the practice of composing an *ekphrasis* on a particular season of the year. Hellenistic rhetorical handbooks traditionally defined *ekphrasis* as speech intended to "bring the subject matter vividly before the eyes."[70]

In these poems, therefore, we find some of the clearest links between Ephrem and Greco-Roman literary traditions.[71] Ephrem's reliance on traditional literary motifs provides further evidence, however slight, of the pre-existing Greco-Syriac literary culture of which he was an heir. Here we find possible evidence that Ephrem drew upon sources—whether consciously or unconsciously—to aid in the composition of his *madrāšē*. Ephrem utilized traditional imagery for springtime and the style of *ekphrasis* composition to evoke a familiar literary picture of the season for his audience, all while interweaving references to the Paschal celebration of the Church and the narratives of the Exodus and Passion. In this preference for rich, descriptive language, Ephrem fits well among other poets of late antiquity.[72]

---

697); and a selection from a homily of Gregory of Nazianzus for the Sunday after Pascha (PG 36.617–620).

69. He roots his argument on the Hellenistic origin of this imagery in an ancient poem from the *Palatine Anthology* (ed. Pierre Waltz and Guy Soury, *Anthologie grecque. Première partie. Anthologie Palatine*, Vol. 8, [Paris: Les Belles Lettres, 1974], 5–6). Rouwhorst also argues that the use of this traditional poetic imagery was intended to support the Council of Nicaea's ruling on the date of Easter, by linking the feast with neutral imagery of spring rather than the Jewish Passover. Although we do not know the exact details of the council's decree on the date of Easter, it is said to have decreed that the feast should never be celebrated earlier than the spring equinox. Rouwhorst speculates that the use of traditional springtime motifs would have helped to solidify the new date of Easter and further differentiate it from the Jewish Passover; see Rouwhorst, "L'évocation," 109–10.

70. On *ekphrasis*, see Ruth Webb, *Ekphrasis, Imagination and Persuasion in Ancient Rhetorical Theory and Practice* (Farnham, UK: Ashgate, 2009), 10. For the composition of *ekphraseis* on the seasons, see Webb, *Ekphrasis*, 40–41.

71. For this subject, see Ute Possekel, *Evidence of Greek Philosophical Concepts in the Writings of Ephrem the Syrian*, CSCO 580, Subsidia 102 (Leuven: Peeters, 1999). See also Edmund Beck, "TEXNH und TEXNITHΣ bei dem Syrer Ephräm," *OCP* 47 (1981): 295–331; Yifat Monnickendam, "How Greek is Ephrem's Syriac?: Ephrem's Commentary on Genesis as a Case Study," *JECS* 23, no. 2 (2015): 213–44.

72. See Michael Roberts, *The Jeweled Style: Poetry and Poetics in Late Antiquity* (Ithaca, NY: Cornell, 1989), 39–41.

One of the traditional springtime motifs Ephrem employs is the imagery of rain and thunderstorms. References to thunder (*r'amā*) and lightning (*barqē*) pervade these poems, with thunder typically functioning as a metaphor for positive sound. In *Res.* 2, this descriptive framework provides Ephrem with a canvas on which to paint an evocative picture of his church's liturgical celebration of Pascha. Like the booming spring thunder outside, the collective voices of the Church "thunder forth" (*r'em*) in praise at the Paschal feast.[73]

> [*Res.* 2.3] See how the earth has thundered forth below,
>   and above, heaven has thundered forth!
> April has mixed voices with voices:
>   exalted ones with low ones,
> voices of the sanctified church mixed
>   with the thunder of divinity,
> and amidst the glow of its lamps
>   are mixed flashes of lightning.
> With the rain, the passion's weeping,
>   and with the field, the fast of Pascha.

In the next stanza, the poet connects the situation of the Church offering worship in the midst of fierce weather to that faced by Noah on the ark, which he imagines as a "type" of the Church.

> [*Res.* 2.4] In the same way, on the ark,
>   every voice shouted joyfully from every mouth.
> Outside were terrible waves,
>   but inside were beautiful voices.
> Pairs of tongues
>   within sang together purely—
> a type of this, our festival,
>   in which virgin men and women
> chant chastely.[74]
>   Glory to the Lord of the ark!

---

73. *Res.* 2.2–3 (ed. Beck, *Paschahymnen*, 83). Cf. *Res.* 4.3, 10.
74. Or "in a holy fashion," a play on another word for the chaste in Syriac (*qaddišē*).

The Power of Fasting

Although the cycle of poems *On the Fast* is actually composed of three distinctive groups of poems (1–5, 6, and 7–10), one theme appears consistently throughout: the spiritual power of fasting. Ephrem presents fasting as the power revealed by Christ, the power to overcome sin and the weakness of the body. The first stanza of *Ieiun.* 1 offers a sort of poetic thesis statement for Ephrem's perspective on the efficacy of fasting:

> This is the firstborn's fast,
>   the first of his deeds;
>   let's revel in its advent:
> for by fasting, he prevailed,
>   though he was able
>   to prevail by all means.
> He showed to us
>   the power veiled
>   in the fast, conquering all,
> whereby one conquers
>   that one who by fruit
>   conquered Adam and devoured him.
> Blessed is the firstborn who compassed
>   our weakness with the wall
>   of his great fast.

Not surprisingly, the Garden of Eden narrative, which equates the primal sin of disobedience with an act of forbidden eating (described by Ephrem as "the food of Adam's house" in *Ieiun.* 1.4), provides Ephrem with an important counterpoint to the benefits of fasting. The most striking example of this is *Ieiun.* 3, in which Ephrem points to the actions of the serpent—the Evil One—in misleading Adam and Eve.

The metaphor of sight is another significant theme in several of the poems in the cycle *On the Fast*. Ephrem presents fasting as a purifying act that "purges the soul," making it able to gaze spiritually upon hidden things, whether upon God (to see the divine beauty) or upon the enemy (to see the dangers of temptation more plainly).[75]

---

75. *Ieiun.* 1.2.

This is the concept of the "luminous eye" popularized by Sebastian Brock's introduction to Ephrem's thought.[76] Ephrem's understanding of optics underlies this metaphor. For Ephrem, vision requires the presence of external light and the eye's capacity for sight. The union of the two—sight coming out of the eye, and external light drawing near—produces vision.[77] In the following stanza of the same poem (1.3), Ephrem speaks of the experience of fasting for the person who has a "luminous eye," an eye illuminated by divine light outside of itself: "The fast is meet and bright / for one who's purified / to be clear with God." As we saw earlier, however, the eye of faith itself must be "purged" by the discipline of fasting and prayer so that internal sight and external divine illumination can combine to bring about the vision of God. In *Ieiun.* 6, for example, Ephrem contrasts the positive illumination of the eye of faith, illustrated by the story of Bartimaeus (Mk 10.46–52), with the opening of Adam's eyes so that he saw his nakedness (Gn 3.7). For Adam, this new illumination proved a curse and a source of shame, but for the faithful, Ephrem argues, it is a source of blessing (*Ieiun.* 6.7–8).

These poems also frequently employ the imagery of weight and lightness.[78] People who gorge themselves on food are, in Ephrem's imagination, weighed down and unable to ascend properly to the

---

76. Sebastian Brock, *The Luminous Eye: The Spiritual World Vision of Saint Ephrem the Syrian* (Kalamazoo, MI: Cistercian Publications, 1992), 74–75.

77. See Ephrem, *Against Bardaisan's* Domnus, in *PR* II, 40, 42; *Fid.* 25.5–6. For a summary of Ephrem's understanding of optics in historical context, see Possekel, *Evidence of Greek Philosophical Concepts,* 207–10.

Ephrem's understanding of optics comes closest to the Platonic tradition and also exhibits some Stoic features *à la* Galen (cf. Possekel, *Evidence of Greek Philosophical Concepts,* 218–20). Also compare the metaphor of giving birth to color in Plato's *Theaetetus:* "as soon ... as an eye and something else whose structure is adjusted to the eye come within range and give birth to the whiteness together with its cognate perception ... then it is that, as the vision from the eyes and the whiteness from the thing that joins in giving birth to the color pass in the space between, the eye becomes filled with vision and now sees, and becomes not vision, but a seeing eye; while the other parent of the color is saturated with whiteness and becomes, on its side, not whiteness, but a white thing"; *Theaetetus* 156d–e, trans. Francis M. Cornford, *Plato's Theory of Knowledge,* 47, quoted in David C. Lindberg, *Theories of Vision from Al-Kindi to Kepler* (Chicago: The University of Chicago Press, 1976), 4–5.

78. *Ieiun.* 3.6, 7.2–4, 10.2–3.

spiritual heights. By contrast, those who fast assiduously, and are less burdened by the "weight" of food, can float upward. The ultimate example of this is Jesus, whom the alternate final stanza of *Ieiun.* 2 identifies as "the light one who lifted the heaviness and bore it on himself."

Biblical Exegesis

As the previous examples have already indicated, Ephrem's poems are rich with biblical allusions and references. Biblical interpretation was not solely the domain of institutions of learning, nor confined to commentaries composed for elite, literate audiences. Rather, the Bible was an ever-present feature of the discourse of Christian Late Antiquity, inscribed on popular memory by constant exposure to its words and narratives.

Ephrem assumed his audiences knew the biblical stories he recounted, cited, and expanded upon. In his publicly performed works, Ephrem sought to bring those familiar stories to life in a variety of ways, linking them to one another and applying them to a diverse spectrum of issues and audiences. In what follows, I will discuss several ways in which Ephrem uses the Bible in these poems.

Biblical Exemplars of Fasting   The cycle of poems *On the Fast* relies heavily on biblical exemplars of fasting. In fact, the marshalling of biblical witnesses to support the practice of fasting is a stated goal of Ephrem's for the composition of these poems. In *Ieiun.* 1.7, he writes: "Let scriptures be for us / just like a mirror; / let's see our fast in them." Some of the poems, such as *Ieiun.* 7–9 (which focus on Daniel and his three companions) and *Ieiun.* 10 (which centers on Moses's ascent of Mount Sinai), primarily explore a single biblical episode or series of episodes.

In *Ieiun.* 10, for example, Ephrem brings together many of the images he associates with fasting to paint a vivid portrait of Moses's fast atop Mount Sinai. In the first two stanzas of the poem, Ephrem presents Moses as an ideal faster, spurning the temptations of the royal table of Pharaoh's daughter to embrace the "fast of the mountain." Moses's ascent of the mountain in stanza 3 hints at the image of lightness, with Moses rising up by means of his fasting. The power of fasting similarly transforms Moses's features: "He fasted and shone, he prayed and prevailed, / in one aspect (*gawnā*) he arose, another came down" (stanza 2). Throughout the remainder of the poem, Ephrem contrasts the fast of Moses with the "greedy" idolatrous feasting of the Israelites at the foot of the mountain. Ephrem presents Moses's fast using medical imagery as a source of "spiritual remedies" for the soul that can heal the "sickness" of gluttony, that "need that / craves novelties" (stanza 7):

> [*Ieiun*. 10.6] Egypt's medicines are distinguished,
>   the artisans there are accomplished:
> Moses shunned the medicine store,
>   the disease not of body but soul.
> He ascended Mount Sinai, God's mountain,
>   there he lingered, gathered, and brought down
> spiritual remedies,
>   restoring the soul's health secretly.

Through this extended exploration of Moses as a faster in dialogue with the parallel narratives of the Golden Calf and the manna, Ephrem provides a detailed biblical model for the Christian practice of fasting. Other poems, especially *Ieiun*. 1–4, do not focus on a single biblical exemplar, but instead present lists of biblical models. The series of biblical figures given in, for example, *Ieiun*. 4 (Esther; Shadrach, Meshach, and Abednego; Jonah and Nineveh; and Moses) may have its origins in earlier, memorized *testimonia* lists.[79] Although, as Robert Murray has noted, Ephrem recites such lists far less frequently than Aphrahat, we can sometimes detect their presence beneath the surface, as it were.[80] When he compiles

---

79. Cf. Aphrahat, *Demonstration on the Fast*, where we find the ascent of Moses up Mount Sinai (*Dem*. 3.3), Naboth's vineyard (*Dem*. 3.4–6), Jonah and Nineveh (*Dem*. 3.7), Esther and Mordecai (*Dem*. 3.10–13).

80. Aphrahat does not use the word "demonstration" (*taḥwitā*) for these texts; however, he does use it when introducing one list of exempla in *Dem*. 3.2: "Listen, my beloved, to a demonstration (*taḥwitā*) of pure fasting" (Parisot, *Aphraatis*, Vol. I, 100). See Robert Murray, "Some Rhetorical Patterns in Early Syriac Literature," in *A Tribute to Arthur Vööbus: Some Studies in Early Christian Literature and Its Environment, Primarily in the Syrian East*, ed. Robert H. Fischer (Chicago: Lutheran School of Theology at Chicago, 1977), 110. Murray argues that these listed examples developed out of the Hellenistic Jewish tradition of *syncrisis*, or the "comparison series" (examples of which can be seen in Sir 44–49 and Heb 11); Murray, "Rhetorical Patterns," 116.

series of biblical exempla, Ephrem tends to flesh them out and add more detail than we find in Aphrahat.[81]

Exodus and Passion, Lamb and Lamb The most noticeable exegetical feature of the Paschal cycles is the frequent juxtaposition of the Exodus and Passion narratives (which Ephrem often characterizes as a contrast between the "paschal lamb" and the "true lamb"). The same theme also appears once in the cycle *On the Fast*.[82] Ephrem regularly compares the events and results of the two narratives in order to demonstrate the superiority of Jesus's Passion. The third poem of the cycle *On the Unleavened Bread* opens by expressly inviting the audience to compare the narrative of the "Passover lamb" (*'emar pashā*) with that of the "true lamb" (*'emar qūštā*) alongside one another: "Let us consider / both lambs, my brothers and sisters, / let us see whether / they are similar or different."[83]

The many references and allusions to the Exodus in all four cycles offer strong evidence that Exodus (along with the Diatessaronic Passion narrative) was read in Ephrem's church during the season of Pascha, and perhaps also during the preceding period of fasting.[84] In this setting, we could envision Ephrem's poems functioning as vivid public commentaries upon the liturgical readings. Ephrem weaves elements of the Exodus and Passion narratives into an interconnected tapestry of "types" (*tupsē*) and "symbols" (*rāzē*). In his writings, Ephrem uses these Syriac terms and several others (for example, *salmā* ["image"] and *maḥzitā* ["mirror"]) to portray the relationship between narratives, phrases, and images from Scripture and future realities—especially the events of the life of Christ and the establishment of the Church. He also employs these terms to

---

81. Other prominent examples of Ephrem's likely use of *testimonia* series include the dispute poems between Death and Satan (*Nis.* 52–59) and Virginity and Chastity (*Arm.* 4–5; 9). Murray describes the "exempla" used by the characters of Death and Satan in the former group of poems as "anti-aretology," and suggests that the listing of negative examples of demonic actions was rooted in exorcism formulae; Murray, "Rhetorical Patterns," 127.

82. *Ieiun.* 5.7

83. *Azym.* 3.2.

84. See Wickes, "Between Liturgy and School," 37–38. Clear references to the Exodus narrative appear in *Azym.* 1, 3 4, 5, 6, 8, 9, 15, 17, 18, 19; *Cruc.* 2, 3; *Res.* 3, 4.

convey the moral instruction or truth about God that he finds in biblical passages.[85] As I will argue below, these two biblical narratives, and the exegetical vocabulary Ephrem uses to frame them, underpin much of the extensive anti-Jewish polemic of these poems.

One of the primary symbolic links Ephrem draws between the Passion and the Exodus is the figure of the "lamb." He regularly returns to Exodus 12 (the instructions for the first Passover), his dominant source of sacrificial imagery, connecting it to the sacrifice of Jesus's death. In line with well-established Christian traditions, Ephrem associates the whole complex of Old Testament sacrificial language and imagery with the Passover sacrifice and its fulfillment in Jesus.[86] *Cruc.* 2 offers Ephrem's most thorough treatment of this theme. The first stanzas of the poem imagine Christ ("the true lamb") instructing Moses ("the Shepherd") on how to eat the Passover meal (the "symbolic lamb").[87] In stanza 2, for instance, Ephrem writes:

> [*Cruc.* 2.2] In the house of Jethro, Moses slaughtered
>   many sheep and lambs,
> and though he learned well, he did not fathom
>   how to slaughter a certain sacrifice.
> It was our lamb who was teaching him
>   how to depict his symbol.
> The sacrifice taught the sacrificer

---

85. Tanios Bou Mansour draws very clear distinctions between these terms, arguing that each of them represents different modes of representation and symbolization. He believes it would be a great mistake to read these terms as largely synonymous. Nevertheless, Bou Mansour's argument has not been widely adopted. Ephrem himself often uses many of these terms synonymously. Bou Mansour is right, however, in cautioning us to consider carefully each of them on its own terms, and I believe that there are some distinctions between these terms. I also believe, however, that the distinctions are primarily in the metaphors that the terms evoke. See Tanios Bou Mansour, "Étude de la terminologie symbolique chez saint Éphrem," *Parole de l'Orient* 14 (1987): 221–62.

86. Cf. *Azym.* 2.2–8; *Ieiun.* 5.6–7. For the development of sacrificial imagery in the Second Temple period and in early Christianity, see Robert J. Daly, SJ, *Sacrifice Unveiled: The True Meaning of Christian Sacrifice* (London: T&T Clark, 2009), 40–98; George Heyman, *The Power of Sacrifice: Roman and Christian Discourse in Conflict* (Washington, DC: The Catholic University of America Press, 2007), 95–159.

87. *Cruc.* 2.1–6.

> how to roast and eat [him],
> how to slaughter [him] and sprinkle [his blood].
> Blessed is he who taught his eaters!

In the course of the poem, Ephrem portrays other Old Testament "sacrifices," particularly Isaac (stanza 7) and Abel (stanzas 8 and 9), as witnesses to the paradox of the sacrifice of Christ. Both figures are "lambs" in the sense that they became (or nearly became) sacrificial victims.[88] In the case of Abel, Ephrem revels in the potential for paradox:

> [*Cruc.* 2.9] For it was a lamb that was offering,
> it was a lamb that was being offered,
> and it was a lamb that was receiving [the offering].
> Praise be to the lamb of God!

The sacrificial image of Jesus's death depicted in Abel's sacrifice is one in which the Son serves as priest, making the offering (*mqareb*); as lamb, the sacrifice itself (*'etqarab*); and as God, the recipient of the sacrifice (*mqabel*). Depending upon the particular themes of individual poems, Ephrem envisions the final fulfillment of this sacrificial imagery occurring at different moments: when Jesus ate the Passover meal at the Last Supper,[89] or when Jesus himself was slain on Passover as the "Lamb."[90]

Ephrem's symbolic readings of the various events of the Passion and Exodus narratives in these poems are often brief and undeveloped. Poems such as *Azym.* 13 and 16 and *Cruc.* 4, 5, 8, and 9 take the audience on a whirlwind tour through incidents and imagery from the narratives, including Jesus's scourging,[91] the crown of thorns,[92] the two thieves,[93] and the crowd's appeal to Caesar.[94]

---

88. The image of Abel as a sacrificial victim of his brother also appears in an anonymous (fifth-century?) Syriac dialogue poem on Cain and Abel. See Sebastian P. Brock, "Two Syriac Dialogue Poems on Abel and Cain," *Le Muséon* 113 (2000): 333–75, especially 346–47.

89. Cf. *Azym.* 6; 19.1–4; *Cruc.* 3.2. Cf. also Cyrillona, *Euch.* 1–20, 111–121.
90. Cf. *Cruc.* 5.18.
91. *Cruc.* 4.11.
92. *Azym.* 13.28–29.
93. *Cruc.* 5.7; 8.8–9.
94. *Cruc.* 4.7–8; 8.3.

These poems give a great deal of attention to the miraculous events surrounding Jesus's crucifixion (the three hours of darkness,[95] the tearing of the Temple veil,[96] and the earthquake[97]). Ephrem tends to compound such references and allusions: where one appears, there are usually many others.

Resolving an Exegetical Problem in Poetry: The Chronology of the Passion in Cruc. *6*   Cruc. 6 is unique among the Paschal cycles. Like many of the other poems, it engages in symbolic exegesis of particular episodes from the Passion narratives, but, unlike those others, it narrows its focus considerably to examine one particular exegetical problem—the chronology of Jesus's death and Resurrection.[98] In Matthew's gospel, Jesus predicts his death and Resurrection by reference to the "sign of Jonah," foretelling that "the Son of Man will be three days and three nights in the heart of the earth" (Mt 12.40). For early Christian interpreters, this saying proved a puzzle. If Jesus died on a Friday afternoon and was raised on a Sunday morning, how did this time frame align with Jesus's prediction of "three days and three nights"?

In *Cruc.* 6, Ephrem draws upon his knowledge of astronomy and his belief that the universe bears witness to its Creator, to argue that the three hours of darkness on the afternoon of the crucifixion—followed by an additional three hours of light before sunset—constituted an additional night and day:

> [*Cruc.* 6.1] Three days were numbered
>   for the Messiah,
>   just as for Jonah.
> Look: it was then preparation day
>   when the light
> of that people had set,
>   and again another,
>   the Sabbath day,

95. *Azym.* 13.22–23; *Cruc.* 1.10; 5.2; 7.4–6.
96. *Cruc.* 4.6, 12; *Azym.* 13.18–21.
97. *Cruc.* 4.13.
98. For more on this poem, see my essay "The Significance of Astronomical and Calendrical Theories for Ephrem's Interpretation of the Three Days of Jesus' Death."

INTRODUCTION 31

> symbol of the rest
> > which put death to rest.
> He who darkens and lightens
> > reckoned [as] a day
> the duration and time
> > when it darkened.

In Ephrem's chronology, then, the first day occurred on Friday morning and lasted until midday. This was followed by three hours of "night," from midday until the ninth hour. Subsequent to this "night of the daytime" (stanza 5) were three hours of light prior to sunset. Following Friday night (the night of the Sabbath and the second of the three nights), came the Sabbath day (the third day). The evening after the Sabbath, then, represented the final of the three nights. Ephrem then speculates that the Resurrection occurred at midnight (stanza 19).[99]

While most Greek Christian writers ignored or failed to recognize the potential chronological issue, Ephrem was not the only Syriac writer to attempt to reconcile the Paschal chronology.[100] His solution, however, and his detailed elaboration of the calendrical and symbolic significance of the extra "day" that occurred on the Friday of the Crucifixion are unique. Ephrem roots his explanation of the chronology not only in Scripture, but in the natural world, arguing that the solar and lunar calendars attest to the inclusion of the additional night and day through their excess hours and need for regular intercalation (the addition of extra time to the calendar for the purpose of keeping it on track):

> [*Cruc.* 6.6] O you symbolic foretelling
> > of three more
> > > hours![101]
> Every four years an entire day

---

99. "Yet perhaps on the sixth hour / of that blessed night / our Lord and our God / was raised." Rouwhorst (*Les hymnes pascales*, v. 1, 196) believes this conjecture reflects the liturgical practice of Ephrem's church, in which the celebration of the Resurrection began at midnight between the Saturday and the Sunday of the Pasch.

100. See Aphrahat, *Demonstration* 12.7; *Didascalia Apostolorum* 21; *Commentary on the Diatessaron* 19.4. For a single fourth-century Greek witness to the interest in reconciling the Paschal chronology, see Gregory of Nyssa, *De tridui spatio*.

101. Lit. "you, O preceding symbol of three more hours."

>   is intercalated:[102]
> it is a great symbol,
>   for he revealed beforehand
>   the three hours
>   that were prepared
>   in order to darken at his murder.[103]
> The Lord of lights
>   inscribed his symbols with a light,
> and the sun went before
>   as his herald.

A considerable knowledge of ancient calendars and timekeeping is essential to make sense of this poem. Yet *Cruc.* 6 does not simply represent an obscure piece of late antique speculation; it is an important witness to the nature of Ephrem's thought and the diversity of his writings. It reflects, first, Ephrem's assumptions as an ancient thinker—that the concepts of "day" and "night" do not describe fixed lengths of time, but instead depend upon the movements of the heavenly bodies. It also reveals Ephrem's persistent effort to demonstrate the fundamental agreement between scripture and nature, an argument he was able to make with reference to late antique scientific knowledge.

This poem challenges many common assumptions about Ephrem, as he draws upon his knowledge of astronomy and the calendar to resolve an exegetical difficulty (the chronology of the Passion), an approach rooted in his rich theology of symbols. The fact that Ephrem's argument relies upon the Roman Julian calendar also reminds us that Ephrem was not so distant from mainstream

---

102. Ephrem mentions the practice of *intercalation,* the addition of extra time to the calendar for the purpose of keeping it on track. Although intercalation is a necessity for both lunar and solar calendars, Ephrem is describing the regular intercalation of the solar calendar. Ephrem's solar calendar appears to have been an adapted version of the Julian calendar, likely what scholars call the Syro-Antiochene calendar (see Sacha Stern, *Calendars in Antiquity: Empires, States, and Societies* [Oxford: Oxford University Press, 2012], 255–57). Like our modern calendar (itself a revision of the Julian calendar), Ephrem's solar year featured 365 ¼ days. Since the ancient day was divided into twelve hours, if a day was intercalated every four years to account for the extra ¼ of a day, that ¼ of a day would equal 3 hours.

103. Contrary to the meter, this line ("in order to darken at his murder") contains five syllables.

Greco-Roman thought as scholars sometimes assume.[104] Finally, this poem is notable for the sophistication of its language, sources, and symbolism. For the modern reader, a great deal of background research is necessary simply to track Ephrem's reasoning.

As I have argued elsewhere, the contents of this poem are far more "scholastic" and sophisticated than many of Ephrem's *madrāšē*.[105] The vocabulary, subject matter, and meter are quite complex. Because it seems better suited to a schoolroom than a congregational liturgy, its origins may be non-liturgical. Indeed, when we apply Wickes's criteria for "liturgical" *madrāšē*, we find that this poem does not reference either liturgical rituals or the Paschal festival. Its subject matter (the Passion chronology) does, however, reflect likely lections for that feast.[106] If this were performed for a liturgical setting, it would push the boundaries of our current understanding of the instructional content of *madrāšē* in liturgy. This is certainly possible, and perhaps there could have been an apologetic motivation for raising this complex issue with the congregational audience. Alternatively, the poem could belong to what Wickes calls a "blurred space between liturgy and classroom."[107] In this view, it would be reasonable, therefore, to suppose that Ephrem composed this particular poem for performance for ascetic literary circles during the Paschal season, as a means of meditating upon a particular exegetical problem raised by the festal lections.

Anti-Judaism in the Paschal Cycles

In Ephrem's understanding of salvation history, the Incarnation, death, and Resurrection of Jesus represented a hinge point in God's dealings with human beings—the establishment of a Church made up of many "peoples" and the rejection of the Jewish "people."[108]

---

104. For this point, see Possekel, *Evidence of Greek Philosophical Concepts*, 8.
105. Hartung, "The Significance of Astronomical and Calendrical Theories."
106. Wickes, "Between Liturgy and School," 37. See above in this introduction, pp. 10–11.
107. Wickes, "Between Liturgy and School," 43.
108. Ephrem frequently juxtaposes the word *ʿammā* ("people" or "nation") with its plural form *ʿammē* ("peoples" or "nations"). He uses the former term for the ancient Israelites and the Jews of his own time, and the latter as the functional equivalent of "Gentiles." Unlike the Greek ἔθνη and the Hebrew גויים, however, the Syriac for the non-Jewish "peoples" simply renders the term for the Jewish "people" in the

The anti-Jewish polemic in these cycles is particularly vehement and has attracted a considerable amount of scholarly interest. Some scholars have questioned whether the polemic reflects Ephrem's own personal hatred of Jews, or a tendency toward insults that consistently undermines his otherwise effective and engaging style of writing and thinking.[109] Such interpretations, while understandable, overstate the uniqueness of Ephrem's polemic against Jews. Ephrem's harsh language and tendency toward vehement polemic belongs to a common trajectory of intensifying anti-Jewish polemic among the Christian writers of the fourth and fifth centuries.[110] Unfortunately, the poems in these cycles fit squarely within a much broader trajectory of early Christian theological discourse, which

---

plural. Cf. Murray, *Symbols of Church and Kingdom*, 41–68; R. A. Darling, "The 'Church From the Nations' in the Exegesis of Ephrem," in *IV Symposium Syriacum 1984: Literary Genres in Syriac Literature*, ed. H. J. W. Drijvers, R. Lavenant, C. Molenberg, and G. J. Reinink, Orientalia Christiana Analecta (Rome: Pontificium Institutum Studiorum Orientalium, 1987).

109. A. P. Hayman and Karl Kuhlmann both argue that Ephrem simply hated Jews on a personal level, a hatred that is reflected in his anti-Jewish comments, which appear at times in surprising and seemingly unnecessary points in his writings. In Hayman's words, Ephrem's "incessant need to bring in anti-Jewish themes reveals how deep-seated was his detestation of the Jews" (431). This interpretation of Ephrem's anti-Judaism, with its sweeping generalization about his personal views, does not do justice to the diversity of Ephrem's corpus. Anti-Jewish polemic is not a universal theme in Ephrem's works, and Ephrem even makes somewhat conciliatory statements about Jews at certain points. See A. P. Hayman, "The Image of the Jew in the Syriac Anti-Jewish Polemical Literature," in *To See Ourselves As Others See Us: Christians, Jews, "Others" in Late Antiquity*, ed. Jacob Neusner, Ernest S. Frerichs, and Caroline McCracken-Flesher (Chico, CA: Scholars Press, 1985); Karl H. Kuhlmann, "The Harp Out of Tune: The Anti-Judaism/Anti-Semitism of St. Ephrem," *The Harp* 17 (2004): 177–83. Dominique Cerbelaud, meanwhile, argues that Ephrem's anti-Judaism reflects a broader weakness in his thought. "Devoid of speculative instruments, the thought of Ephrem, when seeking to mark its opposition, makes recourse to insult rather than argument. This violence is observed elsewhere in the deacon of Edessa, not only vis-à-vis the Jews, but vis-à-vis heretics and notably the three who represent—to use a familiar expression—his 'bêtes noires': Marcion, Bardaisan, and Mani"; Dominique Cerbelaud, "L'antijudaïsme dans les hymnes de Pascha d'Éphrem le Syrien," *Parole de l'Orient* 20 (1995): 201–7, especially 206.

110. See Guy G. Stroumsa, "From Anti-Judaism to Antisemitism in Early Christianity?" in Ora Limor and Guy G. Stroumsa, eds., *Contra Judaeos: Ancient and Medieval Polemics between Christians and Jews* (Tübingen: Mohr Siebeck, 1995), 9–10, 16–17. See also Shepardson, *Anti-Judaism and Christian Orthodoxy*, 65–67.

turned Jews into quintessential "others," "crucifiers" who represented profound threats to the Christian community.

Scholars have debated to what degree such rhetoric can shed light on the actual relationship between Jews and Christians in late antiquity.[111] Was early Christian anti-Jewish polemic a response to real debate and competition with Jews,[112] or was it primarily defensive rhetoric designed to advance Christian self-understanding and identity formation?[113] This question is quite relevant to our consideration of the anti-Jewish polemic of these poetic cycles. Are Ephrem's repeated and strident attacks against Jews reflective of real competition or dialogue with Jewish communities in Nisibis and Edessa, or are they mainly symbolic, intended to bolster the identity of the Christian community through setting it over and against a perceived opponent? Scholars have taken both views.[114]

---

111. For a summary of the debate, see Stroumsa, "From Anti-Judaism to Antisemitism."

112. Marcel Simon was the most well-known advocate of the "conflict theory," arguing that the Judaism of Late Antiquity was engaged in active proselytization, placing itself in direct competition with Christianity. Simon's thesis was highly regarded in the scholarship of the second half of the twentieth century, but it has faced major challenges in recent years. See Marcel Simon, *Verus Israel: A Study of the Relations Between Christians and Jews in the Roman Empire,* trans. H. McKeating (Oxford: Oxford University Press, 1986), 135–425. For a recent defense of Simon's position, see Albert I. Baumgarten, "Marcel Simon's *Verus Israel* as a Contribution to Jewish History," *Harvard Theological Review* 92, no. 4 (1999): 465–78, especially 476–78.

113. Important proponents of the rhetoric/identity formation position include Miriam Taylor, Judith Lieu, and Daniel Boyarin. Taylor argued that anti-Judaism was engrained in the fabric of Christian teaching and contended that the attempt to account for it in imagined social dynamics between Christians and Jews is fundamentally flawed. See Miriam S. Taylor, *Anti-Judaism and Early Christian Identity: A Critique of the Scholarly Consensus* (Leiden: Brill, 1995), 141–42. Pushing the argument further, Lieu and Boyarin have critiqued even the idea of a clear "parting of the ways" between Judaism and Christianity. See Judith Lieu, *Neither Jew nor Greek? Constructing Early Christianity* (New York: A&C Black, 2005), 29; Daniel Boyarin, *Border Lines: The Partition of Judaeo-Christianity* (Philadelphia: University of Pennsylvania Press, 2004), 11–13.

114. Stanley Kazan and Stephen Benin, echoing Marcel Simon, argue that Ephrem's anti-Jewish polemic was a response to Jewish proselytism in Nisibis; see Stanley Kazan, "Isaac of Antioch's Homily Against the Jews (Part 3)," *Oriens Christianus* 47, no. 1 (1963): 89–97; Stephen D. Benin, "Commandments, Covenants and the Jews in Aphrahat, Ephrem and Jacob of Sarug," in *Approaches to Judaism in Medieval Times,* ed. David R. Blumenthal (Chico, CA: Scholars Press, 1984), 143. Kathleen

The problem with historically contextualizing Ephrem's anti-Jewish polemic boils down to a lack of evidence. We know very little about the Jewish and Christian communities in Nisibis and Edessa that could inform our interpretation.[115] In contrast with John Chrysostom's eight infamous homilies against "Judaizing" Chris-

---

McVey puts forth a more nuanced (albeit speculative) version of the conflict argument by drawing upon Jacob Neusner's claims regarding the expansion of rabbinic Judaism in Mesopotamia. She argues that Ephrem's *Hymns on the Nativity* respond to the critiques of a proselytizing rabbinic Judaism seeking to expand its influence among other Jews; see Kathleen McVey, "The Anti-Judaic Polemic of Ephrem Syrus' Hymns on the Nativity," in *Of Scribes and Scrolls: Studies on the Hebrew Bible, Intertestamental Judaism, and Christian Origins Presented to John Strugnell*, ed. Thomas H. Tobin, John J. Collins, and Harold W. Attridge, College Theology Society Resources in Religion (Lanham, MD: University Press of America, 1990), 239–40. Given the lack of evidence, however, Jewish proselytism seems more of an interpretive presupposition on the part of these scholars than a clear implication of the text. One can more easily interpret Ephrem's rhetoric as a response to Christian attraction to Judaism and Jewish practices. It is not necessary to suppose that aggressive Jewish proselytism was the motivation. See Taylor's critique of Simon (Taylor, *Anti-Judaism and Early Christian Identity*, 28–29).

115. The evidence regarding the religious landscape of Ephrem's birthplace of Nisibis and later home in Edessa is sparse. Han Drijvers makes an attempt to reconstruct Jewish-Christian relations in northern Mesopotamia (drawing primarily upon the early fifth-century *Teaching of Addai* and the writings of Ephrem), but his article reveals the inherent limitations to such an inquiry. Drijvers believes that the social context of late ancient cities like Edessa is crucial for understanding their religious communities: "Pagans, Jews and Christians did not live in splendid isolation in an antique town in which a good deal of life was lived in public.... Ideological conflicts and struggles like those between Christians, Jews and pagans found their origin in daily experiences of different religions" (H. J. W. Drijvers, "Jews and Christians at Edessa," *Journal of Jewish Studies* 36, no. 1 [1985]: 88–102). Drijvers concludes that it was precisely this real contact between Christians and Jews that was so threatening to Christian leaders like Ephrem. The strength, and even existence," of the Jewish community in Edessa was "a threat to Edessa's nascent orthodoxy" (101). This is certainly a plausible interpretation of Ephrem's polemic, but, given the sources, extremely difficult to maintain as a portrait of Jewish and Christian relations in Edessa. We have some evidence of the presence of a thriving Jewish community in Nisibis during the first and second centuries. Jacob Neusner, describing the presence of Rabbi Judah b. Bathyra I (a Temple official and likely Pharisee) in Nisibis, writes: "His place in the transmission of tannaitic Judaism to Babylonia was analogous to that of Addai of Edessa in the foundation of Christianity in the Iranian Empire" (Neusner, *A History of the Jews in Babylonia*, vol. 1, 48–49). Manichaeans (Russell, "Nisibis as the Background to the Life of Ephrem the Syrian," 195–97) and traditional polytheistic cults also seem to have been present in the city (ibid., 191–93.)

tians in Antioch (in which John explains the impetus for the delivery of his homilies—namely, Christian participation in synagogue worship and Jewish festivals), Ephrem's writings reveal little about the underlying situation that prompted the polemic.[116] While it is certainly intriguing to envision a strong and active proto-rabbinic Judaism confronting Ephrem's communities in northern Mesopotamia, or even a lingering "Jewish-Christian" synthesis that Ephrem sought to combat, scholars can do little more than speculate.

For this reason, other scholars have put aside the reconstruction of the possible historical setting of Ephrem's polemic and focused on exploring the rhetoric of anti-Judaism and its role in communal identity formation for Christians. Christine Shepardson has pioneered this approach to Ephrem's anti-Jewish polemic, arguing that Ephrem's Jews are largely rhetorical constructions.[117] As a proponent of Nicene orthodoxy, Ephrem employed anti-Jewish rhetoric to emphasize the "otherness" of his non-Nicene opponents.[118] This rhetoric, Shepardson argues, was focused more on bolstering Christian identity than on attacking hostile Jewish rivals.

In order to explore the contours of the anti-Jewish polemic of these cycles, it is particularly important to pay attention to the potential contexts and audiences of the sources. In many of these poems, Ephrem compares the Christian feast of Pascha ($pash\bar{a}$) with the Jewish feast of Passover (also named $pash\bar{a}$).[119] Prior to Ephrem, and perhaps still, the two feasts had been celebrated concurrently,

---

116. For Chrysostom's homilies, see Robert Louis Wilken, *John Chrysostom and the Jews: Rhetoric and Reality in the Late 4th Century* (Berkeley: University of California Press, 1983), 67–68. In some of Ephrem's *Hymns on the Unleavened Bread*, he questions the legitimacy of the Passover celebration and presents the Passover meal as a deadly poison—an approach that suggests that he was confronting Christian participation in Jewish rites. Yet, unlike Chrysostom, Ephrem does not explicitly explain the context for his rhetoric.

117. Christine Shepardson, *Anti-Judaism and Christian Orthodoxy: Ephrem's Hymns in Fourth-Century Syria*.

118. Shepardson, *Anti-Judaism and Christian Orthodoxy*, 107.

119. The clear linguistic connection between the names of the two feast days is lost in English translation (though preserved in several other modern languages), but it shaped Christian discourse from a very early period. See *Melito of Sardis: "On Pascha" and Fragments*, ed. Stuart George Hall, Oxford Early Christian Texts (Oxford: Clarendon Press, 1979).

on the 14th of Nisan.[120] It does not require an imaginative leap to suspect that the common names and roughly concurrent celebrations of the two festivals were significant factors in the especially vehement anti-Jewish polemic of these poems.

Anti-Judaism and Biblical Exegesis   In this contested context, the poems in the *Azym.*, *Cruc.*, and *Res.* cycles give particular attention to the question of exegesis, seeking to expound an integrated interpretation of the Paschal lections from the Exodus and Passion narratives. Ephrem's anti-Jewish argument is primarily one of biblical interpretation. Ephrem concludes *Azym.* 6 after laying out a series of Old Testament "symbols" and "types" of Jesus's death, with a summary explanation rooted in the language of the Johannine Passion narrative:

> [*Azym.* 6.13] All of them were planted
>   and proved true about his fullness,
> for they all proclaimed
>   about his fullness everywhere.
> [14] For in him, the symbols

---

120. Rouwhorst and Shepardson take the view that Ephrem's community had a Quartodeciman heritage, but they assume that the churches in Nisibis and Edessa ceased to be Quartodeciman after the ruling of the Council of Nicaea against celebrating the Pasch on 14 Nisan. Shepardson asserts that Ephrem's rhetoric against "Judaizing" in the Paschal hymns demonstrates that he was attempting to shape Christian behavior to align with the decrees of the Council of Nicaea—namely, against celebrating the Pascha on that date; Shepardson, *Anti-Judaism and Christian Orthodoxy*, 30–31. The portrait of Ephrem as a fierce pro-Nicene partisan, however, is unsupported by his writings, which make no mention of the Council of Nicaea (outside of a single, characteristically vague reference to a "synod" in *Haer.* 22.20). Furthermore, we should note that the canon of Nicaea against the celebration of the Pasch on 14 Nisan has not survived. It is referenced (albeit vaguely) in the first canon of the Council of Antioch of 341 (*Canons of the Council of Antioch*, Canon 1), in a citation of an edict of Constantine (Eusebius, *Vita Constantini* 3.17–20), and in the purported synodal letter of Nicaea preserved by Socrates (*HE* 1.6) and Theodoret (*HE* 1.9). Given the paucity of direct evidence for this conciliar decree, it seems best to adopt an agnostic position on its influence and implementation at the time. Cf. Rouwhorst, *Les hymnes pascales*, vol. 1, 195–203; idem, "Jewish Liturgical Traditions in Early Syriac Christianity," *Vigiliae Christianae* 51, no. 1 (1997): 72–93, 82; Jeffrey T. Wickes, trans., St. Ephrem the Syrian, *The Hymns on Faith*, Fathers of the Church 130 (Washington, DC: The Catholic University of America Press, 2015), 20–22.

> and types were fulfilled,
> just as he concluded:
> > "Behold, everything is finished!"

Ephrem transforms Jesus's dying cry—"it is finished" (*mšallam*)—into an affirmation of the "fulfillment" (*'eštamli*) of the "types" and "symbols." Supplementing the quotation of Jesus with the added word *kul* ("all"), he stresses the totality of that fulfillment.[121]

These poems often go to great lengths to uncover "symbols" or "types" within the events of the Passion narratives that attest to the condemnation and shame of the Jews for their role in those events. In the effort to read the narratives in this fashion, Ephrem even reads Gentile characters as Jewish, creating a consistent target to blame for the suffering and death of Jesus. This is the case in *Cruc.* 8, where Ephrem interprets the "reed" (*qanyā*) that the soldiers (identified in the gospel traditions as Pilate's soldiers) gave to Jesus as a scepter (Mt 27.29–30)[122] as a symbol of the rejection of the Jews by God. Playing on the common use of reeds as pens, for instance, Ephrem imagines Jesus using that reed to write out their official condemnation (8.3).[123] Again, in the face of their intention to shame Jesus, "he made them a broken reed (*qanyā r'iā*)" (8.4).

Anti-Judaism and Praxis Even in his vehement critiques of Jewish practices such as continuing to celebrate the Passover away from Jerusalem, Ephrem often frames his approach as an accusation of unfaithful reading on the part of Jews. In *Azym.* 21, for example, Ephrem alleges that the continued Jewish celebration of the Passover violates the law of Moses:

> [*Azym.* 21.1] As to the Pascha that was commanded
> > to take place in purity,
> > look, the one who eats from it
> > > is a prostitute.

---

121. The P text reads simply *hā mšallam* ("behold, it is finished").

122. There are two incidents involving a reed (*qanyā*) in the Gospel Passion narratives: one in which the soldiers mockingly give Jesus a reed to hold as his scepter along with the crown of thorns (Mt 27.30; Mk 15.19) and the other in which the guards offer vinegar to Jesus on a sponge attached to a reed (Mt 27.48).

123. For a similar interpretive move, cf. Romanos's *kontakia* "On Peter's Denial" (18.7) and "On the Passion of Christ" (20.22). See Krueger, *Writing and Holiness*, 160–61.

[2] The feast that was commanded
   to take place in Zion;
behold, it takes place everywhere
   like nothing at all.
[3] For Moses
   did not permit the people
to celebrate their feast
   wherever they happened to be.

Ephrem continues to develop this argument that the continued Passover celebration defies the biblical commands—a well-known early Christian critique of the Passover—for the remainder of the poem.[124] This sort of bitter anti-Jewish polemic in the Paschal cycles thus fits within a broader theological context. Ephrem reads the Exodus narratives and the instructions for the Passover in light of their Christological fulfillment. Ephrem's attempts to delegitimize Jewish praxis for his audience are not purely symbolic or theological, however. Especially in *Azym.* 18, 19, and 21, Ephrem seems particularly focused on discouraging Christian participation in Jewish festivals. The practice of celebrating the Passover, he argues, ignores the symbolic meaning of the Passover meal.

Azym. 19 warns its audience in quite vivid and shocking language that the unleavened bread of the Passover is "the poison of death" (19.24). He warns his listeners that "the evil people / who desire our death / enticingly offer us / death by food" (19.5). He urges them to "flee … from the unleavened bread / because stench dwells / within its purity" (19.12). As the poem moves toward its crescendo in stanzas 16 through 21, Ephrem argues that the source of the impurity and death in the unleavened bread lies in the fact that those who bake it have their hands stained with the blood of Jesus and the prophets.

It seems clear that through this vehement challenge to the Jewish Passover and its rituals, Ephrem aims to construct firm barriers between Jewish and Christian identities and practices, as Shepardson has argued.[125] If Shepardson is correct, the implication is

---

124. For a detailed examination of this line of argument in the writings of Ephrem, Aphrahat, and John Chrysostom, see Christine Shepardson, "Paschal Politics: Deploying the Temple's Destruction against Fourth-Century Judaizers," *Vigiliae Christianae* 62 (2008): 233–60, especially 250–58.

125. See, e.g., Shepardson, *Anti-Judaism and Christian Orthodoxy*, 31.

that the Passover/Pascha celebrations of Jews and Christians in fourth-century northern Mesopotamia overlapped in many ways. In this instance more than any other, Ephrem's symbolic imagination in which Jews play primarily a villainous role—calf worshipers and "crucifiers"—collides with praxis. Ephrem struggles to make those bright lines between Judaism and Christianity—so vibrant in his theological vision of the world—applicable to his audience.

Notes on Translation

Although translation is necessary to promote scholarship and to make works of the past available to the interested public, it is always problematic, especially when rendering poetry. Ephrem's original Syriac poetry, with its often-complex meters and allusive, polyvalent use of language, is notoriously difficult in this respect. Ephrem seems to take particular delight in wordplay, homophony, and making subtle references to the Syriac biblical tradition. As translators, we cannot hope to convey perfectly the depth and richness of these features of the original poems.

Recognizing the inherent limitations of translation, we have pursued a middle ground between a literal and a more interpretive approach. Through discussion and mutual editing, we have also worked toward a generally coherent style so that our distinct approaches to translation will complement and reinforce one another. Each of the three translators brings a different (although complementary) approach to the task of translation. We believe that our different perspectives and approaches provide the reader with greater insight into the multifaceted nature of Ephrem's poetry than a translation produced by a single scholar. The difficult work of translation has occasionally necessitated minor divergences from the original sense of the Syriac text (such as adding words in English translation or combining two equivalent Syriac terms). In such instances, we have indicated these changes with footnotes.

For the Syriac text behind this translation, we have primarily followed Edmund Beck's published critical editions. In cases where more than one manuscript exists and we chose to follow an alternative reading, we have noted any divergence from the text of the critical edition in the footnotes.

Editorial Notes

Transliteration Conventions

The Syriac text that comprises our source text is consonantal and unvocalized, with the exception of occasional diacritics. This means that it is at times necessary to disambiguate between various possible ways of vocalizing the text, and at other times it is necessary to refer to the word without vocalizing it.

When a given Syriac word is described according to a specific vocalization, it is transliterated using the Latin script in italic type. When a Syriac word is described while suspending judgment about the vocalization, or when there is no vocalization, such as acrostic sequences, the Syriac script is used.

In the case of proper names and place names, the most common forms in the target language are used instead of transliteration, for example, "Jesus" (not "'Išoʿ").

The objective of our transliteration scheme is not to reconstruct the spoken form of the Syriac language at any given place or time, but rather to represent the written form of the Syriac text as clearly as possible, so that scholars working with the material will be able to understand and work with the material at hand without any unnecessary confusion.

For this reason, we do not distinguish between aspirated and unaspirated letters for the consonants ܒܓܕܟܦܬ = *bgdkpt*.

Nor do we indicate when a letter, written once, is doubled in certain pronunciations, for example, ܪܒܐ = *rabā* (not *rabbā*), and ܩܛܠ = *qatel* (not *qattel*).

Quiescent written consonants are placed in parentheses to indicate that they are unpronounced, for example, ܐܢܬܝ = *a(n)t(y)* (not *anty*).

Conjunctions and prepositions that are prefixed to words are joined by hyphenation, for example, ܘܠܕܒܟܬܒܐ = *wa-l-da-b-ktābā* (not *waldabktābā*).

The consonantal *ālap* (ʾ) is indicated when it has consonantal value in the middle of words but not at the beginnings and ends of words, for example, ܐܡܐ = *amā* (not *ʾamāʾ*).

The consonants *waw* (w) and *yod* (y) are not transliterated unless they have consonantal value, including the diphthongs -*ay*- and

-*iw*-, for example, ܟܘܪܣܝ = *kursay* (not *kursai*), and ܫܪܝܘ = *šariw* (not *šariu*).

The Syriac consonants are transliterated using the following characters:

ܐ	→ ʾ	ܠ	→ l
ܒ	→ b	ܡ	→ m
ܓ	→ g	ܢ	→ n
ܕ	→ d	ܣ	→ s
ܗ	→ h	ܥ	→ ʿ
ܘ	→ w	ܦ	→ p
ܙ	→ z	ܨ	→ ṣ
ܚ	→ ḥ	ܩ	→ q
ܛ	→ ṭ	ܪ	→ r
ܝ	→ y	ܫ	→ š
ܟ	→ k	ܬ	→ t

The Syriac vowels are transliterated according to classical East Syriac conventions as follows:

ܳܐ	→ *do*	ܶܐ	→ *de*
ܽܐ	→ *du*	ܺܐ / ܶܐܐ	→ *dā*
ܻܐ	→ *di*	ܰܐ	→ *da*
ܶܐ / ܻܐ	→ *dē*		

Capitalization and Spelling Conventions

Since there is no distinction between upper and lower case in the source language, to introduce such a distinction in the target language would restrict the meaning of the text, especially in the ubiquitous instances of polysemy and symbolic expression in our source text.[126] Ideally, an English translation in a script that does not have a distinction between cases, such as an uncial script, would be the most accurate way to represent this aspect of the source language.

The requirements of current English usage, however, constrain

---

126. For example, if one were to capitalize such words as "Evil" or "Greed," the capitalization introduces personification in English, while in Syriac, personification is not necessarily conveyed. This can lead to problems in maintaining consistency, since not every instance of "evil" or "greed" reads well as a personification. Please see the subsection entitled "Personifications" below.

us to use certain capitalized words, for instance, place names and personal names. Beyond such cases, it is our aim to keep the distinction between upper and lower case to a minimum in the target text. This task becomes especially tricky when working with divine names and personifications in particular. Below is a summary of our rationale for imposing capitalization on certain divine names and personifications.

Divine Names   Pronouns often refer both to God and to the symbol: lowercase tends to retain the significance of both senses, for example, "he," "his," "him," "you," "who," etc., can refer to both the symbol and God, while the uppercase pronouns cut off the meaning of the symbol.

Divine names often overlap with symbols: again, lowercase tends to be more meaningful for both senses. For example, "firstborn" works on two levels: the firstborn of Egypt and the firstborn who is Christ; but "Firstborn" tends to denote the latter only.

We capitalize the bare minimum of divine names as required by common stylistic conventions, for example: "Holy Spirit" and "Elohim."

We always lowercase attributions and epithets, because these abound in our text, and if we capitalize one, we would be compelled to capitalize many for the sake of consistency, leading to much unnecessary distinction between upper and lower case, for example: "the true lamb" and "power."

Personifications   Substantives often switch back and forth between personifications and abstractions, for example: "Evil" when it is functioning as a clear personification and disambiguation is necessary to make sense of the passage, but "evil" when it can function either as an abstraction or a personification, and no disambiguation is needed in the context.

With a few exceptions, substantives qualified by definite articles are in lowercase, because the definite article functions in English to set them apart from the generic sense, and there is no reason to introduce further distinction. For example, "the people" is clearly referring not just to any people, but to the one people of Israel as "the people" that is continually invoked, and the context makes it unmistakable. And "the snake" refers not just to any snake, but to the snake who tempted Eve, as the context makes clear.

Stanzaic Structure and Layout

For Ephrem, symbols were a vital means of communication and the primary medium of his art form. This is especially evident in his use of numbers in constructing a wide range of innovative stanzaic structures and meters that are associated with his *qālē*, or "meter-melodies," ranging from simple couplets to intricate, multifaceted stanzas. His poetry was not merely in words, but in numbers as well.

Some of these stanzaic structures and meters are so complicated that they have vexed scholars through the centuries. In certain cases, the editor of the twentieth-century critical edition of Ephrem's corpus, Dom Edmund Beck, even marked such *qālē* as *"unklar,"* as if throwing up his hands in despair. A few of these very stanzaic structures are used in the *madrāšē* translated in this book, and the burden has fallen to us hapless translator-editors to try once more to make some sense out of them.

To make matters even more complicated, there are often several ways to divide the stanzas into larger or smaller units, due to factors and multiples. For such cases as these, there is no single "right way" to divide the stanzas. Yet it has been common practice in editions of Ephrem's work to indicate the *qālā* with a single "meter."

Fortunately, there was one translator-editor among us who took upon himself the abstruse task of counting syllables and looking for patterns. This task developed into a working method that falsified various hypotheses until some working patterns emerged, and in the best-case scenarios, they passed the criterion of *reproducibility*. That is, a proposed stanzaic scheme is reproducible only if the same method is applied to any given unseen stanza in the same *qālā*, and the same sense divisions obtain.

There are, to be certain, cases where the schemes proposed in this book do not perfectly fit in a given stanza. Anomalies generally fall into one of two categories: (1) a clear departure from the usual sense divisions and/or rhythm in an artful manner that appears to be intentional; and (2) minor discrepancies, usually no more or less than one or two syllables when vocalized according to standard Classical Syriac grammar rules.

In the first category, the poet may have been artfully breaking the rule for the sake of contrast, or for some other effect. This can be observed, for example, in the occasional deviation from the usual pattern of three dyadic lines to two triadic lines (for example, the first and last stanzas of *Ieiun.* 1). Such exceptions to the general pattern are noted in the footnotes.

In this second category, a line may be too short or too long by a syllable or two, and the manuscripts do not indicate whether to add or to subtract a vowel from its usual place. In many cases, it was possible to resolve such discrepancies with recourse to the "poetic licenses" enumerated in the Appendix on Prosody in Arayathinal's monumental *Aramaic Grammar,* but in other cases, these rules failed to describe the phenomena at hand. It is clear that much more work needs to be done on this subject.

The result of this work appears at the beginning of every teaching song translated in this book. It must be emphasized that these proposed stanzaic structures are one way, but not the only way, of breaking down stanzas into larger or smaller units or sense divisions. We hope that future researchers will continue to build on this work and find new ways of dividing the same stanzas, which can reveal more of the intricate mathematical poetry that Ephrem was building.

The following conventions apply to the proposed stanzaic schemes:

Within a given stanza, the largest divisions may be indicated by a hard return. In a stanza that adds up to sixty-eight syllables, for instance, it is common to see two, three, or four main parts.

The next-largest divisions within each of these parts are indicated with a space, followed by a plus sign, followed by a space (" + ") between the clusters of numbers. For example, the spaces between the following two clusters of numbers indicate this kind of division: "6+4+4 + 6+4."

Beyond these divisions are even smaller units, joined by a plus sign with no spaces ("+"), for example, "5+7."

The smallest possible irreducible units of sense divisions are not always indicated. Despite the necessary imperfections of this system, we hope it will convey some sense of how the whole relates to the parts, and vice versa.

The layout of our translations, including line divisions and spaces, are partly informed by our understanding of these stanzaic structures. On the whole, the layout of the translated stanzas follows one of the possible ways to divide the Syriac stanzas. It is possible to lay out lines longer or shorter, depending on whether we are observing the larger or shorter units of sense division.

As a general rule, we avoided letting the lines run over the width of the page, because this interrupts the flow and rhythm of the translations in unforeseen ways. In addition, a layout that looks more like what is associated with poetry may stand a better chance of being read as poetry and not merely plundered for information.

TEACHING SONGS ON THE HOLY FAST

Translated by
JOSHUA FALCONER

ON THE HOLY FAST 1

To the melody: "This is the
Firstborn's Fast"[1]
6+5+5 + 5+5+6
+ 4+4 + 5+5 + 5+7 (or 7+5)
+ 6+6+4 + R: 6+6+4[2]

Refrain:
Blessed is the king who adorns
his holy church with fasting,
prayer, and vigil.

I
This is the firstborn's fast,
the first of his deeds;[3]
let's revel in its advent:[4]

---

1. *This is the Firstborn's Fast.* This *qālā* title appears as *hānaw sawmeh d-bukrā*, "This is the Firstborn's Fast," as the first *qālā* listed in the volume on the fast, according to Sinai Syr. 10, f. 167r. The title is identical to the first words in the first stanza of this *madrāšā*. Beck's edition was published before he became aware of Sinai Syr. 10 and had supplemented the *qālā* title from BL Add MS 14,506 (Beck's MS J[a], a liturgical collection that Wright dates to approximately the 9th or 10th century) as *hānaw nisan bribā* (*sic:* read *brikā*), "This is the blessed April."

2. The stanzaic structure shows exceptions to the general pattern in the first and last stanzas of this *madrāšā*, where the usual dyadic lines 4+4 + 5+5 + 5+7 (or 7+5) turn into triadic lines 4+4+5 + 5+5+7 (or 5+7+5), on the basis of the sense divisions.

3. *the first of his deeds.* Cf. Mt 4.1–11.

4. *let's revel in its advent.* Or, "his advent." Cf. *Ieiun.* 7.1. References to *Ieiun.* pertain to the Teaching Songs on the Holy Fast here in this section of the book; see list of abbreviations in the front matter.

for by fasting, he prevailed,
 though he was able
  to prevail by all means.
He showed to us
 the power veiled
  in the fast, conquering all,
whereby one conquers
 that one who by fruit
  conquered Adam and devoured him.
Blessed is the firstborn who compassed
 our weakness with the wall
  of his great fast.

2

This is the raising fast,
 that dawned from the firstborn
  to raise up the least:[5]
the fast gives rise to
 delight for the prudent one,[6]
  when he sees how he's grown.
Secret fasting
 purges a life[7]
that she might see God
 and grow in his sight,
for earth's heaviness inclines
 her unto the ground.
Blessed is he who gave us
 the fasts, clear wings by which
  we soar toward him.[8]

---

5. *the least*. Cf. Mt 25.45. The same word for "the least ones" (*z'orē*) appears in both P and S.

6. *the prudent one*. Beck's edition marks this word as plural, but the syntax and context suggest a singular reading: *pārošā*, "prudent, discerning, distinguished one." This would account for the singular masculine subject in the clause that follows it.

7. *a life*. Or, "the soul." This is the antecedent of the pronoun "she" in the following line.

8. *soar*. This word also carries connotations of rising, growing, and blossoming, in harmony with the imagery of this stanza.

3

The fast is meet and bright
  for one who's purified
    to be clear with God:[9]
no turbid one who's
  disturbed by anything
    can look at that clear one.[10]
One who acquires
  an unclouded eye[11]
can look at him as much
  as he's allowed to look:
instead of straining wines,
  let us strain the mind,
so we might see the clear one
  who by fasting conquered Evil,
    that perturber.

4

Here's the fast whereby Greed
  disgorged the peoples
    atop the mountain:[12]
one clad in fasts conquered
  Greed, who was covered
    with the food of Adam's house.[13]

9. *to be clear with God.* This reading follows the vocalization *dneḥwar*, "to be clear (of sin)," "to be white (like light)," followed by "with God" or "through God." Another vocalization suggested by the context is *da-nḥor*, "to look upon." The Syriac idiom denotes not only looking upon God but also being attentive to and mindful of him.

10. *clear one.* The word rendered here as "clear one" (with reference to God and perhaps to the purified faster as well) can be vocalized as *šāpyā*, "thorn," "hindrance," "stumbling block" (for which cf. *Ieiun.* 6.8) and also *šapyā*, "strained, filtered one." The wordplay draws an association between the straining of wine and wine as a stumbling block, in that it clouds one's vision, in contrast to the one who strains his mind and obtains an unclouded eye.

11. *an unclouded eye.* Or, "a limpid eye," "a clear eye."

12. *the peoples … the mountain.* This stanza uses some of the same wording found in P Is 2.2, including *'ammē*, "peoples," "Gentiles," "nations," and *b-riš ṭurā*, "on the mountaintop." Cf. Gn 22.1–19, 1 Chr 21.18–30, 2 Sm 24.18–25, Jn 19.17 et par.

13. *covered / with the food of Adam's house.* In this visceral and grotesque image, a contrast is made between the one who was outfitted with the honorable armor of the fast, and, in opposition, the revolting personification of Greed, who was covered with

The victors' chief
  gave us his arms,[14]
and was raised on high
  to be a lookout:[15]
who would not rush toward the arms
  by which God prevailed?
A shame, my brothers, to fail
  by the arms that conquered
    and saved the whole world.[16]

5

Let us purge our mind's eye
  so the concealed foe[17]
    sees that we see him:[18]
when he sees those who
  have never seen him,
    then he can steal from them.
When a life falls
  down in fasting,
the Fast raises her,[19]
  and gives her his friend[s]:[20]

"the food of Adam's house," i.e., the peoples whom he had devoured and shamefully vomited all over himself on the mountaintop.

14. *arms.* This word, *zaynā*, rendered twice in this stanza as "arms," is a homograph of *zayānā*, "provision," "sustenance."

15. *to be a lookout.* Lit. "so that he might be a seer." The meter requires the vocalization *ḥazāyā*, "seer," "watcher," "lookout."

16. *A shame ... whole world.* Lit. "It is a shame, my brothers, for us to suffer defeat (or, be found guilty) by means of the arms (or, in the armor) that overcame (or, cleared of blame) and granted victory to (or, redressed) all of creation." Cf. *Ieiun.* 4.5.

17. *foe.* Or "the adversary," "the enemy," that is, "Satan."

18. *Let us purge ... see him.* On the image of polishing a metal surface until it shines and its comparison to the mind, see Brock, *The Luminous Eye,* 73–79.

19. *When a life falls / down in fasting.* This reading follows the vocalization *mā da-nplat lāh napšā b-ṣawmā,* which in addition to the reading above can also mean "when a life falls into the fast," or in other words, "when a life begins the fast." An alternative vocalization is *mā d-naplat lāh napšā b-ṣawmā,* "when a life casts herself into the fast."

20. *friend[s].* For this word, ܚܒܪܗ, the syntax and meter apparently require a collective noun here, i.e., "company," rendered above as "friend[s]" (see the following note). This is in spite of the fact that the plural form of the word for "friend," *ḥabraw(hy),* is

amidst their surges,[21]
    the secret eye is purged
        so it may see whence came
            the sharpened spears, hidden
                from the sighted.

6

This Fast is a trainer,
    teaching a fighter
        the ways of struggle:
come, grapple with him,[22]
    concentrate, and learn
        the decisive battle.
See him order us:

---

in fact not attested in the manuscript witnesses. Another vocalization, *ḥabārā*, would denote "dark pit." Cf. *Ieiun.* 3.6 for another example of a life that fell into a pit.

21. *their surges*. For this word, *gallayhon*, "their surges," "their waves," there is a near-homophone, *gelyāhon*, "their revelations," which relates to one of the principal themes of this stanza. There also appears to be a textual problem here: this word has a plural masculine pronominal suffix, but it is unclear what its antecedent could be. As Beck notes, the only marked plural masculine noun in this stanza is what comes after it, i.e., *girē šenīnē*, "the sharpened spears (or, arrows)." If this reading were followed, it would result in a reading that does not fit the context. That is, it does not seem to be the case that "waves of arrows" are what cleanse the eye. Beck's proposed correction is to emend the pronominal suffix to singular: *gallaw(hy)*, "its waves." This would address the grammatical problem, but the question of the referent remains. Beck thinks that the singular suffix would refer back to the fast. This, however, does not make much more sense either: what would be meant by "waves of the fast"? The "eye" is also out of the question because it is singular feminine. Another possibility is that no emendation to the text is necessary if we read ܥܕܒܗ as a collective noun meaning, "its company," or "group," a sense that is attested in other Aramaic dialects including JBA, JPA, and PTA. In this case, the masculine plural pronominal suffix would refer back to this collective noun in its plural sense: "their waves," i.e., the waves of the company of fasting. In context, what accompanies fasting could be interpreted as tears, for instance, whose waves or surges would be the means by which the hidden eye is purged. Or, keeping the refrain in mind, the companions of the fast could be prayer and vigil. The translation above follows the interpretation "company," rendered as "friend[s]" because it makes the most sense in context, in lieu of a more warranted alternative. Further lexicographical studies would be needed to verify other instances of ܥܕܒܬܐ in Syriac with the collective sense, "company" or "group." For similar syntactic precedents, see Aray. §92.3 and §303.6.

22. *come, grapple with him.* Lit. "draw near unto him/it," with connotations of drawing near in battle.

our mouth to fast
and our heart to fast,[23]
not to fast from food[24]
and brood on the thought
in which death's poison is hid.[25]
Give thanks in the fast to the firstborn
who gave us living speech
to ruminate.[26]

7

Let scriptures be for us
just like a mirror;
let's see our fast in them:
for they set apart
a fast from a fast,
and a prayer from a prayer.
They chose a fast
and spurned a fast;
some fasters made peace,
and some stirred up wrath;
there's a prayer of sin,
and one that's living medicine.
May our Lord have joy in our fast,[27]

---

23. *our mouth to fast / and our heart to fast.* Jl 2.12–13; cf. Mt 4.4.

24. *food.* In Semitic languages, cognates of the word rendered here as "food" (*l-ḥ-m*) tend to refer to the principal meal or staple food that is epichoric according to each dialect. So in Hebrew, *lachem* means "bread" because it is a staple, whereas in Arabic, *laḥm* refers to "meat," "flesh." For Aramaic *laḥmā*, "principal meal" or "staple food" is one possibility, and "bread" is another. Even though Ephrem does use this word to refer to "bread" in other contexts, such as the eucharistic bread, it seems unlikely that he was referring to mere "bread" as that from which one fasted in cases such as this. It is more likely that the custom of the fast was to refrain from the staple food, such as meat. For a clear example of *laḥmā* referring to a staple food such as meat, in contrast to the vegetarian diet of Daniel and his companions, see *Ieiun.* 7.9.

25. *in which death's poison is hid.* The Syriac term for "poison" is *sam*, which means "medicine" or "drug" in other contexts and is also a near-homophone with *ṣawm*, "a fast." For other examples of this comparison, see *Azym.* 18.15–16; 19.22, 24.

26. *to ruminate.* Lit. "so that we may meditate upon it."

27. *May our Lord have joy in our fast.* Cf. Mt 6.16. It is also possible to read the Syriac text as follows: "May we rejoice in our fast, my Lord …"

as he had joy, my brothers,
  in his own fast.

8

Untainted was the fast
  for the holy one who[28]
    came down and won by it;
another prepares
  a mixture for the fast
    to be tainted when pure.
Consider nature:
  if desirable
fruits inside something
  putrid are spoiled,
they repulse our mind,
  though they be washed many times.
Blessed is the pure one who received
  the fruits that all penitents[29]
    scrubbed and gave him.

9

The turbid one mixes dregs
  with our clearness to make
    our firstfruits hateful:
our prayer and fasting
  he soils with his envy
    that our offering be shameful.[30]

---

28. *Untainted was the fast / for the holy one.* The text appears to use a type-B construction of the "tautological infinitive"; see Gideon Goldenberg, "Tautological Infinitive," in *Studies in Semitic Linguistics: Selected Writings of Gideon Goldenberg* (Jerusalem: Magnes Press, Hebrew University, 1998), 66–115, especially 85, §18: *law gēr meṭmā ṭmā leh / ṣawmā l-qadišā*, lit. "For it was not defiling (that) the fast was defiled for the holy one ..." The theme in the previous stanza indicates that there are different kinds of fasts, both good and bad, and thus the fast can be said to be "impure," yet to the holy one it was not impure.

29. *penitents.* Or "apostates," "backsliders."

30. *offering.* This word, *qurbān*, is the same word used in P Mt 15.5 et par., in describing the hypocritical ritual offering made by the scribes and the Pharisees, apparently to avoid giving financial support to their mothers and their fathers and thus violating the fifth commandment.

Clear your ruses
> out of your fasts,
flung away your taunts
> out of your praises:
let your voices cleanse
> your mouths from duplicity.
Firstborn, grant us the grace
> to root out the hidden
>> weeds from our mind.[31]

10

Simple ones, rely not
> on that deceiver
>> who steals from fasters:
for someone he sees
> abstaining from food,
>> he sates him with anger.[32]
To one he sees
> standing in prayer,
he proffers some thought
> in place of another:[33]
he pilfers and takes from his mouth
> the prayer of his mouth.
Our Lord, grant us an eye
> to see how he snatches
>> the truth by fraud.

---

31. *Firstborn ... mind.* Lit. "Firstborn, grant us with favor (or, mercy) so that we may prune the hidden briars from our mind." This word, "thorny tangle," "briars," "thicket," "weeds," is often used in association with sin, debt, and error.

32. *food ... anger.* There is an association between the words for "food" and "anger" by their similar appearance and sound. ܠܚܡܐ as *laḥmā*, "food," "bread," "principal meal" (the cognate in Arabic, *laḥm*, means, "flesh," "meat"), can be alternatively vocalized as *lāḥmā*, "threatening," "menacing," or *lḥāmā*, "torture," both of which derive from the verbal root *l-ḥ-m*. See note 24 above.

33. *he proffers some thought / in place of another.* Lit. "he hands over (or, extends) something in his thought in place of another thing."

11

Gather in the fast, brothers,
 let's dwell and marvel
  how evil is Evil!
Giving and taking,
 he ruins us by what's his
  and richens not by what's ours.
The truth he steals
 does not suit him,
and the fraud he gives
 to us is stillborn:
like his peer the whore,[34]
 what's not ours is neither his.[35]
Lord, judge between us and him:
 through you, Solomon judged
  between the whores.[36]

12

Let's follow Truth's traces
 in fasting, traveling
  the path of mansions:[37]
the one-eyed people,[38]
 with hubris and astray,[39]
  hurtled through their fast day.

---

34. *the whore.* P 1 Kgs 3.16.

35. *what's not ours is neither his.* This passage compares Evil to the one prostitute who stole the living son of the other prostitute and replaced him with her own dead son in 1 Kgs 3.16–28.

36. *through you, Solomon judged / between the whores.* Lit. "for it was through you that Solomon had judged between the harlots."

37. *the path of mansions.* The same words *urḥā*, "path," and *awānē*, "mansions," appear in the Syriac versions of Jn 14.2–4, and the latter carries the association of heavenly dwellings. Cf. *Ieiun.* 4.11.

38. *the one-eyed people.* I.e., "blind in one eye" or simply "blind," although this is not the usual term for the latter. For other instances of the same expression, cf. *Ieiun.* 5.7–8, 5.10, 6.4. In all of these cases, the context suggests that partial blindness is meant, and especially blindness to spiritual mysteries, in the same vein as Mt 13.10–17 et par.

39. *astray.* Or, "in a trackless waste," in the sense that they had lost the tracks of Truth.

Fasts on their mouths,
   idols in their hearts,[40]
prayers on their lips,
   kismet in their minds:[41]
their bellies bereft
   of food but stuffed with perfidy.[42]
They plunge their hands each day,[43]
   but blood concealed in them
      bellows against them.[44]

13

Happy is he who travailed,[45]
   prevailed, and whose head
      was extolled in his crown,
and, mouth wide open
   like a creditor,
      claimed his pay, unlike me,
who's too frail to fast,
   wretched to keep watch,[46]
      and first to owe debt.
My foe is adept—
   when he beat me, he let me rise
      to hurl me back down.
Mercies' sea, grant me a palm
   of mercies to blot out
      my deed of debts.[47]

---

40. *idols.* Lit. "an idol," or in so-called magical texts, "a demon."

41. *kismet.* This term is *qeṣmā*, "divination," "omen," or "distribution by lots." All of these senses are connected to the idea of fate or destiny.

42. *stuffed with perfidy.* Similar language appears in the Syriac versions of Mt 23.25–27 et par.

43. *plunge.* I.e., "immerse," as in ritual cleansing. It is the same word for "baptize," used here with manifest irony. The same verbal root appears in S and P Mk 7.4. Cf. Mt 15.1–20 et par.

44. *blood.* Cf. *Cruc.* 4.7–8.

45. *travailed.* Lit. "persevered and withstood opposition with fortitude."

46. *to keep watch.* I.e., to keep vigil.

47. *mercies' sea ... of debts.* Lit. "Sea of mercies, grant me a palmful of mercies so that I might blot out the deed of my debts." This is an allusion to Col 2.14 (including some terminology in common with P), a passage that Ephrem frequently echoes (e.g., *Cruc.* 9.2; *Virg.* 46.10–14, 19; *Eccl.* 32.2, 79.23; *Dom.* 12.26; *Pub.* 24).

ON THE HOLY FAST 2

To the same melody
6+5+5 + 5+5+6
+ 4+4 + 5+5 + 5+7 (or 7+5)
+ 6+6+4 + R: 6+6+4

Refrain:
Blessed is the firstborn who gave us
 the fast to dry the spring
  of the passions.

I

He made that Isaiah[1]
 an eloquent herald
  to chew out the fasters,[2]
he shouted and cried:[3]
 the ear, though shut fast,[4]
  is open to silver's voice.
Keep not the fast,
 swallowing the orphan;
wear no sackcloth,
 stripping the widow;

---

1. *He.* The masculine subject is most likely the firstborn, mentioned in the refrain immediately prior to the first stanza.
2. *to chew out.* This verb, *d-nekas* (prefix conjugation from *k-s-s*), means both "to chew" or "break into pieces," and, "to blame," "put to shame." The English idiom (mainly in N. American usage), "to chew out," captures both meanings of this verb.
3. *he shouted and cried.* Cf. Is 58.1.
4. *the ear, though shut fast.* Cf. Is 6.9–10; Prv 21.13.

incline not your neck,
   subjecting the free to the yoke.[5]
A grievous, oppressive fast
   reveals the idols veiled
      in its oppression.

2

Even Cain adorned his
   daughters like blossoms
      for Elohim's sons:[6]
as it is written,
   Cain's two sons invented
      singing and blacksmithing.[7]
Tubal-Cain cast
   lovely cymbals;[8]
Jubal constructed
   beautiful lyres:[9]

---

5. *subjecting the free to the yoke.* Cf. Is 58.5–6.

6. *Elohim's sons.* On the sons of Elohim, cf. Gn 6.1–4. According to the *Comm. Gen.* attributed to Ephrem, the identification of the sons of Elohim with angels or spirits is rejected, while their identification as the sons of Seth is affirmed (*Comm. Gen.* 6.3, *Nis.* 1.4). Cf. *Nat.* 1.48, *Fid.* 46.9, *Haer.* 19.1–8. See the discussion in T. Kronholm, *Motifs from Genesis 1–11 in the Genuine Hymns of Ephrem the Syrian with Particular Reference to the Influence of Jewish Exegetical Tradition,* Coniectanea Biblica Old Testament Series 11 (Lund: Gleerup, 1978), 166–68.

7. *singing and blacksmithing.* The term *qinātā*, "singing," "chanting" (pl.), is similar to *qaynnātā*, "forged metals," and is listed before *ḥešltā*, "forging," "casting." As for blacksmithing, the same tradition appears in later sources, including *The Book of the Bee,* ed. E. A. Wallis Budge (Oxford: Clarendon Press, 1886), ch. 19.

8. *cymbals.* Cf. Gn 4.21–22; *Comm. Gen.* 4.1. The Peshitta version states that Tubal-Cain was "an artisan who worked all manner of bronze and iron," but cymbals are nowhere mentioned in any version of Genesis. The tradition that Tubal-Cain forged cymbals is attested in later sources including *The Cave of Treasures* (ed. Su-Min Ri, *La Caverne des Trésors: Les deux recensions syriaques,* CSCO 486–487, Syr. 207–208, vol. 486 [Leuven: Peeters, 1987], 34); and *The History of al-Ṭabarī* (ed. F. Rosenthal, vol. 1 [New York: SUNY Press, 1989], 338).

9. *lyres.* This term is *kenārē*, "kinnors" (Heb. *kinnor*), also known as lyres or kitharas (Gk. *kithāra*). On the motifs of the cymbals and lyres in both this text and *The Cave of Treasures,* see the discussion in Kronholm, *Motifs,* 169 n. 3, and Su-Min Ri, "La Caverne des Trésors et Mar Éphrem," *Symposium Syriacum VII: Uppsala University, Department of Asian and African Languages, 11–14 August 1996,* ed. René Lavenant, Orientalia Christiana Analecta 256 (Rome: Pontificio Istituto Orientale, 1998), 71–83, especially 76.

the left hand playing
   led captive those on the right.
Seth's sons transgressed and fell
   and ruined their great name
      with the daughters of man.

3

Who could put Sin into
   words: how much she is
      and what she is like?
She mauled the people
   of myriad mouths,[10]
      acrid and murderous.
She spurned the beasts
   of the gorges,[11]
the same animals
   of Daniel's vision:
for by them she rendered
   the breach of heathendom vast.
To the four quarters she turns,[12]
   sparing the height alone
      her ravages.[13]

10. *myriad mouths.* This reading follows the vocalization *d-rebo,* "of ten thousand," "a myriad," answering the question just mentioned in this stanza, i.e., "how many?" Cf. the number *rebo rebon,* "ten thousand times ten thousand," in Dn 7.10 (Dn 7 is referenced later in this stanza).

11. *the beasts / of the gorges.* Lit. "the beasts of the valleys / were disdained by her," following the feminine plural passive absolute participle vocalization *šiṭān* (Aray. §90). Also possible is the active *šayṭān:* "The beasts of the gorges despised her." The rhetorical thrust appears to be something to the following effect: it is the personification of Sin that held the beasts in contempt, in the sense that the monstrosity of Sin is so immense that she looked down on and despised even the apocalyptic beasts of Daniel's vision. The referent for the word for "gorges" (*neḥlē,* "torrents," "valleys") is unclear. Perhaps it alludes to the sea from which the four beasts emerged after the four winds stirred it up in Dn 7.1–8.

12. *the four quarters.* The trope of the four quarters of the earth appears throughout scripture. Cf. the four winds in Dn 7.2.

13. *sparing the height alone / her ravages.* Lit. "it is the height alone that is spared from her damages." Mt 24.15–17 warns of the sign of the abomination of desolation spoken by Daniel and enjoins those in Judea to flee to the mountains or to remain on the rooftops.

4

One, he made himself light[14]
   and won in the contest
      a brilliant victory,[15]
but gloomy, she grieved,
   seeing him spotless:[16]
      her grime did not reach him.
Some in her claws,[17]
   some in her fangs,[18]
the breath from her mouth
   reaches all bodies:
the light one dwelt in and bore
   the weight upon him.[19]
Blessed is he who wore Adam,
   leapt and led him with the tree
      into paradise.

---

14. *One, he made himself light.* Lit. "He is one who lightened his person (*qnomeh*)." The number "one" stands in contrast to the countless broken pieces left by Sin in the context of the previous stanza.

15. *victory.* This term, *zākotā*, "victory," can also mean "innocence," a significant theme in this stanza.

16. *seeing him spotless.* Lit. "since she saw that he was kept from defilement."

17. *her claws.* This term, *teprēh*, "her claws, talons," is the same word used to describe the claws of the fourth beast in both the Aramaic and the Syriac versions of Dn 7.19.

18. *her fangs.* Or, "her tusks." While this exact term (*nibēh*) does not appear in the Aramaic or Syriac versions of Daniel, this passage evokes the "teeth" (*šenēh*) and/or "ribs" (*'el'ēn*) in the mouth of the second beast described in Dn 7.5, in order to portray the personification of sin. According to the *Commentary on Daniel* attributed to Ephrem, "The three ribs that [Daniel] said were in [the second beast's] mouth and between its teeth are the nations (*'ammē*) of the Medes, the Persians, and the Babylonians" (Vat. sir. 103 f. 185r).

19. *weight.* The term "weight" is the rendering for *yaqirā*, "that which is heavy, honored, or glorious."

ON THE HOLY FAST 3

To the same melody
6+5+5 + 5+5+6
+ 4+4 + 5+5 + 5+7 (or 7+5)
+ 6+6+4 + [R: 6+6+4][1]

1

Who has looked out and seen
 both Adam and Eve
  and the crafty snake,
as guile in his heart
 and peace on his lips
  pours forth and beguiles?[2]
Adam is simple,
 Eve is innocent,
the tree blossoming,
 the fruit glistening:
the offense is immense,
 yet justice blooms and is mighty.
Blessed is he who mixed a torrent
 of mercies with his just law
  and spared the guilty.

2

Who can stand to look at
 the honorable couple
  suddenly disrobed?

---

1. The refrain (*'onitā*), usually present in this *qālā*, is missing from the extant MSS.
2. *pours forth*. This verb carries connotations of bloodshed.

Evil stood himself up,
   a glad onlooker;
      Good looked at and watched him.[3]
Who can stand to
   look at Adam
without shedding tears,
   the great one abased,
the chaste one, fastening leaves
   to cover his disgrace?
Blessed is he who spared him leaves,[4]
   and sent a glorious robe[5]
      for his nakedness.[6]

3

Who can shed light upon[7]
   that tree which dazzled[8]
      inquisitive ones?

---

3. *Good looked at and watched him.* This stanza alludes to the tree of the knowledge of good and evil, as described in Gn 2.17 and Gn 3. When Adam and Eve partook of its fruit, their eyes were opened, and they could see their nakedness. In Ephrem's imaginative retelling of this narrative, the eyes of the personifications of Good and Evil are opened, as they look upon Adam and Eve in contrasting ways. Evil arose (or woke up, *qām*), as though from sleep, while Good kept watch over him (*naṭreh*), as though vigilant. Moreover, Evil experiences schadenfreude at the spectacle of the once-honored pair and looks for an opportunity to exploit their weakness, while Good soberly guards them to prevent further misfortune.

4. *Blessed is he who spared him leaves.* Lit. "Blessed is he who had compassion on him with his leaves."

5. *a glorious robe.* On the "robe of glory," and its relation to the exegetical tradition of Genesis, see Sebastian Brock, "The Robe of Glory: A Biblical Image in the Syriac Tradition," *The Way* 39:3 (1999): 247–59. As Brock observes, the early Syriac exegetical tradition understood Gn 3.21 to mean that God had clothed Adam and Eve prior to the fall with garments of light rather than skin. According to the *Commentary on Genesis* (on Gn 2.25), when Adam and Eve ate of the forbidden fruit, they were stripped of their robes of glory, and then they were ashamed.

6. *his nakedness.* The "leaves" evoke the leaves Adam and Eve used to cover their nakedness in Gn 3.7, and the "splendid robe" apparently alludes to the original "robe of glory" prior to the fall in Gn 3.21. See Brock, "The Robe of Glory," 249.

7. *shed light upon.* Or, "interpret," "explain."

8. *dazzled.* Or "bewildered," "led astray," "caused to err."

The target is hidden,
    concealed from pupils,[9]
        and look, it strains archers.
Of knowledge it is,
    and of ignorance,[10]
and knowledge's cause,[11]
    by which mankind grasps
the gift that was lost,[12]
    the hard lesson that followed.[13]
Blessed is the fruit that mingled
    the tree of life's knowledge
        into mortals.

4

The snake looked out and saw
    a dove in paradise,[14]
        for whom he hungered:[15]
that venomous snake,[16]
    utterly accursed,
        acquired the dove's form.[17]
He was from her
    to make her his;[18]

---

9. *pupils.* Lit. "eyes," rendered here as "pupils" as part of a broader effort to compensate for polysemy and paronomasia that is lost in translation elsewhere.

10. *Of knowledge it is, / and of ignorance.* That is, it is not only the tree of knowledge of good and evil, but also of ignorance.

11. *and knowledge's cause.* Or, "and knowledge entered." This word, *'elat,* can be read as a verb, "entered," or a noun, "the cause of."

12. *the gift that was lost.* Lit. "what is the gift that was lost." The word for "lost" can also have connotations of loss of understanding, or going astray from knowledge.

13. *the hard lesson that followed.* Lit. "and the hard lesson that entered." The word rendered here as "hard lesson" (*marduta*) means "punishment," "discipline," and "instruction."

14. *The snake ... a dove.* The allusion appears to be to the serpent and Eve, respectively, in the narrative of Genesis.

15. *for whom he hungered.* Two syllables are missing from this line in Beck's edition.

16. *that venomous snake.* One syllable is missing from this line in Beck's edition.

17. *acquired the dove's form.* Lit. "transformed himself into a dove."

18. *He was from her / to make her his.* Lit. "He became from her, / so that she might become from him."

he dressed in her hue
  to clothe her in his loathing:
he sang a glad tune[19]
  to convulse her with mourning.
Blessed is the father's voice[20]
  that came down, soothing away[21]
    our mother's grief.

5

Let there be no delight
  for Evil when we bite
    our peers in our fast.
A fast they ordained,
  but Naboth they stoned:[22]
    Evil savored their fasts.
O fasters who
  instead of food
consumed a man's flesh
  and, fasting, lapped blood:
since they ate man-flesh,
  they became food for the dogs.
Blessed is he who gives his body
  to make our rabid mouth
    stop from biting.

6

Mercy looked out and saw
  a life in the pit,
    and strained to draw her out:

---

19. *a glad tune.* Or, "a passover song."

20. *the father's voice.* In this context, the "father" in this case could be associated not only with God the Father but also Adam, the father of humanity, who consoles Eve, the mother of humanity. In Ephrem's poetry, the voice of the Father is often associated with the Son.

21. *soothing away.* Lit. "consoling and causing her grief to pass over (or removing her grief)."

22. *Naboth.* The name "Naboth" (ܢܒܘܬ) is an eye rhyme with the verb "to bite" (ܢܟܬ). 1 Kgs 21.12–13.

when his nod could have[23]
   saved her, he bound fast
      his love and went to his work.
Putting on Humanity,[24]
   he attained his youth
to bring her to his mind;[25]
   with his lyre, he sang
his lowly songs to her
      that she might reach exaltation.
His cross raised him on high[26]
   to draw up Eve's offspring
      unto the heights.

23. *his nod.* This term refers to a gesture given by an authority to signal a command.

24. *Humanity.* In order to convey the overall sense of this stanza, it is necessary to emphasize that this feminine word functions as a feminine personification. The same is also true of the word translated as "a life" above. In this case, the personification of Mercy put on Humanity through Mary, in contrast to Eve in stanza 4 above.

25. *his mind.* The same word can also mean, "his knowledge."

26. *His cross raised him.* The sounds of the words are similar and derive from a common root (*zqipeh zaqpeh*).

ON THE HOLY FAST 4

To the same melody
6+5+5 + 5+5+6
+ 4+4 + 5+5 + 5+7 (or 7+5)
+ 6+6+4 + R: 6+6+4

I

See the remedial fast:[1]
  let's desire its reliefs,
    and enjoy its cures,
for the fast came down
  from Sinai's mountain[2]
    to the stricken regiment.[3]
It healed the wounds
  of a secret life,
and bound up the mind's
  great fragmentation:
the fast held up that people's
  collapse in the waste.[4]
Let's acclaim the mercies,

---

1. *See.* Emended to *hā*, "see," "behold," against Beck's supplemented reading from MSS C J(a), *hānaw*, "this is," to fit the meter and the pattern of the first lines of the first half of this *madrāšā*.

2. *from Sinai's mountain.* Only the reading of MS C fits the meter "from the mountain of Sinai" (*men ṭurā d-sinai*), in contrast to Beck's main reading "from Mount Sinai" (*men ṭur sinai*).

3. *regiment.* Or, "camp," "troop," "army." On the organization of the children of Israel into "armies," see Ex 12.51.

4. *that people's / collapse in the waste.* Or, "that people's downfall in the desert." The same verbiage appears in P 1 Cor 10.5.

for the fasts are good for us
   like remedies.

Refrain:
Let's acclaim the firstborn,
   whose fold heeds the scriptures,[5]
      blessed pastures.

2

See the enriching fast:
   let's take from its treasure,
      get rich by its wealth:
for in the beginning,
   Adam fell into debt
      by food and became poor.
See how the fast
   enriches us:
repaying Adam's debts,
   making bellies poor,
stocking a life's treasure-house
   with living merchandise.
Give glory to the firstborn,[6]
   whose good fast is a girdle[7]
      of our weakness.

3

See the releasing fast
   set free the eaters
      from the yoke of Greed:
for the Belly's rule
   is weary and troubled
      and unfit for freedom.

---

5. *heeds.* Or, "hears," "answers with," "holds converse with …" This term plays on the similar sound and appearance of the noun that immediately precedes it: *'āneh,* "his fold," i.e., "his flock." The choice of the verb also suggests that the scriptures were read aloud to the "fold" in question.

6. *Give glory.* Lit. "let us give glory."

7. *girdle.* The traditional sense of this term was a band wrapped around one's waist that held together one's attire. Keys could be attached to it and money and other possessions could also be stored in it, similar to a modern belt combined with a purse or a wallet.

Let the Belly cease
  from her service,
and let the Spirit
  serve with living words,
so fill your stomachs
  with living orthodoxy.[8]
Let's acclaim the firstborn
  whose fold heeds the scriptures,
    blessed pastures.

4

See how the training fast[9]
  musters our weakness[10]
    to rise triumphant;
see sackcloth, her raiment,
  akin to a mail shirt,
    humility like arms.
See it equip
  the feeble heel
with steadfast habits[11]
  to tread down and crush
delicate pleasures,[12]
  where there are serpents lurking.[13]
Blessed is he who gave Eve
  the fast to defeat the snake[14]
    and his craving.

---

8. *living orthodoxy.* Lit. "correct instruction of life."

9. *training.* The sense of "treading" or "trampling" is brought out in this stanza by the image of "the feeble heel" that treads upon the pleasures by means of firm habits. These habits furthermore are instilled by means of training.

10. *our weakness.* Reading with MS C, *rapyutan,* "our weakness," "our laxity." Cf. "our foulness" in stanza 6 below. Adjectives from the same root *r-p-y* also appear in this stanza as "feeble" and "delicate," respectively.

11. *steadfast habits.* Lit. "habits of firmness." Cf. Eph 6.15.

12. *delicate pleasures.* Or, "weak, delicate things," i.e., things that look harmless. Another sense is "weak pleasures," in the sense that the pleasures are not strong.

13. *where there are serpents lurking.* The vocalization represented by the reading above results in an extra syllable in this line. It is unclear whether another reading is possible in this context.

14. *to defeat the snake.* Gn 3.15.

5
See the victorious fast
  that weans both children
    and parents from food:[15]
O Evil's lowness:
  he even flings girls
    down with him in the fight.[16]
See the fast, heaped
  with hidden crowns,
rise and distribute
  to the fasting crowd:
see Evil lament when he sees
  the camp resplendent.
Give glory to the firstborn
  who by fasting prevailed
    and saved his fighters.[17]

6
See the adorning fast
  call forth our foulness
    to spoil it with its frills:[18]
see tears streaming forth,
  for cleansing our filth
    and washing out our stains.
In sackcloth is veiled[19]

---

15. *food.* Or, "staple food," "bread." Cf. note 24 in *Ieiun.* 1.6.

16. *flings ... down.* This reading takes the personification of Evil as the subject of the verb in the *ap'el* stem, *napel*, "flings down" and "seduces." Another possible reading takes "girls" as the feminine plural subject of the verb in the *p'al* stem, *nepel*, "fall down."

17. *saved.* Lit. "granted victory to," "cleared of blame," or "defeated." *his fighters.* Cf. *Ieiun.* 1.4. This could refer to the contestants (*atletē*) on either side, of the firstborn or the evil one. The reading above follows the former possibility. If interpreted according to the latter possibility, the meaning would change to "who was victorious over and defeated his (i.e., the evil one's) fighters."

18. *to spoil it with its frills.* Lit. "so that its (masculine: i.e., fasting's) adornments might spoil (i.e., ruin or put an end to) it (feminine: i.e., our foulness)."

19. *sackcloth.* This term, *saqā*, "sackcloth," is a near-homophone of *sāq*, "to breathe," "inhale," and *sawqā*, "breath," "sense of smell," a theme emphasized in this stanza.

a splendid robe;[20]
from its ashes exude
a scent of verdure:[21]
O sordid ones, get dressed
in fine vestments at no cost.
Blessed is he who summoned us[22]
to the pure and high feast
of that beauty.

7

In fasting, high-born ladies
shun frills and dainties[23]
that bud like blossoms:[24]
that royal vesture
possessed by Esther
was earthly in her eyes.
She fled to the fast;
it passed down to her[25]
celestial beauty,
spiritual splendor:
thus she came seeking
life for the dead from the king.[26]
Blessed is the king who arrayed
his holy church with fasting,
prayer, and vigil.[27]

---

20. *a splendid robe.* Cf. the note on the "splendid robe," known elsewhere as "the robe of glory," in *Ieiun.* 3.2 (n. 5).

21. *verdure.* Lit. "vitality."

22. *summoned us.* Lit. "summoned and called us."

23. *shun frills and dainties.* I.e., "despise." The notion suggested here is that if the elite or proud ladies in Ephrem's audience are truly refined, then they will consider such ephemeral "frills and dainties" (lit. adornments and delicacies), to be beneath their dignity. For a similar comparison, cf. *Ieiun.* 10.2.

24. *blossoms.* This word is not marked as plural in Syriac but is rendered plural in English to aid in the comparison.

25. *it passed down to her.* Lit. "and it (i.e., the fast) cast down and granted her."

26. *life for the dead from the king.* Est 4.16.

27. *and vigil.* To meet the requirement of the meter, Beck supplied [ܘܥܝܪܘ] "and watchfulness" from MSS C and P.

8

Have no shame in sackcloth[28]
nor in its garments,
   that shine as armor:
for it wears down Evil[29]
by testing and trial[30]
   of lowliness, all-blameless.[31]
Sackcloth cast down
   haughty Haman;
before that lowly one,[32]
   fasting made appeals:
an insatiate mouth
   to a faster who was silent.[33]
Blessed is he who gave us the fast
   that fought Haman's people[34]
      with his mouth against them.[35]

---

28. *Have no shame in sackcloth.* Lit. "Let us be unashamed therein in sackcloth." As in stanza 6 above, this stanza hints at the near-homophone of *saqā* as "sackcloth" and *sawqā* as "breath, inhaling," given how it draws on exemplars of the actions of the mouth during the fast, including lamentation and keeping silence.

29. *for it wears down Evil.* Cf. Eph 6.13. The phrase *šqil leh gēr l-bišā* can have a few different meanings, including: "for by it, the evil one is abolished," and "for by it one is clad and clothed." There is wordplay in the multiple ways to read ܠܒܝܫܐ, including *lbišā*, "clothed," or *l-bišā*, "for the evil one" or "evil one" as a direct object.

30. *testing and trial.* This reading requires an additional preposition (*b-*) for *b-beqyānā w-nesyānā*. The preposition (*b-*) is sometimes omitted before another (*b-*), as appears to be the case here. Another possible reading that fits the meter is *b-qinā w-nesyānā* "with lamentation and the trial."

31. *all-blameless.* Lit. "overcoming all," or "being clear of all blame."

32. *that lowly one.* On the sackcloth and fasting of the "lowly" Mordecai, see Est 4–6, especially 4.1, 16.

33. *an insatiate mouth / to a faster who was silent.* Beck proposes adding a preposition to the text for the reading "through a mouth." This emendation is unnecessary because the syntax of this part of the stanza can be read as an instance of parataxis, and the translation above reflects this interpretation. On Esther's petitions, see Est 5.3–8, 7.2–4. On Haman making petitions for his life, see Est 7.7–8. In our extant text, the word for "faster" (*syāmā*, "one who fasts") is masculine, not feminine as we might expect if Queen Esther were the intended faster in question.

34. *Haman's people.* According to Haman's traditional name, "Haman the Agagite," he was a descendant of Agag, the king of the Amalekites. On the slaughter of the enemies of the Jews, including the ten sons of Haman, see Est 9 passim. Cf. *Ieiun.* 5.9.

35. *them.* The pronominal suffix is singular and apparently refers back to Haman's people.

9

You young men, be heedless[36]
  of your bodies' attire
    at the time of your fasts:
for the three youths could
  be donned in all attire[37]
    within Babylon's midst.
Hating gold, they
  became like gold;
the forger cast them[38]
  in the great furnace:
the fasters proved fair,[39]
  like tested gold in the fire.
Blessed is he who gave us the fast,
  that purges the dirt of greed[40]
    from our senses.[41]

10

See the passing-over fast[42]
  that can, by appeal,
    subdue necessity:[43]
for Jonah pronounced

---

36. *be heedless.* Lit. "disdain" or "neglect" (imperative).

37. *be donned in all attire.* Lit. "they could be clothed in all adornments." According to Dn 3.21, when the three youths were cast into the blazing furnace, they were wearing several kinds of garments, including their baggy trousers (*šarbālayhon*, cf. Persian *šalvâr*), leg or foot wrappings (*peṭšayhon*), long outer garments (*naḥtayhon*), and hoods (*qubayhon*).

38. *the forger.* Or "cheater," "liar." This term, *zēpānā*, is from Akkadian *zīpu*, "mold, cast coin." In this context, the forger in question is King Nebuchadnezzar, who both made the image of gold and ordered the three youths to be cast into the blazing furnace, as recounted in Dn 3.

39. *proved fair.* Or, "they were beautiful," "bright," "pleasing."

40. *that purges the dirt of greed.* On this image, see Brock, *The Luminous Eye*, 73–79.

41. *senses.* Lit. "mind," "sense," "intelligence."

42. *passing-over.* Or, "brightening," "pacifying," "gladdening," "bounding over." The root of this word, *mapshānā*, is behind the word for Passover / Pascha. In this context, this sense is also suggested as the "passing over" of divine judgment, applied to both Nineveh and the Israelites in Egypt (cf. Ex 12.13).

43. *subdue necessity.* Or, "be blameless to necessity."

like a tribunal,[44]
  Nineveh is guilty!
She imposed a fast[45]—
  he knew the schemes[46]—
the crafty defense
  came, spoke, and was clean:
it silenced Jonah
  and repealed the king's sentence.[47]
Glory to the mercies that made
  the inner mouth appeal
    for penitents.[48]

II

See, Moses, Elijah,
  and our blessed Lord
    trod on fasting's path:
measuring, paving[49]
  a path for the weak,
    they passed beyond measure.
Of a power
  beyond nature,
sustained not by bread,
  nor food by nature,
the strong man vaulted

---

44. *a tribunal.* Only the plural vocalization, *bēt dayānē*, "house of judges (or tribunal)," fits the meter.

45. *She.* The feminine subject refers to Nineveh.

46. *he.* The masculine subject refers to Jonah and perhaps God, the divine judge, by implication.

47. *the king's sentence.* The king's decree of judgment may refer doubly to (1) God's judgment on Nineveh (Jon 3.4) and (2) the decree of the king of Nineveh to fast in repentance (Jon 3.7–8).

48. *the inner mouth.* Perhaps this image suggests the way that abstaining from eating is an action that speaks for itself without words, as in the case of Nineveh's fast. In contrast, an example of the "outer mouth" is Jonah's proclamation of judgment.

49. *measuring, paving.* This rendering follows the vocalization *w-kad mašaḥ(w) w-ṭakas(w)*, "and when they measured and ordered." An alternative vocalization (against the meter) is *w-kad mšaḥ(w) w-ṭakas(w)*, "and when they anointed and appointed."

and crossed the path to its mansions.⁵⁰
Let's acclaim with fasting⁵¹
   the mercies that gave arms
      to our weakness.

12

Who can plead a defense
   to pardon someone
      subdued by his belly?⁵²
For the daily fast⁵³
   is a little mile,⁵⁴
      while its reward abounds.
If weeks passed by
   the finishers,⁵⁵
and part of the weeks
   the middling as well,
then let not the weak
   lose even a brief moment.⁵⁶
Let's acclaim the firstborn,
   who in all measures wills
      to sustain all.

---

50. *and crossed the path to its mansions.* Lit. "and crossed the path and to its (f.) mansions." The feminine pronominal suffix refers back to the feminine noun *urḥā*, "path," so "the mansions of the path" is meant. Both "mansions" and "path" allude to Jn 14.2–4. Cf. *Ieiun.* 1.12.

51. *with fasting.* Or, "in the fast."

52. *subdued by his belly.* This reading follows the vocalization *da-zkē l-karseh*, "who is subdued by his belly." Fitting the same meter is the alternative vocalization *da-zkā l-karseh*, "who has subdued his belly." The rhetorical question poses a conundrum in any case. That is, if one is subdued by his belly, then the presumption of guilt is manifest, and who can rise up to defend him? If, on the other hand, he has subdued his belly, then his innocence is manifest, so what need is there to make an apology?

53. *the daily fast.* Or, "the fast of a day."

54. *a little mile.* Cf. Mt 5.41.

55. *the finishers.* This term, *kašīrē*, "successful ones," "diligent ones," is often applied to ascetics.

56. *a brief moment.* This rendering follows the vocalization *ṭawrā karyā*, "short (or sad) interval (or measure)." Were it not for the dot, the word ܛܘܪܐ would look identical to the word for mountain, *ṭūrā*. Associations with this homograph are brought out by several words relating to various heights in the same context, including ܫܦܠܐ, here read as *špālē*, "weak, lowly, humbled, cowardly, feeble ones" but can also mean, "lowlands."

ON THE HOLY FAST 5

To the same melody
6+5+5 + 5+5+6
+ 4+4 + 5+5 + 5+7 (or 7+5)
+ 6+6+4 + [R: 6+6+4]¹

I

Look, they raised heavy fasts
  to become the guides
    of the king's bride,
that she be borne and brought
  to the white wedding feast,
    to bathe in it and be bright.²
Let her crowns stem
  from her regimen,³
    her gems from her fasts;
let her ride upon palms;⁴

---

1. The refrain (*'onitā*), usually present in this *qālā*, is missing from the extant MSS. This *madrāšā* also contains at least three clear diversions from the pattern of sense divisions in the first, fifth, and eighth stanzas, where the usual dyadic lines 4+4 + 5+5 + 5+7 (or 7+5) turn into triadic lines 4+4+5 + 5+5+7 (or 5+7+5). There may be additional stanzas that deviate in this way, but they are less clear. See the note on stanzaic structure at the beginning of *Ieiun.* 1.

2. *to bathe in it.* Or, "so that she might be baptized in it." The image is connected both to the Christian ritual of baptism and to the Jewish custom of *mikveh*, wherein the bride would take a ritual bath prior to her wedding. *and be bright.* Lit. "and so that she might be bright in it."

3. *regimen.* Or "her ways of life," "customs," "diets," "manners."

4. *ride.* Lit. "go forth," "proceed," or "behave." *upon palms.* This denotes both "with hosannas" and "upon palm branches."

let a lamp shine before her
   with steadfast oil.[5]
Blessed is he who sent and raised
   his firstborn's bride to attain
      the bridal chamber of his light.

Refrain:
Glory to the Son who adorned
   his holy church with fasting,
      prayer, and vigil.

2

See the encouraging fast
   muster its regiment[6]
      to wage war with Greed:
by having eaten,
   that fighter was beaten,
      whose strength weakened with food.
The tempter took
   from the first one
to take down the last one[7]
   and drew near to test him:[8]
the scent of his fast[9]
   diffused his greed, and he was stunned.

---

5. *steadfast oil.* Cf. Mt 25.1–13.

6. *regiment.* Lit. "camp," "army," "force."

7. *first one ... last one.* The "first one" may evoke Adam, and the "last one" may evoke Christ.

8. *drew near to test him.* Mt 4.3 et par.

9. *scent.* The Syriac word as it appears in Beck's edition is ܪܗܐ, but this exact spelling is unattested for the sense he gives in his translation, "der Duft," which would require ܪܝܗܐ *rihā*, "scent" (for which, see *Ieiun.* 7.8), or even ܪܐܗܐ *rāhā*, "odor." The reading is thus uncertain. It could be a scribal error or defective orthography hitherto unattested. Other possible readings include the following: (1) ܪܗܐ *rhē*, "millstone" (in the absolute state), which could echo the allusion just mentioned of the temptation of Christ during his fast to command the stones to turn into bread (Mt 4.3 et par); and (2) ܪܗܐ *rahā*, a word listed without a definition in Audo's lexicon (p. 501), where he says it is not in use as such, as far as he is aware, but there are other words deriving from it that are related to the senses "to go around" and "to circle," often in the context of an encircling wall. See Thomas Audo, *Treasure of the Syriac Language: A Dictionary of Classical Syriac,* Kiraz Historical Dictionaries Archive (Piscataway, NJ: Gorgias Press, 2008), 501.

Blessed is Mercy who gave us
the fast that dries the spring
of the passions.

3

The bow of Evil is raised:
let us go to war—
to arms, everyone!
The Spirit's mail shirt
is able to take
the point of the sharp darts.
Grave is the peril
should one be grazed,[10]
for Fire remains
in the one smitten:
consuming, she delights him,
for sweet is that Fire.[11]
Blessed is Good who gave us
the fast that can put out
his blazing darts.[12]

4

Weak is one ill-equipped
with Freedom's power,[13]
whose arms are her will:
divided is one who
can't conquer Concord,
whose assembly is his wholeness.

---

10. *grazed*. In this line, the poet plays with the double meaning of the verb *blaʿ*: "swallow," "devour," "be absorbed," or "be wounded." This suggests that by eating, one could be wounded by the evil one. The English "grazed" comes closest to capturing the senses of both "swallow" and "be wounded."

11. *consuming, she delights him, / for sweet is that Fire*. Lit. "for it is the burning (that) delights him, of that sweet Fire."

12. *his blazing darts*. Lit. "the coals of his darts."

13. *Weak is one ill-equipped / with Freedom's power*. This tautological parallelism implies that fasting equips one with the power of freedom, but one who is ruled by the belly is not supplied with this power.

A side as one[14]
   is a vast ocean;
together, it prevails,
   but divided, it fails:[15]
if its union comes undone,
   it is absorbed and gone.
Blessed is he who gathers peoples
   divided and makes them a people
     undivided.

5

Blessed is he who gave us
   an image as our mirror
     if only we gaze in:[16]
let's see our covered
   concord, my brothers,
     in manifest symbols.
Let's look at rennet:
   if covered up
     within liquid milk,
its liquidity
   no more will be spilt,
     having curdled with firm strength.
Blessed is he who gave us love,
   mingling covered strength
     with our weakness.

6

In fasting, remember
   what fools committed
     during their own fasts:
it's dreadful to pass
   the holy one's shame
     through our mouth and our ears.

---

14. *A side.* Reading *gabā*, "side," or "wing (of an army)." Another possible vocalization is *gābē*, "choosing."

15. *divided, it fails.* Cf. Mt 12.25 et par.

16. *as our mirror / if only we gaze in.* Lit. "which, if it is (that) we should gaze upon it, (then) it turns into our mirror."

The Lord of Pascha
   they killed at Pascha;
the Lord of feast days
   they slew at the feast:
they hanged God upon the tree[17]
   and gave rise to wrath.[18]
The mouth that cried, "Crucify him!"
   stood at Pascha to read
      holy scriptures.

7

At Pascha, they would read
   how they had slaughtered
      the lamb in Egypt:
O one-eyed people[19]
   who read, not knowing,
      and explained, not perceiving.[20]
They read in scriptures,
   "they hanged on a tree,"[21]
types within volumes,
   Truth upon the tree:
they hanged and gallowed the true lamb,[22]
   pierced and roasted the lamb.
The pierced lamb silently
   had witnessed the hanged lamb:[23]
      see the fulfillment.

---

17. *they hanged God upon the tree*. Some MSS, including Beck's MS B, omit "God." Its redaction and/or addition could reflect the sensitive and controversial debate in early Christianity over whether God could suffer.

18. *gave rise to wrath*. Lit. "they raised (him), and they provoked (him) to wrath."

19. *one-eyed people*. In this case, the people are "one-eyed" in the sense of partial blindness, in that they can read and interpret the scriptures, but they do not understand or perceive their true meaning. Cf. *Ieiun.* 1.12, 5.8, 5.10, 6.4.

20. *who read, not knowing, / and explained, not perceiving*. Cf. Mt 13.13 et par.

21. *"they hanged on a tree."* This phrase (*tlaw 'al qaysā*) appears verbatim in P Est 8.7 and 9.14 with reference to the death of Haman and his ten sons upon the gallows. Cf. Antiphon Fifteen of the Great and Holy Friday Matins in the Triodion: English translation in *The Lenten Triodion*, translated by Mother Mary and Kallistos Ware (South Canaan, PA: St. Tikhon's Seminary Press, 1994), 587.

22. *they hanged and gallowed*. Or, "they crucified and hanged."

23. *the lamb in Egypt ... the true lamb ... the lamb ... The pierced lamb ... the hanged*

84   ST. EPHREM

8
One-eyed, soused with envy,
    they hanged, were flustered,[24]
        and went all askew:[25]
they had alleged that
    the law it was that
        transgressed the firstborn.[26]
The law in him
    they turned to coals[27]
        and broke by their deeds:[28]
their mouth accused them,
    the hand wrote he was guilty,
        but the mouth reneged.
The fools broke and quickly

---

lamb. All five instances of the word rendered as "lamb" (*ēmrā*) in this stanza can also be read as "saying" or "word" (*ēmrā*) with reference to the scriptures, conveying the double action of slaughtering both the lamb and the word. Here, as in other instances of polysemy, the implication is that the "one-eyed people" can perceive only one of the possible senses, but not the other.

24. *hanged.* This term, *zqap(w)*, if taking an object, would mean, "they crucified [someone]" or "they hanged [someone]." In this line, however, there appears to be no object, so the sense seems to be, "they were crucified or hanged" or "they arose." In English, "crucified" can only be transitive, while "hanged" can be both transitive and intransitive, like the Syriac *z-q-p*.

25. *went all askew.* This verb can also mean "to forget," as in forgetting the law, in contrast to the theme of remembrance in the previous stanza.

26. *the law it was that / transgressed the firstborn.* With *l-* taken as marking the direct object (i.e., "the firstborn"), this is a humorous transposition of the expected subject and object, spoken by the one-eyed people, who meant to allege that "the firstborn transgressed the law," but they jumbled their speech in their drunken state and said the opposite instead, that it was the law that transgressed the firstborn.

27. *they turned to coals.* This verb means, "they turned into coals," "they fulfilled," and "they perfected." The masculine pronominal suffix can refer back to both the law and the firstborn. Cf. Mt 5.17. On the semantic development of this term, see Sebastian P. Brock, "Fire from Heaven: From Abel's Sacrifice to the Eucharist: A Theme in Syriac Christianity," *Studia Patristica* 25 (1993): 238 (reprinted in *Fire from Heaven: Studies in Syriac Theology and Liturgy*, ed. Sebastian Brock, Variorum Collected Studies Series [Aldershot, UK, and Burlington, VT: Ashgate, 2006]).

28. *broke.* The word ܫܪܐ is repeated three times in this stanza with varying nuances that depend on the context. It can be vocalized as either *šraw* or *šar(w)*, from two different verbal roots. Options include: "they were proved true," "they dismissed," "they broke," "they destroyed," and "they lodged with."

dismissed that which they broke
through Pascha's deeds.[29]

9

With visible crucifiers,
a spiritual assembly,
invisibly standing,
compassed the firstborn:
culprits with their taunts[30]
and prophets with their scrolls.
Moses standing,
stretching out his hands,
his staff above his chest,[31]
a wonder at the crest:[32]
hand stretched and staff raised,
as above the Place of the Skull.[33]
Their own witness bellows[34]
above them: here's the symbol[35]—
it razed Amalek.[36]

29. *One-eyed... Pascha's deeds.* This stanza, at least as it survives in the manuscript tradition, appears to be missing about twelve syllables from the usual pattern, give or take a few depending on vocalization options. About eight syllables are missing from the beginning part, three from the middle part, and none from the last part. Breaking the pattern may emphasize such themes as drunkenness, brokenness, and loss through the abrogation of the firstborn.

30. *culprits.* Lit. "wicked ones." *their taunts.* Depending on the aspiration of one letter, which is not marked in our text, this word may be *ḥesdayhon* (with an unaspirated *d*), "their reproaches," or *ḥesd(h)ayhon* (with an aspirated *d*), "their kindnesses." This word choice conveys a certain irony in the apparent "kindnesses" of those "wicked ones," who represent the antithesis of the prophets.

31. *his staff above his chest.* Ex 17.8–13.

32. *the crest.* Lit. "at the top of the mountain."

33. *the Place of the Skull.* Lit. *gagoltā*, "Golgotha."

34. *Their own witness.* Lit. "a witness who is from them." The word for "witness" also means "martyr."

35. *above them.* Or, "against them." In this stanza, the position "above" is repeated three times for emphasis.

36. *razed.* This word can be read in two antithetical ways for ironic effect: "defeated," in the sense that Moses prevailed over the Amalekites through the lifting of the staff (Ex 17.8–16); and "granted victory to" or "justified" the enemies of the Israelites. Similarly, "razed," although not strictly literal in either sense, approximates this antithesis by contrasting the sense of "crushed" with the homophone "raised."

10

The Mosaic covenants
  are just like a mirror—
    she gazed on our Lord[37]—
and every person
  whose mind they entered,[38]
    saw he was there and here.
He sees at hand[39]
  the symbol in a voice;[40]
here too, he beholds
  Truth in a servant:[41]
Just-Truth, who shouts[42]
  even to the one-eyed, "I'm here!"
The blind felt him and gained sight,
  the sighted touched him and went blind,
    for they crucified the light.

37. *she gazed.* The antecedent of the feminine singular subject of this verb appears to be the personification of the mirror, to which the covenants of Moses are likened.

38. *they entered.* The antecedent of the masculine plural subject of this verb, *'alu(hy)*, is unclear. The logical subject would appear to be "the Mosaic covenants," or "every person," although the former option is typically feminine, and the latter option is typically singular.

39. *at hand.* Or, "the future," "that which is to come."

40. *the symbol in a voice.* Cf. Dt 4.12. In this context, the "voice" may refer to the notion that the symbols in the Mosaic covenants were spoken in words, anticipating the Incarnation of the Word, who took the form of a servant.

41. *in a servant.* The meter requires the reading *ba-ʿbādā*, "in a servant," as opposed to *b-ʿabdā*, "in deed," although there can be no doubt that the latter reading, "the truth in deed," is hinted at as well, given the comparison between the symbol that was spoken in a voice and its fulfillment. Of course, the identity of "the servant" must be "the servant of God," i.e., Christ incarnate. Cf. Lk 22.27 and Phil 2.6–7.

42. *Just-Truth.* This term, *qušṭā*, is also used for fairness and justice, in contrast to *šrārā*, the other term for the personification of Truth in the previous line.

ON THE HOLY FAST 6

Again on the fast
To the melody: "My Master, You
Have Composed It"
5+6 + 7+4 + 4+4 + 4+5 + 5+6[1]

1

In the fast, gather
  and turn into merchants,[2]
for the scriptures are
  a divine treasury,
and with the key
  of that holy voice,[3]
see them open
  before the hearers.
Blessed is the king who opened
  his treasuries to his paupers.

2

In them are garments
  for the wedding guests,

---

1. This song is an acrostic that spells out the author's name, Ephrem, using the first letter of each stanza.

2. *merchants.* The root of this term denotes acquiring and profiting through business trade.

3. *that holy voice.* In Ephrem's corpus, the "voice" (*qālā*) is often associated with Christ, who in this interpretation unlocked the treasures of the scriptures through the Incarnation. Another possible reference is the *qālā* of a teaching song, which interprets the scriptures and thus unlocks their meaning for the audience.

in them are sackcloth
    and tears for all penitents,
in them also
    is an armor[4]
for fighters as well:
    they are full of all riches.
Blessed is he who prepared
    all benefits for all.[5]

3

Shrewdly open, my brothers,
    and take from it with prudence,
for this treasury is common
    to all mankind.
See, the holder of all
    mankind is also his key:[6]
who would not be wealthy
    like a treasurer?
Blessed is he who released
    the reasons for our poverty.

4

Huge is the gift that
    streams down before our blindness,

---

4. *armor.* Reading *zaynā*, "armor," "weapon," against *zayānā*, "sustainer," "preserver," "protector," because the former fits the context, even though the latter fits the meter. See the following note.

5. *In them ... for all.* The scansion of this stanza exhibits two or three irregularities against the meter and stanzaic structure of the rest of the poem. The first hemistich contains four syllables instead of the usual five, and the third hemistich contains six syllables instead of the usual seven, and the sixth hemistich contains three syllables instead of the usual four if we read *zaynā*, "weapon," "armor," which fits the context more straightforwardly than the only alternative that fits the meter, *zayānā*, "sustainer." In addition, the style of this stanza sticks out as somewhat one-dimensional, in contrast to the telltale signs of the master poet's subtle craft. There is thus some reason to doubt the authenticity of this stanza, but we include it here as an important part of the manuscript tradition.

6. *the holder of all / mankind.* Or, "every human being holds his key." The expression *aḥid kol*, "the holder of all," is a common epithet roughly equivalent to "the omnipotent one."

while every one of us has
    a pair of eyes each.
Few are they who
    have ever seen
what the gift is
    and from whom it is.
My Lord, spare the one-eyed[7]
    who only see gold.

5

O Jesus who opened
    Bartimaeus's pupils,[8]
you opened what were blinded
    while he was unwilling.
My Lord, open the eyes
    that were blinded
while we are willing,
    to magnify your grace.
Your mud, my Lord, taught that[9]
    you are our maker's Son.[10]

6

Who compares to you,
    ennobler of our visage?[11]
You spat on the dirt,
    not faces, to raise our image.
As for us, our Lord,
    spit on our faces,
and open the eyes
    that our free will had shut.
Blessed is he who gave
    the mind's eye that we blinded.

---

7. *spare*. Or, "have compassion on." *the one-eyed*. Cf. *Ieiun.* 1.12, 5.7–8.

8. *Bartimaeus's pupils*. Mk 10.46–52, Jn 9.

9. *Your mud*. Jn 9.6.

10. *our maker's Son*. The same root from which the word for "maker" (*gabol-*) derives is behind the word for "(God) made," or "formed" (*gbal*), Adam from the dust in P Gn 2.7.

11. *visage*. This term, *parṣopā* (Grk. πρόσωπον), also means "person," "face."

7
Who would not marvel
    at Adam and his opening?
For his eyes' opening
    greatly wounded Adam.
As for us, our Lord
    greatly aided
our eyes' opening
    which Evil had shut.
Blessed is he who closed
    and opened eyes to give aid.

8
Who would not curse him,
    the sharp one who betrays us?[12]
He lied and opened Adam's eyes,
    and he saw his disgrace.
As for us, he beguiled us,
    and look, he dulled our eyes,[13]
lest we might see
    our great nakedness.
My Lord, may he be most cursed,
    that you might be most blessed.

---

12. *the sharp one.* See the note to *clear one* in *Ieiun.* 1.3 (n. 10). The same semantic range applies here as well.

13. *dulled.* Or "besmeared," "plastered over." In a metaphorical sense, "stopped up the eyes from seeing."

ON THE HOLY FAST 7

Again on the fast. To the
melody: "God in his Mercies"
3+2+3 + 3+2+3
+ 3+2+3/4 + 3+2+4
+ 5+5 + 5+5
+ 3+3 + 3+3+3
+ R: 3+3+3

I

Let's look forward to our blessed fast:
    a treasury opened by the prudent,
the heart's delight for the intelligent,[1]
    the mind's repast, the sages' quarry.[2]
By it shines brighter a life that's prudent,
    and wiser the spirit that heeded the ancients;
for fasting bestows her[3]
    with Moses's and Elijah's armory.[4]

Refrain: Blessed are you whose fasts have prevailed.

---

1. *the heart's delight for the intelligent.* Or, by ellipsis: "the heart's delight (is opened) by the intelligent."

2. *the mind's repast, the sages' quarry.* Lit. "the quarry (i.e., hunted prey; prize; sustenance) of the wise ones." Or, *ṣēd* can be read as a preposition, "with," "to," yielding an alternative reading: "the mind's supplies with the wise ones."

3. *her.* Both *napšā*, "life-breath," and *rūḥā*, "spirit," are feminine nouns.

4. *Moses's and Elijah's armory.* The meter requires the vocalization *haw zaynā d-bēt mušē w-eliyā*, lit. "that weapon of the house of Moses and Elijah."

2

Put flesh on a fowl on trial:
    if she abounds eating heavy,
her pinion she fills and weighs down,
    and cannot soar as once she had done.
Higher than all, an eagle, if greedy,
    can glide no more as once he had glided:
the light one is weighed down[5]—
    as heavy as he eats, he weighs down.

3

Since Daniel's company ate vegetables,
    they grasped and expounded in Babel:[6]
their fellow youths were insatiable[7]
    for that mortal king's delectables.
Prince of the left with his wine was desirous
    to weigh down heart and mind of the righteous:
through fasting, the youths weaned
    their mouths from his kingdom's high table.

---

5. *the light one.* Or, "the one that is light," or "the one who is swift." The connotation of swiftness anticipates the imagery in stanza 4 below.

6. *grasped and expounded.* Following the reading of Beck's MS D, *šma'(w) wa-praš(w)*, "they grasped (also, 'heard,' 'obeyed') and expounded (also, 'discerned,' 'interpreted')," against the reading of Beck's MSS J(a) J(c) P *šman(w) wa-špar(w)*, "they grew fat and fair." The issue at stake is not that fatness and fairness would be regarded as qualities that would be out of place in such a text as this (on the contrary: see, e.g., *Ieiun.* 9.1). One reason in favor of the D reading is that this stanza centers on the correlation between the vegetable diet of Daniel and his companions and their lucidity of heart, mind, and speech. The variant reading can be attributed to a scribal misreading of the *'e* in *šma'(w)* as a *nun* and a transposition from *praš(w)* to *špar(w)*. The first two lines literally mean, "Daniel and his companions grasped and expounded, / since they had eaten vegetables in Babylon's midst." *Babel.* Or, "Babylon." This term is rendered "Babel" throughout this translation for its resonance with the theme of the division of languages, to maintain the terse rhythm, and to preserve the wordplay with "El."

7. *fellow youths.* This reading follows the vocalization *ḥabrayhon ṭalāyē*, "their young companions." Other possible readings include *ḥabārayhon*, "their abysses," "pits," "conjurors," and *ḥebrayhon*, "their darkness," "gloom," "fog," "mist." The English expression "bottomless pit," with reference to someone who is incessantly hungry, is perhaps fitting here.

ON THE HOLY FAST

4

Yet those lads who were sustained well
   had strained their mind-heart with training,
and when they came to the trial,[8]
   they could not keep up with the fasters.
Weighed down by food, they lost in the contest—
   faster-youths had them beat as they ran past:
fasts and vegetables defeated
   the royal delectables and tasters.

5

Daniel and his fellows loathed wine
   that troubler of sharp ones in its stillness:[9]
wits grew in those who unloved it,
   taste dulled in those who grew used to it.
Cedars—Zion's kin—drank water, foliated,[10]
   Babel-bound people in their shade resided:
came brooding on their boughs—
      like a dove on an olive—the Spirit.

6

And even that vine from Egypt,[11]
   on kings and priests spread her vine-shoots:[12]
compare them with cedars that bore her,[13]
   yet the vine that left from Egypt's midst,
Babel had choked her in her heathen shade.[14]
   Daniel's companions were the cedars there:
in Babel they bore her,
      like Moses and Aaron in Egypt.

---

8. *and when they came to the trial.* Lit. "but when they came so that they might reach the trial."

9. *sharp ones.* See the note for *clear one* in *Ieiun.* 1.3 (n. 10). The same semantic options are possible here also.

10. *Cedars.* Or, "symbols," "mysteries." This applies in the other instances of "cedars" below. Cf. Ezek 17.22–24.

11. *that vine from Egypt.* Ps 80.9.

12. *her vine-shoots.* The same word appears in P Ps 80.11.

13. *cedars.* For the comparison between the shoots of the vine and the cedars, see Ps 80.10. Alternatively, this word can be read in the perfect, "he/it compared them," with the implied subject being God, scripture, or Asaph.

14. *her heathen shade.* Lit. "in the shade of her heathendom."

7

Yet Babel envied those cedars[15]
  that bore up the vine that spread out;
she hurled them in Fire for burning;
  they sprouted and stretched out within the flame.
Since they spurned liquor, there they subdued Fire;
  since they loved fasting, there they earned power:
dew flowed in the furnace[16]
  for the fasters refraining from wine.

8

Then Fire closed in and sniffed at[17]
  that flesh of fasters purified:[18]
a dire whiff of their fasts snuffed it,
  and Greed was shut off from their bodies.
She fasted from fasters, feasted on gluttons;
  those eating, she ate; those fasting, she guarded:
they fasted with Daniel—
  the wild beasts who fed on the greedy.

9

The blessed youths repulsed and hated
  the king's table and his dainties:
Fire did not touch their bodies,
  for they had not touched his choice foods.
They loathed the staple food more but ate pulses[19]
  and changed their natures, thus Fire also
exchanged her own nature:
  those outside, not inside, she consumed.[20]

---

15. *cedars.* See note 10 on *cedars* in stanza 5 above. This may be rendered also as "symbols" in this context.

16. *the furnace.* The pericope of the fiery furnace in Daniel 3 is explored at length here and in the stanzas that follow.

17. *closed in.* Or "approached," "drew near." The same word with a preposition is rendered as "touched" in the following stanza.

18. *purified.* I.e., "refined" or "cleansed."

19. *the staple food.* See the note for *food* in *Ieiun.* 1.6 (n. 24).

20. *those outside, not inside, she consumed.* Lit. "instead of that which was inside, she had consumed the outside ones."

10

Now three had fallen in Fire,
  they grew to be four in her core:
and that Fire consumed many;
  the few abounded inside her greed.
Fire, oppressor, constant despoiler,
  failed to turn pledge and trust into cinders:[21]
her greed was overcome—
  both pledge and interest she had repaid.

11

Fire was a land, in symbol,
  furrowed for seed and arable:[22]
for she was tended sevenfold,[23]
  harrowed over and over to sow.
Into her midst they sowed those who ate seeds[24]
  in their fasts, and those who fasted with seeds
like seed they abounded,
  in Fire wherein many were brought low.[25]

---

21. *pledge and trust.* I.e., "principal and deposit." In this case, the three young companions of Daniel were the principal and deposit paid down but not recompensed by the personification of Fire.

22. *arable.* The literal meaning of this expression is "useful for seed's offspring."

23. *tended.* The primary sense of the root *š-g-r* is "to fire," "to heat," "to stoke," and it is the same root found in P Dn 3.19. Additional senses include "cause to flow" and "to cultivate." Thus the word choice evokes both heating a furnace and cultivating a land, brought together in a common symbol.

24. *seeds.* In this stanza, the poet plays with several variations of the root *z-r-ʿ*, rendered here as "seed" but elsewhere as "vegetables" or "pulses," as the principal diet of the fasters in the Daniel 3 narrative.

25. *were brought low.* Or "became few," "became small," "diminished," or "reduced." The word rendered here as "many" can also mean "great ones," which could be an allusion to the mighty men in the army of King Nebuchadnezzar, who bound and cast the three young men into the furnace and were slain in Dn 3.20–22. The image is also paradoxical: Fire reduces everything she burns into a tiny heap of ashes, yet the fasters did the opposite in the fire by growing and multiplying like the seeds they had eaten. Thus the few (three) became many (four) in the midst of the fire, and, in turn, the many became few again when the three young men exited the fire unscathed. The root of this word is *z-r-ʿ*, which also stands behind the word rendered as "seed(s)."

12

That Fire Elijah also sent down
  devoured many atop the mountain:
the faster sent her down by command;
  consumers and gluttons she consumed.
Fire repaid the faster's deficit:
  by her fall, slew many of Greed's prophets,[26]
hired by the Belly
  to steer the simple from Just-Truth.

13

The prophets were hired by food;
  the liars turned profits by greed:[27]
with trusty names they were vested[28]
  and sold the just-truth for daily food,
taking a mouthful, preaching a mouthful[29]—
  blessed is the faster whose mouth is not venal.[30]
My brothers, fear the Belly,
  lest her dominion rule over you.

14

If Daniel had also fallen
  with his three fellows in the furnace,
the tyrant would have deemed the fourth one,
  who appeared in the fire, a splendorous
sight of his god—for he gave his idol's name
  to Daniel by fraud—thus by not willing
to discredit his god,
  he gave way for Truth to be illustrious.[31]

---

26. *slew many of Greed's prophets*. According to 1 Kgs 18.19, there were 450 prophets of Baal and 400 prophets of the groves who were slain.

27. *turned profits*. Lit. "were bribed." The reading "turned profits" is one of the attempts in this translation to compensate for puns in the Syriac text that are lost in translation elsewhere.

28. *trusty names*. Lit. "names of reliable officials" or "trustees."

29. *taking*. Or "since they take."

30. *whose mouth is not venal*. Lit. "whose mouth was not bribed."

31. *thus by ... be illustrious*. The implication is that the tyrant could have thrown Daniel into the fiery furnace with his companions, but the reason he did not do so is the fact that the king gave the name of his idol, Belteshazzar, to Daniel (Dn 1.7),

15

To that Error who lost on one side,
  he gave no other for her to win:[32]
for if she deemed that splendorous sight[33]
  the idol that saved through Daniel,
then Error who had lost could have cleared her
  shame through the image and win in the furnace,[34]
but Truth made light of her[35]—
  from every place her crops failed to yield.[36]

---

and thus the king did not wish to bring ignominy to his deity by casting him into the furnace. Ironically, by attempting to save face for his god, Nebuchadnezzar gave an opportunity for the true God to show his splendorous manifestation as the fourth person who appeared in the midst of the furnace (Dn 3.25), instead of Daniel, who would have been the fourth person if he had been cast into it.

32. *he.* The last-named singular masculine agent is the personification of Truth from the previous stanza.

33. *that splendorous sight.* Again, the fourth person who was seen in the fire in Dn 3.25.

34. *could have cleared her / shame through the image and win in the furnace.* This is an apodosis of a counterfactual conditional, lit. "(then) she would have been able to be vindicated, / who was put to shame by means of the image, and she (would have been able to) be victorious (or vindicated) in the furnace." An alternative reading, albeit less certain: "(then) she would have been able to prevail, since she would have put to shame through the image and prevailed in the furnace." This reading seems less likely because these verbal stems usually take objects.

35. *made light of her.* Lit. "mocked," "ridiculed," "derided."

36. *her crops.* In Beck's edition the pronominal suffix has no dot above it, indicating a masculine pronoun, but at least one manuscript that the present translator could consult (BL Add MS 14,571, f. 13v) clearly shows the feminine marker. The immediate context further supports this reading. If read as masculine, the antecedent would be the personification of Truth, and the vocalization would be ʿelātā-, "pretexts" or "allegations": "(Truth's) allegations ceased," but this reading would be rather forced, since the allegations would be those that Truth made. So the question arises: how would it fit the context of this stanza to say that Truth stopped making allegations? The feminine pronoun, on the other hand, makes sense with reference to the feminine personification of Error. The reading "crops" follows the vocalization ʿalātā-, which can also mean "fruits," "harvests," and "increases." In combination with the verb *pāseq hwā* (with a feminine plural subject), it takes the meaning, "her crops stopped producing." Cf. other imagery of crops in stanza 11 above. There is also a pun in the Syriac text with the similarity of sounds between ʿalātāh, "her crops" (i.e., the fruits of Error), and a word that is repeated twice in the previous stanza, alāheh, "his god."

ON THE HOLY FAST 8

To the same melody: "God in his Mercies"

3+2+3 + 3+2+3
+ 3+2+3/4 + 3+2+4
+ 5+5 + 5+5
+ 3+3 + 3+3+3
+ R: 3+3+3

I

Was it not Sin who fired the furnace
   to incinerate Just-Truth therein?
Heedless, she made a hearth wherein[1]
   Just-Truth's fairness would glow illustrious.
His fire in her criers burned and bared their shame,[2]
   for outside, her own turned to cinders and flame:
Just-Truth in the triad[3]
   emerged bright as gold and victorious.[4]

---

1. *a hearth*. This is another word for "furnace" or "kiln."

2. *her criers*. The subjects of this line are described as *kārozēh*, "her heralds," "her harbingers," "her forerunners," the feminine possessor thereof being the personification of Sin (whereas the personification of Just-Truth is masculine). The "criers" and "her own" appear to be associated with the attendants who cast the youths into the furnace (Dn 3.22). Outside of the furnace, they are exposed and turned into ash and flame, in contrast to those three youths within who go out unharmed. *bared their shame*. Lit. "they were exposed," or "they were laid bare."

3. *Just-Truth in the triad*. The personification of truth among the three persons is evocative of the fourth person in the midst of the fiery furnace whose form is described as the Son of God (Dn 3.25). Cf. *Ieiun.* 7.14.

4. *emerged bright as gold and victorious*. Lit. "was victorious (or shone), and was bright as gold, and went out."

Refrain:
Blessed is he who shone through the youths in Babel.[5]

2

Now while the vainglorious king's[6]
 idol and kingdom were idle,[7]
Media, mother of simpletons,
 had taken Babel, daughter of Chaldeans,
simple and artless Medes then defeated[8]
 Chaldean mediums, seers, and palm-readers:[9]
Babel's sons were abased,
 a single demise took the lot of them.

3

Chaldeanness was mortified,[10]
 heedless that her old flames were killed:[11]
disgraced and shamefaced in the ire,
 for sorcery failed to revive herself.
She served a cup of ire to all kings;[12]
 dregs of that cup were left for her to drink:[13]
  by serving the first ones,
   those dregs in the last befall oneself.

---

5. *shone.* Another sense: "was victorious."

6. *the vainglorious king's.* Lit. "the king who was haughty." An allusion to King Nebuchadnezzar.

7. *were idle.* Or "ceased" or "ended."

8. *Medes.* Cf. Dn 5.30–31.

9. *Chaldean mediums, seers, and palm-readers.* Elsewhere in Ephrem's corpus, "Chaldean" is associated with esoteric wisdom and magic with negative connotations. Cf. Dn 2.27, 4.7, 5.6, 5.11.

10. *Chaldeanness.* This term is synonymous with divination in association with ancient Chaldean magic. *mortified.* Or, "greatly put to shame."

11. *that her old flames were killed.* Lit. "of the murder of her beloved ones," referring back to the "mediums, seers, and palm-readers" in the previous stanza. The idiomatic rendering "old flames" attempts to draw on senses from two possible vocalizations: *ḥbibēh*, "her beloved ones," "her friends," "her kith," and *ḥabibēh*, "her white-hot ones," "her kindled ones." The meter favors the former option as the primary reading. Another possible translation that attempts to capture the wordplay is "kith and kindled."

12. *served.* Or "gave to drink."

13. *cup of ire ... dregs.* The language is reminiscent of Ps 75.8 and Is 51.17.

4

The faster read and expounded
    the judgment writ for Chaldeans:
in plaster signed by heaven's finger,
    in signs inscribed to be deciphered.[14]
Seeing the writings, at once, feasters wondered,
    read without grasping; in reading, they wandered:
the wise and greedy were shamed when
    the faster came, read, and deciphered.[15]

5

At the feast where a legion was lodging,[16]
    they brightened Satan with libations:
he rushed and settled in their goblets,[17]
    as blasphemy spouted from their secrets.[18]

---

14. *signs*. The term "signs" is preferred in this case because it denotes both graphemes and indicators. The term *pelāwātā* can also mean "parables," "proverbs," "allegories," "enigmata," "riddles," and "dark sayings." *in plaster ... be deciphered*. Lit. "the finger of heaven wrote on plaster, / inscribed it in signs, that they might be interpreted." Dn 5.5.

15. *came*. This word can also mean, "he penetrated the secret truth."

16. *a legion was lodging*. Reading *lēgyon šrē hwā*, "a legion was unloosed," or "a legion was lodging." The same verbal root *š-r-y* appears in the final line of the same stanza with the former sense. The term *lēgyon* (a Latin loanword via Greek: see Aaron Butts, "Latin Words in Classical Syriac," *Hugoye* 19 [2016]: 132–33) can refer to a legion of soldiers, a mob of people, or the name "Legion," associated with the host of demons who possessed the demoniac in Mk 5.9 and Lk 8.30. From this sense, there is another possible reading: "At the feast where Legion was released." As is the case for other Syriac authors, Ephrem frequently uses this word to refer to demonic forces either directly or indirectly. In this context, however, "legion" may simply refer to the group of feasters mentioned in the preceding stanza.

17. *settled*. Reading *šken*, "he rested," "he settled." The same word is used in scripture to describe the Spirit of God "resting" or "settling" on the tabernacle. In this stanza, there seems to be a sort of twisted reversal of this familiar image. The sense of "settle" is also analogous to the way in which dregs settle to the bottom of the cup.

18. *their secrets*. This term, *kāsayhon*, is a homonym for "their cups" and "their secrets." The word is repeated in Syriac but rendered here in English using a distinct sense on each line. Lit. "he hastened to rest upon their cups (or secrets) / for it was blasphemy that their secrets (or cups) uttered."

See how the hand stirred up their feasters,[19]
and through the faster, troubled their mixtures;[20]
unseated amidst them,
he came and uncrowned them by his reading.[21]

6

The fair faster who had not fallen
in the furnace, fell into the lions' den,[22]
that on all sides Truth might be victorious,
that it be above all, and in all, manifest.
For when the idol and its name had ceased,
greedy ones cast the faster to wild beasts,
that in both den and furnace,
the victors' rescuer might be illustrious.

7

The faster had fallen to wild beasts,
his fast's scent aired out the lair's midst:[23]
the prayers' soft whisper outmastered
the fearsome roar of lionesses.
That roar was silenced by a moan of entreaty,[24]
chants of the lowly calmed down the mighty,
the wild beasts were dumbstruck
by Daniel's fasting and lowliness.

---

19. *the hand.* Lit. "the palm of the hand." This alludes to the hand of that "sublime finger" in stanza 4 which wrote on the plaster on the wall in Dn 5.5, where the exact expression *pastā d-idā*, "the palm of the hand," appears in P.

20. *through the faster.* While *b-idā* means "through," its components literally mean "through the hand," echoing "the palm of the hand" in the previous line. *stirred up ... troubled.* The renderings "stirred up" and "troubled" follow the perfect-tense readings *šagšat* ("threw into confusion," "made turbid," "muddled") and *daḥlat* ("terrified," "agitated").

21. *he ... uncrowned them.* Reading *šrā ... tāgayhon*, lit. "he unloosed their crowns." The same verbal root appears on the first line in this stanza.

22. *the lions' den.* Dn 6.

23. *his fast's scent aired out.* Reading *paḥ* as third masculine singular, lit. "his fast's scent diffused." The third feminine plural reading, taking "wild beasts" as the subject, would mean, "they breathed out the scent of his fast."

24. *roar ... moan.* The words for "roar" and "moan" derive from the same root: *n-h-m* (*nehmtā* and *nehmā*, respectively). In this case, "moan" should be read as a soft groaning, since the term denotes "moaning," "murmuring."

ON THE HOLY FAST 9

To the same melody: "God in his Mercies"

3+2+3 + 3+2+3
+ 3+2+3/4 + 3+2+4
+ 5+5 + 5+5
+ 3+3 + 3+3+3
+ R: 3+3+3

1

See fasting that put forth two beauties,
   adorning both soul and body:
it glorified the soul before watchers,
   it beautified the body before the embodied.
Hunger, by which beauties' beauty withers,
   in fasting, made the youths fatter and fairer:[1]
they gazed on Moses in his fast,
   whose brightness alighted on the greedy.[2]

Refrain: Glory to you, for in your fast they shone.

2

All that takes place with joy of heart,
   even heaviness to bear is lightness,[3]

---

1. *in fasting, made the youths fatter and fairer.* Dn 1.1–20.
2. *alighted.* Ex 34.29–31. In this line, "alighted" stands for two asyndetic verbs: *nḥet*, "came down," and *'azleg*, "shone forth."
3. *lightness.* Lit. "cheerfulness."

and all that takes place in sorrow,
  even honey to eat is bitterness.[4]
Fasting with joy, thereby the heart shines,
  when cheerful, the spirit lights up the face:
the youths were thus joyful
  in their fasts, as their faces shone with brightness.

3

Like the taste for repasts of one greedy,
  so Daniel's taste for the fast grew as greatly:[5]
when he forged on, he felt urged to press on—
  he could not wean himself from his custom.[6]
An infant forgets the milk of its nurse
  at the time of its weaning—how wondrous
that Daniel could not wean
  his old age from the fast of his young years.

4

The fast of Daniel was desired[7]
  like a thirst that binged upon wines:
he remembered the fast and grew younger,
  and three weeks he fasted, one after another.[8]
Though his beauty withered, the elder in his fast
  was desirable, as Gabriel cried out, to manifest[9]

---

4. *all that ... is bitterness.* Cf. Prv 17.22.

5. *Like the ... as greatly.* Lit. "Daniel greatly acquired a taste for fasting / like a greedy person who has acquired a taste for banquets."

6. *he could ... his custom.* This line continues the comparison between the greedy person and Daniel, in the sense that the habit compelled each to continue in his ways whenever he persisted in feasting or fasting, respectively. Lit. "When he persisted (i.e., abstained), he was overcome (by the emotion) to go on— / the habit was unable to wean itself off (fasting)."

7. *was desired.* Given the context, the fast was desired, or desirable, not only to Daniel, but also to the angels.

8. *three weeks.* Dn 10.2–3. This reference to Daniel's fast for three consecutive weeks could also be a reference to a fasting practice attested in early Christianity. According to the fifth-century historian Sozomen, for instance, some churches fasted three alternate weeks or three consecutive weeks immediately prior to the Feast of Pascha (*Historia ecclesiastica* 7.19).

9. *Gabriel cried out.* Dn 9.20–23. The same adjective *rgig*, "desirable," "pleasant," also appears in P Dn 9.23.

his vintage was desirable[10]
   through the fasts, and his youth through vegetables.

5

For weeks, the elder bore fasting,
   one day was hard for the young men:
he knelt and bore their three burdens,[11]
   a merchant, his wealth on his shoulders.[12]
He despised his desire of food most desired,[13]
   thus to the highest, he became desired:[14]
the heavenly host desired him
   since he could not bear earthly desires.[15]

6

Once pure were the names and bodies
   of the youths, styled with bynames:
idolatrous names had been married[16]
   to names consecrated and worshiped.
For Daniel's marred name proclaims El's judgment,[17]

---

10. *his vintage.* Lit. "his old age."

11. *their three burdens.* The feminine plural possessive pronominal suffix appears to refer back to "weeks." In this case, the burdens would point to the three weeks of Daniel's fast in Dn 10.2–3. Cf. the previous stanza for the three weeks' fast. Daniel was kneeling to pray three times each day in Dn 6.10.

12. *a merchant, his wealth.* The absence of subordination in this line is an instance of parataxis.

13. *food.* In Dn 10.3, Daniel abstained from "bread (or food) that is desirable." The same wording appears here.

14. *the highest.* I.e., the heavenly beings, the exalted ones in the heights. Dn 9.20–23.

15. *he could not bear.* This is an idiomatic rendering for the generic term "he detested" or "he hated." The idiom is introduced as an element of compensation for wordplay lost in translation elsewhere.

16. *idolatrous names had been married.* Lit. "the names of idolatry had joined in wedlock." Dn 1.1–7.

17. *marred.* There are two possible readings of ܓܝܪ here. The first is the particle *gēr*, "for," "indeed." The second is the passive participle *gir*, participle of *g-w-r*, "adulterated," functioning as an adjective modifying *šmeh*, "his name." The latter reading is foregrounded as "marred" because the context favors it, in the sense that the sacred name "Daniel" was adulterated by being married to the idolatrous name "Belteshazzar" in Dn 1.1–7. Another reason for "marred" is that, in the spirit of Ephrem's wordplay, this word conceals the divine name "Mār" (Syriac for "Lord") within it. *El's judgment.* In Hebrew, Daniel's name translates as "El is my judge," from

Babel shrank from that name lest he judge her:
the judge judged her and gave[18]
her kingdom to Media and Persia.[19]

7

Insidiously, Sin held captive
 that fearful fame over Daniel
to a feeble name of idolatry
 that an idol might hold down the victor, El.
Held down below, that name still compounded
 its power, a blow that compelled the captor
to bow to the captive,[20]
 and priestlike, he offered him sweet incense as well.[21]

8

By being worshiped, the name El,
 symbolically placed upon Daniel,
returned his worship within Babel
 to show among his oppressors his due praise.[22]

---

dān- "judge," *-i-* "my," and *-ʾel*, "God." In Biblical Aramaic and Syriac, the series of unvocalized consonants ܕܢܝܐܠ, standing for Daniel's name, is compatible with the etymological interpretation, *din-*, "judgment," *-i-* "my," and *ʾēl*, "God." In this passage, the meter requires the vocalization *dineh d-ēl*, "(his) judgment of El" (where "El" is interpreted as a subjective genitive), rather than *dayāneh d-ēl*, "that El is his judge."

18. *the judge.* Again, there are two possible readings of ܕܝܢ here. The first is the particle *dēn*, "but," "however." The second is the active participle *dayān*, functioning as an agent noun, "the judge," identified with the masculine El. The latter reading is also foregrounded not only because the context favors it, but also because the meter requires it. In this stanza, the poet is playing with two words that look like common enclitic particles at first glance, but they turn out to comprise a polarity of adultery and judgment upon closer inspection.

19. *her kingdom to Media and Persia.* Dn 8.20.

20. *to bow.* Verbs derived from the root *s-g-d* are alternately rendered in the following stanzas as "worship" and "bow."

21. *he offered.* Dn 2.46. The reference is to King Nebuchadnezzar as the captor and Daniel as the captive, but in this stanza, it is the feminine personification of Sin who is the captor and the name "Daniel" who is the captive (by being replaced by "Belteshazzar"), upon which is set the formidable glory of El, described in the previous stanza.

22. *praise.* In addition to "praise," *neshānā* also denotes "heroic deed," "victory," and "trophy."

Babel's king, who thought he burned the house of worship[23]
   and wiped out the worshipers, turned in his own place
to bow to the captive,
   whose name, placed upon him, was worshiped.

9

Another name worthy of worship
   El symbolically placed upon Mishael:[24]
Sin dealt insidiously with the worshiped name
   that he fall and bow before an idol.[25]
Mishael pondered the name placed upon him:
   how could the worshiped name bow to an idol?
Not bowing to Error,
   the erring bowed to the true one with him.[26]

---

23. *who thought he burned the house of worship.* A reference to the destruction of the Jewish Temple by the Babylonians. In 2 Kgs 25.8–10, Nebuzaradan, the head of the guards and servant of King Nebuchadnezzar, besieged and burned the house of the Lord in Jerusalem.

24. *Mishael.* Dn 1.6–7. The unvocalized consonantal form of the name appears as ܡܝܫܐܝܠ in the Aramaic and Syriac scriptural versions of the Book of Daniel, but as ܡܝܫܐܠ in the manuscripts that preserve this *madrāšā* with the exception of Beck's MS B, which agrees with the scriptural spelling. It is unclear whether the variant spelling was drawn from an unknown version or was an intentional departure from the scriptural spelling. The Hebrew name perhaps means, "Who is equal to El?" The variant spelling in Syriac suggests the interpretation, "touch of El" or "El has searched closely," depending on the vocalization.

25. *he fall.* Dn 3.11. The subject of this line could be the name of El or the name of Mishael. The sense seems to be that if Mishael were to bow down to the idol, then the name of El set upon him would also bow to idolatry.

26. *the erring.* The identity of the erring ones is unclear. One possibility derives from the narrative of Daniel 3, to which this stanza clearly alludes. In this chapter, Mishael, also called Meshach, along with his two companions, refused to fall down and worship the idol (cf. "not bowing to Error"). They then were sent into the fiery furnace, and they fell down into its midst (Dn 3.23). After the three youths emerged unscathed, King Nebuchadnezzar blessed their God who delivered them so that they might not worship any god except their own God (Dn 3.28). Following this reading, the context suggests that the erring ones are to be associated with King Nebuchadnezzar and his company who join Mishael and his companions in their worship of the true God. Another possibility is that the erring ones are personifications of the pagan names Belteshazzar, Shadrach, and Abednego, that bowed along with Meshach to the truth, i.e., the true one, El, whose name was symbolically placed into the names of Daniel and Mishael.

10

Now let us leave off appellations
    symbolically placed upon fasters:
no time remains to repeat their names,
    it is time to repeat their vegetables.[27]
Let us look on their fasts, which became their keys
    and unlocked the Holy Spirit's great treasury:
he unlocked, took the vision,[28]
    and interpreted the dream and its riddle.

11

Satan was divided against his kingdom,[29]
    for he started blaming his own side:[30]
Fraud reneged, dooming his debtors,
    for Sin was divided against her minions.
Error and Knowledge fell into battle:
    Error was put to shame through the old men,
yet through the young men,
    Truth was crowned; he also crowned them.

12

See Zion's penitents, with vegetables,
    revive and save Babel's prodigals:[31]
a blade went to lay waste the sages[32]
    but was dulled by the fast of Hananiah's kin.[33]
For fasters spared the Belly's ministers,[34]

---

27. *their vegetables.* More specifically, this word denotes pulses such as lentils, beans, peas, and seeds. Dn 1.12.

28. *he unlocked.* Dn 2.31. The implied subject is most likely Daniel, since the Holy Spirit is typically feminine in Ephrem's corpus.

29. *Satan was divided against his kingdom.* Mt 12.26 et par.

30. *own side.* Lit. "sons of his side," which denotes his "followers," "associates," and "comrades."

31. *prodigals.* Or "gluttons," "intemperate ones," later referred to as the "slaves of the belly."

32. *a blade went to lay waste the sages.* Dn 2.12–13.

33. *Hananiah's kin.* Lit. "the house of Hananiah," referring to Hananiah and his associates.

34. *spared.* This word, *ḥan(w)*, "they had compassion," "they had mercy," plays on Hananiah's name. Verbs derived from the root *ḥ-n-n* signify acts of compassion and mercy.

>   but rabid was Error who captured her preachers,
>   for Error herself erred,
>   as she turned to attack her own [men].³⁵
>
>   13
> Arioch roared and left in a furor,³⁶
>   the goats and black [sheep] were scattered:³⁷
> the flocks of the left were left in terror,³⁸
>   for this arm's love does not endure.³⁹
> The sheep of the right ran, bolted fast the furor,⁴⁰
>   hurtled to put on the fast, victors' armor,
> of Moses' and Elijah's kin,
>   who shut and opened heaven with prayer.⁴¹

---

35. *turned.* This word is the same as the word used in the previous stanza with the sense "reneged."

36. *Arioch.* Dn 2.14. Arioch's name is a near-homophone of *'aryāk,* "your lion," suggested also by the verb, "roared." In Dn 2.12–13, it was King Nebuchadnezzar who became furious and sent Arioch to slay the wise men.

37. *black [sheep].* Cf. *Cruc.* 3.14 and *Nat.* 18.16 for comparable instances of "black [sheep]"; Kathleen McVey, *Ephrem the Syrian. Hymns on the Nativity, Hymns Against Julian, Hymns on Virginity and on the Symbols of the Lord,* The Classics of Western Spirituality (New York and Mahwah, NJ: Paulist Press, 1989), 162. In this context, the goats and black [sheep] may be interpreted as the wise men of Babylon in Dn 2.12–13.

38. *the flocks of the left.* Despite the fact that the terms "right" and "left" were shorthand for good and evil, respectively, this line merits comparison with the pericope of the last judgment. The verb of P Mt 25.33 *wa-nqim 'erbē men yamīnēh wa-gdayā men semālēh,* "And he shall make the sheep stand on his right hand and the goats on his left hand," is echoed in the following line in this stanza.

39. *this arm's love does not endure.* Lit. "the charity of this forearm (i.e., the left forearm) is not made to stand," or "does not endure." This reading follows the vocalization *'amā,* "arm," but it may also be vocalized as *'emā,* "mother," in which case the following interpretation would result: "for she is a mother whose love does not endure." In this case, the feminine agent would refer to the left hand (*semālā*), which is also feminine.

40. *bolted fast.* Or, "they restrained," "they closed." It is the same verb commonly used to describe the closing-up of the heavens from rain. The allusion seems to be to Elijah's prayer that the sky cease from raining in 1 Kgs 17–18 and Jas 5.16–18. In the context of Dn 2, it is the wrath of the king that is restrained through prayer.

41. *who shut and opened heaven with prayer.* Ex 32.11, 1 Kgs 17.1, Dn 2.17–19, Jas 5.16–18.

ON THE HOLY FAST 10

To the same melody: "God in his Mercies"

3+2+3 + 3+2+3
+ 3+2+3/4 + 3+2+4
+ 5+5 + 5+5
+ 3+3 + 3+3+3
+ R: 3+3+3

1

He grew at the breast of Pharaoh's daughter,
  the Egyptians' feasts he would order:
she spoiled him with the best of the kingdom,
  in milk and honey was his pleasure.
He left Pharaoh's daughter who drew out and raised him[1]
  but loved Jacob's daughter who withdrew and debased him:
he loathed and rejected her riches,[2]
  for he sensed that all-enriching treasure.

Refrain: Blessed are you, fasters who prevailed.

2

Moses, first of fasters, looked down[3]
  on Pharaoh's daughter's full table:[4]

---

1. *drew out and raised him.* Ex 2.10.
2. *her riches.* The feminine singular possessor of these riches is not clearly specified. Possibilities include Pharaoh's daughter, Jacob's daughter, or both.
3. *first.* Or "chief," "height," "head."
4. *looked down / on.* I.e., "despised." This comparison conveys how Moses's taste was so refined that he deemed even the sumptuous fare of the daughter of Pharaoh to

he cast out the feast of the kingdom,
    the fast of the mountain he was craving.
He fasted and shone, he prayed and prevailed,[5]
    in one aspect he arose, another came down:[6]
an earthly aspect arose,
    he donned that heavenly glow and came down.

3

See April of the fasts at the mountain:[7]
    Moses climbed it, fed, and grew fatter;
for him, the fast became a banquet;
    his prayer, a fount of living waters.
The discerning man, his atoning fast,
    came down, spied the calf, set up amidst[8]
the people: the plow-bull[9]
    burned full of wrath at that idle sin-calf.

4

At the peak, as Moses was entreating,
    that blind people was greedily seizing:
for Moses, the fast of atonement,
    for the people, the feast of idolatry.
Moses at the height, the people at the calf,
    Spirit in Moses, Legion in the people:

---

be beneath his dignity. Only the fast would satisfy his desire, and he would settle for nothing less. For a similar comparison, cf. *Ieiun.* 4.7.

5. *prevailed*. Ex 34.29. The primary sense of this verb, *etnaṣaḥ*, is "he prevailed." It also evokes light imagery in the sense that "he was glorious," and in other stems deriving from the same root, e.g., *nṣaḥ*, "he shone." The same root appears in the response.

6. *aspect*. The polyvalent Persian loanword *gawnā*, here rendered "aspect," refers to surface, color, species, complexion, appearance, kind, manner, and medicine. In this context, the primary sense is the complexion of Moses's face in Ex 34.29–35, before and after its luminous transformation. The same term reappears with various nuances in stanzas 8–10 of this *madrāšā*.

7. *April*. Nisan is roughly equivalent to April, when the Passover and the Feast of Unleavened Bread take place.

8. *came down, spied the calf*. Ex 32.19.

9. *the plow-bull*. The term *palāḥā* describes Moses, "the ox" or "the bull," as "plowing," "serving," and "worshiping."

the fasts were healing salves
    for the erring ones stricken by the calf.

5

See how the cast calf gave rise to
    ruptures in the camp, standing idle:
for with the horn of idolatry concealed,
    it secretly gored and killed its worshipers.
Moses gored its worshipers with a sword[10]
    to show the death of souls through the corpses:[11]
they beheld the calf in the sword;
    through revealed things, he showed them concealed things.

6

Egypt's medicines are distinguished,
    the artisans there are accomplished:
Moses shunned the medicine store,
    the disease not of body but soul.[12]
He ascended Mount Sinai, God's mountain;
    there he lingered, gathered, and brought down spiritual remedies,[13]
    restoring the soul's health secretly.

7

The glutton's odious habit
    is a sickness, killing the taste buds:
the habit kills inside his mouth
    the sweetness of ordinary meals.
Greed's habit is to eat with complaining,
    drink with grumbling, a sickness of being difficult: his need that
    craves novelties is insatiable.

---

10. *Moses gored its worshipers with a sword.* Ex 32.27–29.

11. *souls.* This is another instance where the contrast with the bodies suggests the sense "souls," although it can also mean "lives," or "life-breaths." Cf. *Ieiun.* 9.1–2.

12. *soul.* See note 11 in the previous stanza on *souls*. The same rationale applies here and at the end of this stanza.

13. *remedies.* This term literally means "herbs" or "roots" used as medicines, here qualified as "spiritual."

8

Consider the people who with grumbling
  had eaten heavenly manna:
its color, the aspect of crystal,[14]
  its flavor, the taste of honeycomb.
That manna he compared with many images[15]
  to depict for the hearers' ear its qualities:
through the mouth of revealed things,
  for us he announced its concealed tastes.

9

He compared it with crystal to show
  that it rivaled light in its color,[16]
coriander he called it to make known
  in savor and taste it was seasoned.[17]
With oil and honey he compared it:
  with oil, to show it was a fat source,[18]
with honey, to make known
  that it was a wellspring of sweetness.[19]

---

14. *crystal.* Nm 11.7 and Ex 16.31. Cf. Wis 16.20. The term for crystal is the Syriac *berulā*, "beryl" or "crystal." In classical Syriac literature, the term is used to describe rock crystals and gemstones, usually white and translucent, while crystals and gems of other colors are sometimes mentioned as well. P Nm 11.7 reads as follows: "And manna is like the seed of coriander, and its color is like the color of *brulḥā*." Possible senses of *brulḥā* include "crystal," "pearl," and "white gemstone." According to RPS, cols. 606–7, *brulḥā* can have the same meaning as *berulā* and the Arabic *mahā* ("rock crystal"). Possibly of interest in this regard is the fact that the *Commentary on Numbers* attributed to Ephrem also explains *brulḥā* as *glidā*, meaning "ice," "frost," or "crystal"; J. S. Assemani, ed., *Sancti patris nostri Ephraem Syri Opera omnia quae exstant*, 6 vols., vol. 1 (Rome: Vatican, 1732), 256.

15. *he compared.* The subject is unspecified, but the implication is either scripture or Moses.

16. *it rivaled light in its color.* The background to this image is the hoary color of manna described in Ex 16.31.

17. *it was seasoned.* Nm 11.7. The participle *mtabal*, "it was seasoned," from the root *t-b-l*, "to spice," is attested in Jewish Babylonian Aramaic and Christian Palestinian Aramaic, but is rarely attested in Syriac. Cf. Arabic *t-b-l*, *mutabbal*, "seasoned."

18. *with oil.* Nm 11.8.

19. *with honey.* Ex 16.31.

10

This manna, then, was arrayed thus,
    in color, scent, and flavors:
the gluttons, sick with appetites,
    ate with malaise, a sign of the ailing.
Moles, the earth's offspring, ate bread unleavened,
    bitter herbs to remember—with grumbling
they ate heavenly manna,
    for they were used to Egyptian onions.[20]

11

What then shall satisfy the faster
    who curbs his mouth willingly?[21]
Though hungry, he sees, yet wants not,
    though thirsty, he sees, yet does not crave.
When he could eat, the fast gives him delight,
    when he could drink, the thirst makes him joyful.[22]
Most blessed is the Rewarder of all
    who feasts him at the table of his kingdom.[23]

The end of the ten madrāšē *on the forty days' fast.*

---

20. *Egyptian onions.* Ex 12.8, Nm 11.5. This passage contrasts Moses's heavenly diet of manna to the moles' earthly diet of bitter herbs, unleavened bread, and onions. The moles are to be identified with the "sons of the earth," or "sons of the land," an epithet for the sons of Israel. The term "remember" takes no object in the Syriac text, but the ironic implication seems to be that the sons of the land had eaten unleavened bread and bitter herbs, not to remember the bitterness of their captivity in Egypt, from which they were delivered, but to remember their former life in Egypt with longing and nostalgia for its cuisine, which included fish, cucumbers, melons, leeks, onions, and garlic (Nm 11.5–6). By singling out onions among these foods, Ephrem may be drawing on their association with bitterness and tears.

21. *What.* The first word, ܡܐ, here interpreted as *man*, "what," could also be a pun for "manna," evoking the Hebrew spelling *mān* with the same two consonants.

22. *gives him delight ... makes him joyful.* The two participles in this line evoke rich imagery through their multiple meanings: *mabsem*, "makes sweet-smelling," "causes delight," and *marwez*, "causes to flourish," "causes to rejoice."

23. *Rewarder of all ... feasts him.* Again, two Syriac participles are especially worth noting in this multifaceted sentence: *pāraʿ*, "the rewarder," "he who yields forth" (of leaves, flowers, fruit); and *mabsem* (with the accusative *leh* referring to the one who has fasted), "feasts him," "makes him sweet-smelling," "causes him delight."

TEACHING SONGS ON THE CRUCIFIXION

Translated by BLAKE HARTUNG

ON THE CRUCIFIXION 1

To the melody: "God in His Mercies"
8+8 + 8/9+9 + 10+10 + 6+9

1

O Lord of David, who rode a donkey
    and came unto the Daughter of Zion,[1]
happy was the procession before the bridegroom,
    when hosannas resounded from all sides.
The blind shone before him, the lame were stunned and danced.[2]
    The procession of the Daughter of Zion in the cultivated land[3]
        was greater
than that procession that took place
    for the Daughter of Sarah when she went out of Egypt.

Refrain: Blessed is the firstborn who endured all passions!

2

The feast[4] and April are two brothers,
    resplendent messengers of good news.

---

1. Cf. Zec 9.9.

2. Ephrem is engaging in a vivid poetic depiction of an already familiar biblical tableau (reminiscent of the ancient Greek literary practice of *ekphrasis*). The word choices add additional and less expected nuances: the blind "shone" (not only were their eyes opened, but they became a source of light by which others could see), and the lame were "stunned" (not only were they made to walk, but they were paralyzed by astonishment, or moved in the sense of being startled).

3. Ephrem contrasts the "cultivated land" (*šaynā*—an interesting word that in its most basic sense means "peace") of Jerusalem with the wilderness of the Exodus, implied in the final line, a relationship that strengthens the superiority of Jesus's "procession" over and against the "procession" of the "Daughter of Sarah" out of Egypt.

4. Probably an allusion to the feast of Pascha, celebrated in the month of April.

They ran and brought news to the daughter just as to her mother:
> "Look! The bridegroom is at the gate! Come out to meet him!"[5]

She saw him, but he did not please her. She was grieved, for he was holy;
> she trembled, for he was the Savior; she wondered, for he was humble.

He delayed his victorious deeds[6]
> and mixed strength with gentleness.

3

In the presence of his glorious virtues (which displeased her),
> she was especially grieved by his chastity,

for like her mother, she was familiar with adultery.
> In lying, she [even] surpassed her mother!

She knew that there was no pretext[7] that could conquer his purity,
> except one: to say, "he is a stranger."[8]

Craftily she blasphemed
> her betrothed to serve adulterers.

4

Within her mouth is the rebuke of her mother,
> she who cunningly crafted[9] the calf.

For she was oppressed by hidden love of it,[10]
> but was not able to possess it openly.

She came to the treasure house, the treasure of guile,
> and chose for herself a pretext that suited her.

---

5. An allusion to the parable of the five foolish virgins. See Mt 25.6.

6. Probably an allusion to the bridegroom's delay in Mt 25.5, which in the P and S has *'awḥar*, "he delayed."

7. Or perhaps "way" or "ruse."

8. The Daughter's error (representing Jesus as a "stranger") takes on far greater significance in light of Ephrem's persistent critiques of Marcionite theology. The Marcionite sect was a significant force in northern Mesopotamia well into the fourth century and was a frequent target of Ephrem's polemic. Marcionites believed that Jesus was the manifestation of a higher God, "the Stranger" (*nūkrāyā*), who came to deliver humanity from its bondage to the Creator. In this context, Ephrem's words subtly portray the identification of Jesus as a "Stranger" as a misrepresentation originating in the Passion narrative.

9. Or "served," "worshiped."

10. Probably refers to the calf.

With fraud toward Moses,
> she made[11] the molten image, by which she was put to shame.

5

The daughter also is stamped with the likeness
> of her mother.[12] She is cunning in hateful deeds:

she held her betrothed as a stranger,
> and mocked her bridegroom as a foreigner.[13]

She cried out and accused him
like Joseph's lady, who perversely cried out against that holy man.[14]
Overcome were the upright by the voices
> who cried out perversely against them.

6

She led him down to the judgment hall,
> there to kill him and gain favor for herself.

She considered the retinue of that chaste one,[15]
> like the debauched retinue of the house of Herod.

So she cried out before his gate to captivate his attendants,
> like a chaste maiden. She cunningly took refuge with Caesar

to murder and commit adultery
> and to perform both deeds, the one through the other.[16]

---

11. Or "served," "worshiped."

12. Lit. "that mother."

13. The last word of the stanza presents a textual problem. While the MS reads *giyorē* ("foreigners," "aliens"), Beck corrects it to *gayārā* ("adulterers"). Beck is not without justification in suggesting this change, given this hymn's emphasis upon the theme of adultery. There are, however, strong reasons to adhere to the MS reading. First of all, Ephrem is making a twofold accusation against the "Daughter": that she identified Jesus as a "stranger" and that she adhered to "strangers" instead of to Jesus. Furthermore, Ephrem does not identify the "Daughter" as "serving" adulterers (as Beck's reading would have it); rather, he calls them adulterers themselves.

14. See Gn 39.13–15.

15. Probably an allusion to Pilate.

16. Perhaps the sense of this is "perform both in the same action."

7

He greatly reproached her before the peoples,
>when the chief of the peoples washed his hands.[17]

For he saw that she had set two snares,
>one snare for murder, the other for hunting.

The second Herodias lay in ambush for Pilate,
>that like Herod, he too would soil his hands.[18]

He washed his hands of the blood
>of which the foolish one, like her daughter, had borrowed.[19]

8

Impure are the daughters of shadow,
>for their works love darkness.[20]

When she[21] saw the Lamp[22] who accused her,
>the daughter became her mother's breath.

She blew and extinguished [the lamp]. She bore it in solemn procession.[23]

>Unwittingly, her hands became her lampstands:
she lifted up the lamp at the banquet,
>by which it exposed them all the more.[24]

---

17. Mt 27.24.

18. Mk 6.19–24. Just as Herodias sought the head of John the Baptist through her daughter's request to King Herod, so the Daughter of Zion seeks the death of Jesus.

19. In light of the stanzas that follow, this line seems to draw a comparison between the debt incurred by the Daughter of Zion for the blood of Jesus and the debt incurred by Herodias and her daughter for John's death. Herod "washed his hands" of responsibility for the deed, just as Pilate would later do.

20. Cf. Jn 3.19.

21. Lit. "that one" (probably still Herodias).

22. Probably an allusion to John the Baptist.

23. Lit. "she bore and lifted up." The latter verb is typically used to describe a religious procession.

24. The scene evoked by this stanza works as a double reference to John's execution at Herod's birthday banquet and to the Crucifixion of Jesus, both "lamps" that the "daughter" "extinguished" and "lifted up" at a "banquet" (in Jesus's case the Passover, or Feast of Unleavened Bread). Ephrem makes this parallel clearer in the following stanza.

9

Now when this other [daughter][25] saw the Sun
    who drove away the darkness (which is useful to her),
who rolled back and dispelled the thick fog[26]
    that had unfurled over her[27] foul deeds,
she was ashamed that her[28] secrets had come to light.
    Though wishing to obscure the Light with wood,
she lifted him up[29] on the wood,[30]
    so that his rays might be cast over all humanity.

10

The sun too saw the other strong
    Sun that shone on Golgotha,
and was eclipsed and engulfed by his rays,[31]
    that what is visible would point to the Hidden.
It especially exposed the adulteress, so that her hands
    struck her breast and her mouth was filled with woe.
She grew frightened that her secrets were exposed
    before the Light that was exalted [on the cross].

11

The debauched one clung to Caesar
    and called out his name, but he did not hear her.
She put on the names of a stranger,
    and took off the names of the holy Messiah.
When she saw that the chiefs of the peoples scorned her,
    she desired the brigand[32] who was akin to her in everything,
since he bore her images,[33]
    and she also was fully stamped with his [images].[34]

---

25. Probably to be understood as the Daughter of Zion.
26. Lit. "who rolled back and rolled back."
27. The Syriac possessive is not pointed as feminine, but it makes the most sense that the reference would be to the "daughter."
28. See preceding note.
29. Cf. Jn 3.14; 8.28; 12.32.
30. I.e., of the Cross.
31. Cf. Mt 27.45.
32. I.e., Barabbas (Mt 27.15–17 et par).
33. MS lacks feminine pointing here.
34. Ephrem unpacks the shared "images" (the common characteristics) of Barabbas and the Daughter of Zion in greater detail in the following two stanzas.

12

The brigands[35] saw and welcomed one another.
> Their love for one another welled up and spilled over.

He[36] held his sword against the merchants,[37]
> [she held] her blade[38] in her hand against all the righteous.[39]

He[40] robbed in the wilderness like a simpleton,
> but she[41] robbed in her temple like an expert.

She put on lengthy prayers,[42]
> but stripped anyone who was clothed.

13

The simple brigand was like the disciple,
> robbing with simple youths.

She[43] who was the baroness of bandits
> became quite famous through mournful fasts.

When she fasts, she swallows up the orphan and the widow;[44]
> guilefully she even gives [her] alms to the poor,

that [her alms] might become her net,
> with which to catch the poor and their treasures.

14

Openly she raced to kill her Betrothed,
> openly she raced to embrace a bandit.

Her brazenness surpasses the brazenness of beasts,
> for she was not ashamed to murder openly and commit adultery.

She was like her mother, who before the eyes of seventy elders,[45]
> denied the Most High, and under the holy

---

35. I.e., Barabbas and the Daughter of Zion.
36. I.e., Barabbas (lit. "the sword of that one [masculine]").
37. Syriac singular.
38. I.e., the Daughter of Zion (lit. "the sword of that one [feminine]").
39. Cf. Mt 23.34–37.
40. Lit. "that one (masculine)."
41. Lit. "that one (feminine)."
42. Lk 20.46–47.
43. Lit. "that one (fem.)."
44. See Mk 12.40.
45. Ex 24.9. Cf. Mt 27.20, in which the people deny Jesus before the presence of the elders.

pillar of cloud,
   openly engaged in impurity.[46]

15

And when her mother went mad in the wilderness,
   her hand did not reach the Holy One.
Since her arms were too short to reach him,
   she stretched out her blasphemies to reach him.
His nature and his place conquered the prostitute,
   for his place is lofty, and his nature is unsullied.
No one can rise to his height,
   nor touch or take hold of his substance.[47]

16

Her eyes[48] desired a visible image[49]
   instead of the secret and invisible splendor.
God saw her weakness,
   that she loved visible things[50] [more] than the Invisible.
He gave her her desires: he sent his beloved
   to come[51] and put on a body, that she might see him visibly,
and exchange visible things for that Invisible,
   who in his love became visible.[52]

---

46. Ex 32.

47. Beck opts for "his self" as a rendering of *qnōmā*, but in the context of describing God's "height," a word with physical connotations, it seems best to translate this also as somewhat physical at least in imagery. Just as God's "height" cannot be reached, so his "essence/substance" cannot be touched. We are also avoiding the translation of "person" preferred by Rouwhorst, because it carries later Trinitarian connotations (the word would become the common translation of *hypostasis*). In Ephrem's time, however, this technical sense of the word was still far from established.

48. Lit. "her eye."

49. In the immediate context, the allusion is to the replacement of God by the Golden Calf, but it also alludes more broadly to the idolatrous habit of preferring "strangers" in God's place. Ephrem highlights this point with wordplay: the word "visible" (*d-gelyā*) sounds like "false" (*daglāyā*).

50. "Visible things" (*d-gelyātā*) sounds like "false things" (*daglyātā*).

51. The sense of the Syriac is altered slightly here to convey better the shift in subject from God to "the Beloved."

52. Ephrem repeats a similar idea in *Nat.* 21.12, 22.16.

17

Strangers are delightful to the foolish one,
  her husband is detestable in every way.
Worthy of love, her betrothed accepts[53] her,[54]
  even this infamous unclean one.
Very[55] detestable in her sight was the Truth in all respects![56]
   He was great, and she did not desire him; he became small,
     and she did not love him.
He was invisible and she replaced him.[57]
   He became visible, and she vilified and murdered him.

---

53. Or "supports."

54. In *Cruc.* 1, Ephrem depicts the Jews as turning away from Jesus (like their ancestors in the wilderness) in order to follow after "strangers." Thus the appellation "stranger" takes on dark and idolatrous overtones. The subtle anti-Marcionite critique is not difficult to discern: by serving a "stranger," the Marcionites follow in the path of the Jews. These examples have demonstrated that some of Ephrem's anti-Jewish polemic could serve several purposes. In addition to accusing the Jews of the Passion whose actions led to the death of Jesus, his assaults upon the Jewish culpability for the Passion could point forward to his own time, to his contemporaries who reject the Son in favor of a "Stranger." Ephrem associates the very term "stranger" with the willful, adulterous rejection of Jesus, subtly portraying the biblical Jews as proto-Marcionites.

55. There is also wordplay with *ṭab*, read adverbially above, but which can also be "the good one, the famous one," in contrast to the infamous adulterer.

56. Because of the lexical range of the Syriac word *šarbā*, the phrase *b-kul šarbīn* could be taken several ways: "in all respects," "in all generations," or "in all stories."

57. This probably refers to the worship of the Calf.

ON THE CRUCIFIXION 2

The second on the Crucifixion
To the melody: "The Infants were Slain"
7+7 + 7+7 + 7+7 +7+7 + 7+7[1]

1

O hidden lamb, who slaughtered
   the visible lamb in Egypt,[2]
and gave the staff to Moses
   by which he might tend[3] an old flock.[4]
The old man tended the old flock,
   but the lamb tended both of them!
The lamb fed and nourished:
   he fed his shepherds,
so that they fed on him, and he fed them.

Refrain: Blessed is the lamb who tended his [own] flocks!

2

In the house of Jethro,[5] Moses slaughtered
   many sheep and lambs,
and though he learned well, he did not fathom
   how to slaughter a certain sacrifice.
It was our lamb who was teaching him
   how to depict his symbol.

---

1. Ephrem also uses this meter for *Res.* 2 and 3; *Haer.* 22–24, 48; *Nis.* 17–21; and *Nat.* 23–24.
2. See Ex 12.6.
3. Lit. "to shepherd" (*ra'ā*).
4. See Ex 4.2.
5. Ex 3.1.

The sacrifice taught the sacrificer
   how to roast and eat [him],[6]
how to slaughter [him] and sprinkle [his blood].
   Blessed is he who taught his eaters!

3

The new lamb taught
   the shepherd—who had grown old with the flock—
how to engrave his symbol
   on a lamb of the herd, his type.
He commanded him to gather bitter herbs,
   to spread[7] mourning for him among those who ate them.[8]
The lamb warned his slaughterer
   that he should not break a bone in him,[9]
who himself has bound up the broken.[10]
   Thanks be to the Lord [who] binds up all!

4

The lamb taught Moses
   that he should not be boiled in water,[11]
for the spit is a sign of his wood,[12]
   and the roasting a type of his bread.
He also commanded those who ate him
   that none should be left over,[13]
lest that which is as resplendent as the medicine of life,
   be neglected like some ordinary and transitory food.
Blessed is the lamb who made his symbol resplendent!

---

6. Ex 12.8.

7. The text reads *da-b-'ebleh*, but Beck comments that it seems right to correct to *d-'ebleh*. This correction fits the sense of the passage as well as the meter.

8. The Syriac for "bitter herbs" (*mrārā*) is singular, but the sense in English is plural.

9. Ex 12.46; Nm 9.12; Jn 19.36.

10. See Is 61.1; Lk 4.18. The P of Is 61.1 reads "bind up the broken." In the citation of that passage in Lk 4.18, however, the P reads "heal the contrite of heart."

11. Ex 12.8.

12. I.e., the cross.

13. Ex 12.10; Nm 9.12.

ON THE CRUCIFIXION

5

Concerning his symbol, the lamb commanded
   that they should eat it with unleavened bread,[14]
new bread and new meat
   to depict a symbol of its newness.
When the leaven of Eve
   —that aged one that aged all things[15]—was disseminated,[16]
all things grew old and wore out.
   By means of the unleavened bread that renewed all,
the leaven that ages all things has failed.
   Blessed is the bread which renews all!

6

The rest of the commandments, too,
   the true lamb commanded,
concerning the symbol of the temporal lamb,
   that no one should eat it while sitting down[17]—
a symbol of his holy body—
   for who could eat it while sitting down?
Since before him, the seraphim are fearful,
   and veil their faces from him,[18]
let [his] partakers fear and be holy!
   Blessed is he who has taught a resplendent symbol!

7

Come see the living lamb
   who has chosen his own shepherds,
and has chosen also his own slaughterers.
   For he made Abraham take a knife
to kill a sheep, his symbol.[19]
   He killed his symbol and redeemed his symbol:
he redeemed a lamb but killed a ram.
   With his symbol, he redeemed his symbol,

---

14. Nm 9.11.
15. Syr. singular.
16. Or "spread," "broke forth." Lit. "flew" (*praḥ*).
17. Ex 12.11.
18. Cf. Is 6.2.
19. Gn 22.10. Isaac is the "sheep."

to become the completion of symbols.[20]
   Blessed is he who has come and completed[21] symbols!

8

This first lamb
   chose its own first shepherd.[22]
The firstfruit [chose] the firstborn,
   poured some of his likenesses over him,
and stamped upon him some of his images.
   He unrolled over him a parable of his execution.[23]
Since Abel was a shepherd and a sacrifice,
   through him our shepherd and sacrifice depicted
his shepherding and his sacrifice.
   Glory to you, depicter of his symbols!

9

Our lamb taught Abel
   first to make himself perfect
that a lamb might offer a lamb,
   but offer himself first
and only then offer the other [lamb]—
   great was the wonder there!
For it was a lamb that was offering,
   it was a lamb that was being offered,
and it was a lamb that was receiving [the offering].
   Praise be to the lamb of God!

10

In every generation, the firstborn was killed
   through the symbolic deaths of his saints.

---

20. Gn 22.12–13. In a footnote to his own translation of this hymn, Sebastian Brock observes that Ephrem's writings reflect two distinct interpretations of the offering of Isaac: (1) that Isaac symbolizes humanity, delivered by Christ; and (2) that Isaac and the ram *both* represent Christ (which is what we find here); *Ephrem the Syrian: Select Poems*, ed. Brock and Kiraz, 133.

21. Or "ended." Same root as *sākā* ("end") above.

22. Cf. Gn 4.4.

23. Syr. *pras ʿallū(hy) pellat qaṭleh*. The imagery seems to be that of the unrolling of a scroll, possibly alluding to the unrolling of a scroll in a synagogue service.

Through prophecy, the lamb became
   like a herald[24] of his readings.[25]
Something that would come to be
   (though distant), was brought near.[26]
His servants came first, clothed
   in names in accordance with his deeds,[27]
so that [future] generations might read his names.
   Blessed is he whom prophecy has proclaimed!

24. MS plural; Beck omits plural pointing.

25. If *'āmrā* is understood as "it is said," this would read: "For just as it is said in the prophecy, according to the proclaimers of its readings / that which would come to pass: even while distant, it was brought near."

26. In other words, the Old Testament testimony to Christ made known something that was still in the distant future.

27. Or "realities" (*sūr'ānē*). In other words, titles like "sacrifice" and "lamb" for Old Testament figures were a means for Christ to reveal his titles to those who would later read those accounts.

ON THE CRUCIFIXION 3

Meter: Each stanza contains eight lines;
the meter is otherwise indiscernible. To the melody:
"Blessed are You, Ephratha." Meter unclear[1]

I

On the fortieth [day] he slaughtered the paschal lamb
  "between the suns,"[2] as it is written:
It was inscribed beforehand that it would be sunset,[3]
  so that even his time was prophesied about him.
The true lamb
  who was slain teaches us
How perfect is his time: on the fifteenth,[4] he was slain,
  the day on which the pair
    of luminaries[5] were full.[6]

Refrain: Blessed are his symbols that proclaimed him!

   1. This particular poem is metrically very problematic. It may follow the metrical pattern 8+8 + 9+8 + 5+7 + 7+5+5 + R: 5, but we have not yet fully tested this hypothetical structure to our satisfaction.
   2. Syr. *bēt šemšē;* Beck corrects his German translation to "in the evening," following the P of Lv 33.5 (*bēt ramšē*). The expression quoted in the hymn, however, appears in the P of Ex 30.8 to translate *beyn ha'arbayim* ("between the lamps"). Variations of this phrase can also be found in the Targum Neofiti, Ps-Jonathan, and Onqelos readings of Ex 30.8, as well as Ex 12.6 and Lv 23.5. See Rouwhorst, vol. 2, 55, n. 1.
   3. *'rāb* ("sunset") sounds like *'erbā* ("lamb").
   4. Beck takes this to be an error and corrects his translation to "fourteenth." Because this interpretation of the Paschal chronology would contradict Ephrem's usual placement of the Crucifixion on the fourteenth of Nisan, Rouwhorst suggests that the authenticity of this line poses some problems (Rouwhorst, vol. 1, 34).
   5. I.e., the sun and moon.
   6. See *Cruc.* 4.15, *Eccl.* 51.6. Ephrem is likely referring to a simultaneous full moon and spring equinox, as described in the Targum Neofiti, Ps-Jonathan, and Onqelos versions of Exodus. See Cassingena-Trévedy, *Hymnes Pascales*, 208, fn. 1.

2

Blessed are you, final evening,[7]
  for the evening of Egypt was perfected in you.
In you, our Lord ate the small Pascha,
  and became the great Pascha.
Pascha was mixed
  with Pascha, and feast with festival.
A Pascha which has passed away was mixed
  with another Pascha which has not passed away:
    symbols and fulfillment!

3

Blessed are you, Place, for in you a scale
  of truth was set up: on the two sides
were two Paschas and two lambs,
  two peoples and two salvations.
The people were like their Pascha:
  their lamb was temporal, and just like its time, it came to an end and grew cold.
The salvation of the peoples
  is an unfading truth,[8]
    because [its] lamb will never pass away.[9]

4

Blessed are you, [place] where his two disciples were sent![10]
  They came and marked you out for his supper.
Despised was the temple that Solomon built,
  and the palaces of the house of Herod.
Purity was chosen by him,
  and in you he saw holiness,
and in you he found faith:
  he gave the abundant overflow[11] of his blessing,
    the wages for your service.

---

7. Cf. Mt 26.60; Jn 13.1.
8. Or "has not abated." The unknown meter makes it impossible to say for sure.
9. Another possible rendering might be "for it is said that it (i.e., salvation) will not pass away." Cf. P Is 51.6: *w-purqān(y) l-ʿālam nehwē w-zadiqut(y) lā teʿbar*.
10. The upper room of the Last Supper. See Mk 14.13, Lk 22.8.
11. Or "excesses." "Leftovers" or "remainders" also makes sense, like crumbs falling from the table of the Last Supper.

5

Blessed again are you! You are the place of the just one,
    for in you our Lord broke his body.[12]
A small place became a mirror
    for the whole creation, which was full of him.[13]
A small covenant was given
    by Moses from a glorious mountain,
a great covenant
    went out and filled the earth
        from a small house!

6

All the things done by Moses
    were weak, like parables,
and it was fitting that they become greater, lest they be despised,
    until—look—they reach their fullness![14]
For it was fitting that[15]
    the greatness of our Savior should become small,
since the glorious nature cannot
    be seen by his creatures
        without weakness.

7

In you also he appeared[16] to Abraham,
    as he brought[17] a calf to the watchers,[18]
but the seraphim trembled when they saw the Son,
    putting a linen cloth on his waist,
and washing feet in a basin[19]—
    the filth of the thief who betrayed him.[20]

---

12. *Pagreh qṣā hwā*, reminiscent of the wording of 1 Cor 11.24: *hānaw pagr(y) dʿal ʾappaykōn metqṣē*.
13. Or "for it was filled up by him."
14. Or "until—look—their perfections arrive."
15. Swapped with the following line.
16. Or "it was shown to Abraham," or "he was seen by Abraham."
17. Lit. "carried and came" (*tʿin w-ʾetā*).
18. Gn 18.8. Or "to the Watchers, / the Seraphim. But they were frightened ..." or "to the Watchers. / The Seraphim were frightened ..."
19. Jn 13.4–5.
20. I.e., Judas.

Every mouth is too small,
   and every tongue too weak
      to enumerate his revelations!

8

Our Lord cleansed the body of the brothers
   in a basin, which is a symbol of unity.
Through that symbol also the limb was cut off,
   that cut off itself and betrayed itself.[21]
In the womb[22] of water, we are assembled anew:
   let us not be divided limbs,
that dispute against themselves,
   and are unaware
      that they strive against their own love.

9

Blessed are you, Place! When your smallness
   is set in comparison to the whole creation,
the whole creation is filled by
   what was in you, and too small for it!
Blessed is your dwelling, in which was broken
   that bread from the blessed sheaf.[23]
In you was pressed
   the grape from Mary,
      the cup of salvation.

10

Blessed are you, Place! For no one has seen,
   nor will see, what you have seen:
when our Lord was made the true altar,
   the priest, the bread, and the cup of salvation.
In his own person[24] he was sufficient for all.
   None other was capable of this:

---

21. I.e., Judas. The line can also be read, "the dirt of the place that he filled up" or "completed."

22. Or "bosom," "breast" (*'ubbā*). "Womb" seems most appropriate for the context of the rebirth of baptism. It also anticipates the next stanza, which speaks of Jesus's Incarnation through Mary.

23. Feminine (i.e., the Virgin Mary).

24. Syr. *qnōmā*. See note 47 for *Cruc.* 1.15.

altar and lamb,
>   sacrifice and sacrificer,
>> priest and sustenance.[25]

11

Blessed are you, Place!
>   Within you the Paschal Lamb
welcomed[26] the True Lamb.
For the wearied symbol entered and found rest
>   in a restful[27] chest, and was completed therein.[28]
Blessed is your dwelling, in which was served
>   that Pascha, of which there was no equal!
The temporal lamb lifted up[29]
>   its authority and gave [it]
>> to the Lamb of God.

12

Blessed are you, Place! For never has a table
>   like yours been set among kings,
nor even in the sanctuary of the Holy of Holies,
upon which was set the showbread.[30]
In you the bread was first
>   broken, so that you
became his church: the firstborn of altars,
>   which first bore his offering,[31]
>> appeared first in you.[32]

---

25. Syr. *met'aklānā*. I.e., a sacrificial meal.
26. Or "met" (*aqbel*).
27. Or "gentle" (*nihā*); same root as verb "to rest" above.
28. The "chest," "breast," "bosom," or "womb" (*'ubbā*) could refer to the room itself, but in this case the more likely reading is the "bosom" of Christ, into which the Paschal Lamb entered through the consumption of the paschal meal.
29. Syr. *šqal* (there are a number of options that seem to fit the sense of the passage). Potential renderings include "took," "received," or "relinquished."
30. Syr. *lḥem appē*, the wording of Ex 25.30 (P).
31. Or "which served the first offering (or 'Eucharist') (*qurbānā*)."
32. Or "was first seen..." Robert Murray notes that the word *bukrā* ("firstborn") may have had a particular Eucharistic connotation in Ephrem's time, as it was later used to describe the consecrated bread in the East Syrian liturgy; Murray, *Symbols of Church and Kingdom*, 64.

13

Blessed are you, Place! For within you
   the crown of the brothers encircled[33] the Son,[34]
but one fine virgin Flower,[35]
   because it refreshed him, was placed upon his breast.[36]
And though they all were praiseworthy flowers,
   the holy Blossom was desirable.
The stinking Weed[37] departed from there,
   so that his stench
      departed with him.

14

In you, Place, was also depicted the sundering:[38]
   that precise one which will take place.
For in the night, the Son of Darkness[39] departed,[40]
   and put on the darkness befitting him.
The Black one grew angry, got up, and left,
   the chief of the goats[41] did not return.[42]
At the judgment, the goats,
   those of his stock, will be separated
      from the lambs of light.

15

In you again was an invisible mystery revealed
   by the visible bread which he gave him:[43]

---

33. Or "wrapped around," "enwrapped" (*krak*).

34. In a lovely image, Ephrem envisions the disciples around Jesus as a crown of flowers.

35. A reference to John, the "disciple whom Jesus loved." Cf. Jn 13.23; *Azym.* 14.5–8, 12.

36. Jn 13.25.

37. I.e., Judas (Jn 13.30).

38. Or "separation," "division" (*puršānā*). A reference to the final judgment, the separation of the "sheep" from the "goats" (Mt 25).

39. I.e., Judas.

40. Or "The Son of Darkness went out into the night."

41. See Mt 25.32. According to Beck, Ephrem's version of that verse gives the animals as *gdayyā* (goats, kids) and *'emrē* (lambs), while the P reads *'erbē* (sheep, rams).

42. A reference to Judas's departure from the Upper Room (Jn 13.30).

43. I.e., Judas (Jn 13.26).

he concealed himself to teach how much he loved him,
  and he revealed to let him know that he knew him.[44]
He concealed himself and announced without anger,
  he rebuked[45] and scorned him.[46] How he withheld!
Did the kind one say to him:
  "It is you"?
    Nay rather, "You have said [it]."[47]

16

In you, Place, again was dismay[48]
  among the disciples over what they heard.
Labor pangs never seized a mother
  like what seized the twelve.
They were wanting to be silent, but could not,
  they were seeking to speak, but were afraid.
The Sheep beckoned[49] to the Lamb:
  "Teach us:
    Who is the Wolf?"[50]

---

44. This stanza explores Jesus's subtle words and actions toward Judas in the Upper Room, where he both "reveals" that he knows Judas's intentions and "conceals" the full truth of it from the other disciples. The wordplay in these lines is difficult to replicate in English. The roots we have translated as "invisible" and "concealed" are identical in Syriac, as are "visible" and "revealed."

45. Wordplay: the root of *akes* ("he rebuked") sounds similar to that of *ksī* ("he concealed"). It also sounds like *kseh* ("his cup"). Likewise, the root of the second verb meaning "he rebuked."

46. Wordplay: sounds like *besreh* ("his flesh").

47. Syr. *att 'emart*, Jesus's response to Judas (Mt 26.25) in both the P and the S versions.

48. The word *bolhāyā* has a fairly broad range of meaning: "stupefaction," "distress," "wondrous things" (pl.), or "quickness."

49. Jn 13.24, in which Peter "gestures" or "beckons" (*rmaz*) to the beloved disciple.

50. I.e., Judas. This is an interesting retelling of the narrative of Jn 13.24–25, in which the Lamb (*'emrā*) applies to the beloved disciple, while the Sheep (*'erbā*) applies to Peter, and the Wolf (*dēbā*) applies to Judas. This echoes Lk 10.3, when Jesus sends forth his disciples as lambs (*'emrē*) before wolves, commanding them not to carry any provisions with them (OS and P: *kīsē*, *tarmālē*, and *msānē*). This anticipates the following stanza, where Jesus is identified as the provider (*zayānā*) for the lambs. Cf. *Azym.* 14.22.

17

He said, "Take purses,"[51] since he took
   the form[52] of mortals who perished in Sheol.
He showed that he would be slain like a human being
   and although he was the provider, he would not be able to provide.[53]
He returned again and was resurrected to teach them
   that it is he who feeds all flesh.
He rested like one dead, and he returned like one living,
   he provided to teach
      that he died and was alive [again].

18

Blessed are you, Place, for in you the word[54] "justice"
   was explained by the word[55] "swords."
With the sword he cut off that law,
   when it cut off the ear that despised his words.[56]
But the merciful one came and healed it,
   then gave leave to the sword, and it was sheathed—
the strong man who was restrained
   by the rising[57] of the gentle one,
      is a symbol of the law.

19

He said, "Take away the swords"[58] to teach [them] all the more,
   that not even with a staff should a person become violent,[59]

---

51. Lk 22.36.

52. Syr. *ṭupsā* ("type").

53. Lines 3–4 indicate that Jesus had been sustaining the disciples as long as he was alive, but because he was preparing to die, he would no longer be able to provide for them. From then on, they would need a source of provision, represented by *kisē*, "purses," "moneybags," or "wallets," because Jesus "would be slain like a human being."

54. Lit. "name" (*šēm*).

55. Lit. "name" (*šēm*).

56. A reference to the cutting-off of the ear of the servant of the high priest (identified in John as "Malchus") in the Garden of Gethsemane. See Jn 18.10–11 et par.

57. Or "rising" (*denḥā*) like the Sun.

58. Jn 18.11 et par. Cf. Lk 22.36, which has *nessab*, "let him take," in P; Jn 18.11, which has *sim*, "put (away)," in P and *'ahpek*, "put back," in OS.

59. Cf. Mk 6.8 et par.

for see how he held back the sword of Simon:
   with the sword he cut off the wrath of the sword.
He showed "legions of angels,"[60]
   that he was not in need of men.

. . .[61]

60. Mt 26.53.
61. Lacuna.

ON THE CRUCIFIXION 4

Poem 1 of the cycle found in MS D

Again[1] on the Crucifixion

To the melody: "The King's Bride"

6+4+4 + 6+4

4+4+4 + 4+4

5+5 + 5+3

R: 5+5 + 5+3

I

My brothers, a slave[2] struck
  the cheek
    of the slave-freeing master!
  How gentle was the one who wished to free even that
    slave who struck him.[3]
The master of the accursed
  slave grew sad
    that he struck [his] cheek
    and did not accept his freedom.[4]
For the relief of the burden
  of the slave being freed,[5]

---

1. In MS D, this word, *tub*, connects the selection of hymns *On the Crucifixion* with the previous two hymns *On the Unleavened Bread*.

2. Beck comments that the singular "slave" (*'abdā*) probably refers to Jn 18.22, where the P, C, and S read *mḥā 'al pakkā*. Ephrem repeats this same phrase without the *'al*.

3. Lit. "him."

4. Or "emancipation."

5. The unclear meter makes the correct reading difficult to determine.

here, the freer of all
>> was struck.

Refrain: Heaven and earth and all that is in them are too small to give thanks for this!

2

Though insane, they clothed him
>> with royal garments
>>> and made him king.[6]
Though brazenly mocking their Lord
>> like simpletons,[7]
they symbolically worshiped him.[8]
>> With the crown of thorns
>>> they placed upon him, they showed
and attested that he removed
>> Adam's curse.
Whenever they wished
>> to deny his words,
his truth was crowned
>>> by [their] lies.

3

We have heard that
>> "they went in and brought out
>>> the covering of the altar."[9]
They searched deeply[10] for a pretext
>> of accusation.

---

6. Or "changing his garments, they made him a king with royal garments."

7. Reading uncertain (Beck takes it as singular, but I am rendering it as plural since it seems to refer to a group).

8. Reading uncertain.

9. Introduced with *lam,* the customary marker for indicating quotation (hence the quotation marks). Ephrem, however, is not quoting from the biblical text, but apparently is referencing an extra-biblical tradition that predates the composition of this hymn. Although we cannot know the exact details of this tradition and its origin, Ephrem's words here and in *Azym.* 5.6 ("The priests took the veil from the holy place, / and they cast pure purple upon him") attest to a Christian narrative expansion on the guards mockingly robing Jesus in purple.

10. *'ameq* (lit. "to go deep").

That they might put on him
>> the sign of kingship,
>>> they had gone in and uncovered
the holy altar,
>> and clothed him with it, that he would die.
Through the coverings of the holy place,
>> he took the kingship,
like the ephod which David
>> also put on.[11]

4

An ordinary person who touched the altar
>> or its vessels[12]
>>> must surely die.[13]
"In our law," they said,
>> "he deserves death."[14]
But so that they would not be found guilty
>> by the kingdom
>>> that subjugated them,[15]
they did not explain
>> the pretext of this—
of those things[16] with which they had clothed [him],
>> they had feared to disclose it:[17]
They accused [him] cunningly,
>>> since they were afraid.

5

For they wanted to set
>> two snares
>>> for the one who examines all:

---

11. 2 Sm 6.14.
12. Or "garments."
13. Cf. Nm 4.15, 20.
14. Jn 19.7.
15. I.e., Rome.
16. I.e., the coverings of the altar.
17. Apparently referring to "the pretext of this."

With cunning, they put[18] upon him
    the sign of kingship,[19]
and put[20] upon him
    the robe of glory,[21]
        so that "either," they said,
"by one or the other[22]
    he will be given over to death."
So, by two things they took him captive,
    [and] by two things he took them captive,
for he took the kingdom
    and the priesthood.

6

They handed him over to the judge,[23]
    but did not perceive
        that they were condemned by him.[24]
Through the voice that tore it,[25]
    the curtain[26] spelled out
the final destruction:
    when they conquered the conqueror,
        they became greatly indebted,
their debt became
    the cause of destruction.
Who has ever seen a master
    whose slave sat in judgment over him,
and [then] wrote out, nailed in, and proclaimed
    his kingdom?[27]

---

18. Lit. "cast," "throw."
19. A reference to the purple robe.
20. Lit. "cast," "throw."
21. Probably a reference to the covering of the altar.
22. Lit. "by this one or that one."
23. I.e., Pilate.
24. This probably refers to Jesus or God.
25. An allusion to the dying cry of Jesus (Mt 27.50).
26. Syr. *apay tar'ā* ("the veil of the door"), the wording of the C, S, and P of both Mt 27.51 and Lk 23.45.
27. A reference to the sign nailed above the cross, which declared Jesus "King of the Jews."

7

Caesar, whom the condemned[28] chose,
   he destroyed
      their dwelling place.[29]
Again, when they cried out to that judge[30]
   to hand [him] over to them,
the bribe did not
   blind the just man,
      for he declared innocent the innocent one,
having become a prosecutor
   against the scribes.
With water he washed his hands
   of that living blood,[31]
which the house of Cain hid
   among their nation.[32]

8

Now all their generations copied a pledge,
   one after another,
      [one] generation to the next,
for they feared what they had perceived—that debt
   is filled with wrath.[33]
But because they were divided,
   one generation did not wish
      to allow the other to escape,[34]
since like thieves,
   they betray one another.

---

28. This is the same root as "indebted" and "debt" in the previous stanza.

29. A reference to the destruction of Jerusalem and the Temple in 70 CE.

30. I.e., Pilate.

31. See Mt 27.24.

32. On one level, Ephrem is arguing that the Jews played the part of "those of the house of Cain" by covering up the living blood that they had spilled, "within their nation," just as Cain concealed the blood of his brother Abel in the earth. The implication, of course, is that the curse came upon the Jews from within their own nation, just as the curse came upon the house of Cain from the earth.

33. In other words, the incurring of this debt would bring wrath upon them.

34. In other words, the people who cried out, "His blood be on us and our children" (Mt 27.25), knew that there would be judgment for their actions and sought to implicate future generations for the deed as well.

Like murderers
  who were judged and found guilty,
  they did not wish for their companions
    to be delivered.

9

And when they cried out against him and scourged him,[35]
  they did not realize
    that he was repaying the scourging
    of that heir[36] who was corrupted
    and sinned in Eden.
You are the Lord,
  who had compassion on his slave
    lest he be scourged,
  and presented your Son
    and scourged him in his place.[37]
Heaven and earth,
  and everything in them,
  are too small to give thanks
    for this!

10

And at the pillar[38] where they brought him,
  they showed a symbol
    of the downfall of the people,
  for unlike Samson, who seized[39]
  and brought down the pillars,

---

35. Jn 19.1 et par.
36. An allusion to Adam.
37. Cf. *Azym.* 1.8. Ephrem applies the language of debt-payment to the scourging of Jesus, through which Jesus "repaid" (*praʿ*) Adam's scourging. Ephrem appears to mean that Adam incurred punishment through his debt, and out of compassion, the Son accepted this on his behalf. We should not interpret this as an abstract endurance of the "wrath" of God, as in some later western theologies. Instead, Ephrem's language implies something much more concrete, that the punishment Jesus suffered in Adam's place was the physical endurance of "scourging."
38. *ʿamudā*. The "pillar" at which Jesus was scourged is an old tradition but is not mentioned in the four Passion accounts.
39. *ʾettali/ʿettli* can also mean "hung up," "suspended," and thus likely carries an allusion to the Crucifixion.

ON THE CRUCIFIXION

the Lord of Samson
   was himself
      the true column
of the holy city,
   and [when] he abandoned it, it collapsed.
The Chaldeans tore it down,
   but they returned and rebuilt it.[40]
When it denied its pillar,[41]
   it was cast down.[42]

11

When they scourged him with whips,
   through his pain they depicted
      a symbol of their pain,
that he cut off[43] and removed the kingship,
   the priesthood,
and the prophethood,
   for he extracted
      the three ribs
from the mouth
   of the cruel beast.[44]
He smashed its horns,
   pulled out its rib and cast it aside.
He took its strength from it,
   and it was vanquished.

12

The curtain[45] that was torn
   was a cry of pain
      for the holy place,

---

40. A reference to the return of the Judean exiles to Jerusalem and the building of the Second Temple following the Babylonian exile (538–516 BCE).

41. Probably an allusion to Jesus.

42. For more on the use of the Temple's destruction in early Christian polemic, see Christine C. Shepardson, "Paschal Politics: Deploying the Temple's Destruction Against Fourth-Century Judaizers," *Vigiliae Christianae* 62 (2008): 233–60.

43. A play on words: *gzar* can also mean "to circumcise."

44. See Dn 7.5.

45. Syr. *apay tarʿā*, the wording of the C, S, and P of Mt 27.51.

a cry of mourning, that it would be uprooted
and destroyed.[46]
The temporal priest
tore his tunic,
a symbol of the priesthood
that the true priest
came and put on.[47]
The sanctuary tore its veil,
a symbol that—look—he put on
even the holy altar
for his service!

13

When the earth quaked, it showed
the destruction
of their dwelling places,[48]
and when it shook their feet[49]
to remove
and clear them away,
at once it cast them
to the four corners
and scattered them
in wrath.
The people were scattered
so that the peoples might be gathered together.
The temple is destroyed,
and our sanctuary is built.

14

And the sun, the lamp
of humankind,
obscured itself.
It took and spread across its face
a veil of darkness

---

46. See Mt 27.51 et par.
47. See Mt 26.52 et par.
48. See Mt 27.51.
49. Lit. "their foot."

so that it would not see
    the disgrace of the sun
        of righteousness,[50]
in whose light shine
    the watchers above.
Creation reeled
    and heaven doubled over;
Sheol vomited and spat out
    the dead.[51]

15

The luminaries also served him
    on the day of the passion:[52]
    they were both full,
a symbol of his fullness, for in him there is no
    deficiency.[53]
The sun showed
    a symbol of his lordship,
        the moon showed
a symbol of his humanity:
    both of them proclaimed him.
In the morning, the moon
    met[54] and beheld the sun;
a symbol of his flock
    met him.

16

And the tomb into which they brought him
    was new,[55] for
    it was a symbol of the peoples,
who were baptized, washed, purified,
    and made new,

---

50. See Mal 4.2 (3.20 LXX).
51. See Mt 27.52–53.
52. Or "suffering."
53. For the same idea, see *Cruc.* 3.1. There, Ephrem identifies this day as April 15.
54. Or "faced."
55. Mt 27.60 et par.

and the body and blood
> symbolized the murder
>> of the king:
they have mixed him into
> their bodies with love.[56]
On the third day,
> he rose and left the tomb:
his death in us is life
> forever.

17

When the exalted angel rolled away
> the stone of his tomb,
>> it was in the image of a slave
who reverently opened a door
> before his master.
At his tomb,
> three watchers saw
>> that he had been raised.[57]
On the third [day],
> three proclaimed him!
Mary, who saw him,
> was a symbol of the church, which is first
to see the sign
> of his coming.

18

His shrouds also proclaimed
> his way of life,
>> which gleamed and shone,
for that darkness could not
> overtake him.

---

56. These lines (beginning with "and the body and the blood") do not fit the metrical pattern outlined above but seem to be laid out as 5+4+3 + 4+4. For future reference: it would be worth testing if we should emend the breakdown of the stanzaic structure as follows: before: 4+4+4 + 4+4; after: 4+4+4 (or 5+7) + 4+4.

57. Combining the single angel of the accounts of Matthew (28.1–8) and Mark (16.1–8) with the two angels of Luke (24.1–10). This change may have originated with the Diatessaron.

ON THE CRUCIFIXION

The shrouds remained
  in the tomb,
    but the body did not remain,
so that his body might proclaim
  the resurrection of bodies.
The embalming of his body
  is a symbol of the word of truth,
which preserves the life
of souls.

ON THE CRUCIFIXION 5

To the same melody

I

The crucifiers were put to shame, since they made him ride
  the glorious wood,[1]
    clothed in symbols!
For how many glorious beings did he make
  from flashes,
and a chariot
  from rays [of light],
    like that chariot
of the cherubim,
  girded with lightning bolts?[2]
Blessed is he who yoked together[3]
  the cherubim and luminaries:
their bridles are set
  at his signals.[4]

Refrain: Praise be unto you, my Lord, and through you, to
  your sender,
by the lambs who have conquered[5] through your cross.

---

1. I.e., of the cross.
2. Likely the exact wording of Ezek 1.13–14.
3. Or "subjugated," "subdued."
4. Or "winks," "gestures" (*remzē*).
5. Or "shone."

ON THE CRUCIFIXION

2

Even the day and its evening[6]
>are a great symbol
>>and an amazing type:[7]
in the evening of the day, Adam
>was found guilty
>>— a great symbol—
>for the sun turned back
>>and the light set[8]
on Adam,
>and he was buried in darkness.
He was in darkness,
>but the light returned:
a day which grew dark, then brightened
>and became light.[9]

3

Again, when they mounted him upon the wood,
>see how the wood
>>is the occasion[10] for mercy,
for through his cross
>he abolished crucifixion,[11]
so that vicious people
>are no longer crucified.
>>O sweet one,

---

6. The Syriac word *pānyā* literally means "turning" (in this sense, the turning of the day into night), which connects to the other imagery of "turning" later in this stanza.

7. A reference to the Friday of the Crucifixion. Ephrem returns to his interpretation of the day of the Crucifixion in greater detail in *Cruc.* 6.

8. *'rēb* can also mean "sift," and is related to the noun *'arbā* ("surety," "pledge"), a relationship which resonates with an alternate translation for the previous clause ("Adam was found guilty")—"Adam became indebted."

9. More typically "was interpreted." For this rare sense of the verb, see Sokoloff, s.v., ܬܘܪܓܡ. Michael Sokoloff and Carl Brockelmann, *A Syriac Lexicon: A Translation from the Latin: Correction, Expansion, and Update of C. Brockelmann's Lexicon Syriacum* (Winona Lake, IN: Eisenbrauns, 2009).

10. Or "sacrifice."

11. Lit. "the cross" or "crucified one."

see how even the accursed
   bear your[12] blessing!
Through his cross, he abolished
   the idols of that people,
and abolished crosses
   from among the peoples.[13]

4

And when they raged, clothed him,[14]
   and divided
      his chaste garments,[15]
those proud
   scribes reproached themselves,
as [if] they had never
   heard the report
      of that psalm
which the true scribe
   interpreted through his garments.[16]
The secrets waited for
   the scribe of treasures,
to come and reveal
   hidden things.

5

Were the circumcised unashamed
   to mock
      the Lord of the circumcised?
If he were uncircumcised, they would have had
   a reason to kill him.[17]
The completer of all came:

---

12. Lit. "his."

13. In this stanza, Ephrem describes two benefits of the Crucifixion. First, it brought about the end of crucifixion as a method of execution within the Roman Empire. In addition to this, in a rare positive gesture toward the Jews, Ephrem argues that the Crucifixion has ended the practice of idolatry among the Jews. For this point, see also *On Our Lord* 5.3, 6.1.

14. I.e., with the purple robe and crown.

15. See Jn 19.23 et par.

16. Ps 22.18.

17. Lit. "there would have been a cause for death."

he completed the law,
>   but the people were found wanting:
the commandments were fulfilled,
>   but the proud were drained out.[18]
Because [the people] scorned the circumcision
>   when he was hung up in their land,
the house of the peoples scorned
>   the contemptible [land].[19]

6

His undivided tunic[20]
>   is a great symbol
>   >   of the faith.
The apostles spread it into the world,
>   while not dividing it.
The other garments
>   that were divided[21]
>   >   indicated
the divisions and schisms[22]
>   found in his flock.
The symbol of his tunic
>   extolled the faithful,[23]
the schismatics were rebuked by
>   his garments.

7

When they raged and placed him
>   between thieves,
>   >   they indicated themselves,[24]
for the one on the left is their symbol:
>   with him they were abandoned,

---

18. The contrast in these two stanzas is between the images of *fullness* and *emptiness:* Jesus *completes* or *fills up*, while the people are *empty;* he *fills* the commandments, while the proud are *depleted*.

19. An allusion to the Roman destruction of Jerusalem in 70 CE.

20. Lit. "his garment, which they did not tear." See Jn 19.23–24.

21. Jn 19.23.

22. Syr. sing.

23. Lit. "the true ones."

24. See Mt 27.38 et par.

since he[25] chose the peoples,
    who ran and took refuge
        in his crucifixion,
like the thief
    who robbed our Lord.[26]
His Lord saw that he was hungry,
    he opened his treasure before him,
and he[27] robbed and took from him
    the promises.

8

Again, when they shook
    their heads and laughed at him,[28]
        they did not understand
that he brought down their heads[29]
    among the peoples.[30]
They worshiped
    a pagan king and thought
        they would be exalted through him,
but through him their heads[31]
    were bowed even more.
This pledge[32]
    bowed [their] heads then,
just as they will bow [their] heads again
    at [his] coming.

---

25. I.e., Jesus.
26. I.e., the believing thief on the cross (Lk 23.40–43).
27. I.e., the thief.
28. Lit. "before him." See Mk 15.29–32.
29. Syr. "their head" (sing.).
30. The sense is "he made them bow their heads [in disgrace/humility]."
31. Syr. "their head" (sing.).
32. Likely an allusion to the crowd's pledge: "We have no king but Caesar" (Jn 19.15).

9

Furthermore, the vintners[33] harvested, pressed,
    and gave him the bitter [wine]
        of the vineyard to drink,[34]
the vine of Egypt,[35] that cut off
    the strong boughs[36]
of the house of Abraham
    and grafted
        the bitter shoots
of the Sodomites
    onto its branches.[37]
One small shoot[38]
    that sprouted and came out of it—
see how it overshadows the world
    with its grape clusters!

10

Their sponge of vinegar[39]
    also proclaims
        the cancer[40] of [their] souls,

---

33. *Palāḥā* can also mean "laborer," "farmworker," or, vocalized differently, even "artisan" or "soldier," but in this context I have interpreted it as vineyard workers.

34. See Mt 27.34 et par.

35. See Ps 80.9 (i.e., Israel, the vine that God brought up out of Egypt).

36. The word *šabṭē* can also mean "tribes." Ephrem likely intends the double connotation.

37. There is a rich tradition of vine, vineyard, and grape imagery in early Syriac literature. Here, Ephrem alludes to the grafting in of the Gentiles (Rom 11.11–31), whom he associates with the "vine of the Sodom" (Dt 32.32) and the "vine of Egypt" (Ps 80.8). Ephrem likely based this association of texts on a testimony series (like the ones appearing in Aphrahat's *Demonstrations*—*Dem.* 11.1, 14, 19). For Ephrem's use of this tradition, see *Haer.* 39.9–10; *CD* 16.19; cf. Isaac of Antioch, *Against the Jews* 473–76 (ed. Stanley Kazan, "Isaac of Antioch's Homily Against the Jews," *Oriens Christianus* 45.1 [1961]: 30–53, especially 53).

38. The word "shoot" (*nurbā*) can be found in Is 11.1—the "shoot of Jesse."

39. Lit. "the sponge of their vinegar." See Mt 27.34 et par.

40. *Ḥallā* ("vinegar") sounds like *ḥalāditā* ("cancer," "gangrene").

for [their] error is speculative[41]
    and subtle.[42]
[Their] fraudulent books
    vomit forth death
        from every line,
and their works are produced with gall.
Since our Lord did not taste
    the vinegar from the sponge,
you should not taste the gall
    of [their] teachings!

11

That reed on which
    they stretched out[43] the sponge
        is also a symbol of the teachings,
for look, with a reed they write
    deathly gall.[44]
See what Mani's reed
    has written:
        his book has become
a vessel[45] full of
    hidden gall.
Bardaisan's reed
    is the companion of Marcion:

---

41. The root *'qab* basically means "follow" or "tread upon," but can also mean "to search out" or "investigate." Ephrem is highly critical of theological "speculation," "inquiry," and "investigation" (*'uqābā*) elsewhere in his writings, particularly in the *madrāšē* cycle *On Faith*. For this terminology, see Wickes, trans., *The Hymns on Faith*, Fathers of the Church 130, 49–50.

42. Or perhaps "refined." It could also mean "insignificant" or "small," given that this is one of the senses of the verbal root *qtn*.

43. MS D attaches a third person feminine singular suffix to this verb, but we follow Beck's suggested reading, a third person masculine plural without a suffix. The verb "they stretched out" is the same as that found in the Peshitta of Mt 27.48.

44. Cf. *Fid.* 87.13–14, in which Ephrem compares the reed that they extended to Jesus with the reeds the subordinationists use to write their theological works. For this hymn, see Christine Shepardson, "Exchanging Reed for Reed: Mapping Contemporary Heretics onto Biblical Jews in Ephrem's *Hymns on Faith*," *Hugoye: Journal of Syriac Studies* 5.1 (2002): 15–33.

45. Ephrem is engaging in some wordplay between the name *Mani* and the word *manā* ("vessel," "cup").

they have stretched out gall to us
  through [their] books.

12

But that reed they handed him[46]
  is the opposite
    of another reed:
the one, those scribes
  were handing [him],
but the first,
  Truth
    handed him
when it decreed[47] rejecting
  the adulterous tribe.
Through David's tongue
  our Savior's reed
wrote out its promises
  for the daughter of the king.

13

And again, since they struck him
  with a reed,[48] a royal reed
    struck them,
for kings issued a decree to enslave
  and to demand tribute
from the people, when they[49] wrote
  that they should not enter
    their land, and if [the people] would enter,
a hidden power
  would descend and strike [them].

---

46. Mt 27.29. Ephrem's use of the verb *awḥed* ("handed") follows the Sinaiticus version, but the word does not appear in the Peshitta text.

47. The verb *gzar* also means "to circumcise."

48. See Mk 15.19, Mt 27.30. The verb used here for "to strike" is different in the C, S, and P.

49. Lit. "he wrote," but the reference appears to be to the "kings," unless the specific reference is to Hadrian, who banned Jews from entering Jerusalem around 135 CE, following the Second Jewish Revolt.

I too, in my turn,
> strike [the people] with a reed,
when I write and recount
> their blows.

14

Instead of the one reed that struck him,
> learned reeds
>> have struck them,
for all languages write of
> their abuses:
some a proposition,
> others a disputation,
>> one [writes] a commentary,
others write homilies
> against them.
The books of the writers
> are a forest of reeds,
striking the crucifiers
> with their writings.

15

When they raged and foamed at the mouth, and their spit
> reached the face
>> of that holy one,
the insane ones proclaimed that he had wiped
> the disgrace
from the house of Adam.
> When the serpent,
>> one of their family members, foamed at the mouth,
and smeared on Eve
> the gall of his mouth,
the fig tree had mercy
> and gave them[50] [its] leaves,
but Zion stripped
> the one who clothes all.

---

50. I.e., Adam and Eve (see Gn 3.7).

16

The mixture of hateful things
> has depicted and shown us
>> a symbol of [false] teachings—

vinegar, gall, and a mixed balm[51]—
the Pharisees are a symbol
of the bitter herbs, for they are foul and mixed together,
though the strength
> of different types of error is one.

Our Lord did not taste
> the savor of their symbols,

but fools have gathered to lap up
> their gall.

17

Furthermore, when they slaughtered him in keeping with
their custom,
> the fools showed
>> he was the true lamb.

Since they lifted him up on Golgotha,
> they bore witness to his height

for he was the Lord of heights,
> and since they brought him down to bury him,
>> his tomb testified
>>> that he is
>>>> Lord of the depths.

Through these things the sweetener of all
> uttered[52] his truth.

They dipped their hands and tasted
> his truth.[53]

---

51. The Syriac here—*ḥallā mrārā w-ḥunṭtā ḥliṭā*—likely reflects a Diatessaronic harmony of the words used in the different gospel accounts. Cf. Mt 27.34 (P): *ḥallā d-ḥliṭ b-mrārtā*; Mt 27.34 (S): *ḥamrā kad ḥliṭ b-mrārtā*; Mk 15.23 (P): *ḥamrā d-ḥliṭ beh murā*; Mk 15.23 (S): *ḥamrā d-mbassam b-besmā*; Lk 23.36 (P): *ḥallā* (the reference to the drink is absent in the C and S versions of Lk 23); Jn 19.39 (P): *ḥallā*.

52. Or "bestowed," "expressed," "offered."

53. This echoes the wording of the P of Mt 26.23, where Jesus indicates that the betrayer will "dip his hand with me" (*d-ṣāba 'ideh 'amm[y]*). The implication is that they "dipped their hands" in Jesus's blood by killing him.

18

Their unleavened bread, finally, is a witness
   that they have left[54]
      their land:
Through the symbol of the bitter herbs that they eat,
   he embittered their teeth.
And on the feast
   when they release a man,[55]
      they killed a man:
The custom showed
   that he was the lamb of truth.
They had never killed
   a man on the feast:
he whom they slaughtered with the lambs
   was an offering.

---

54. This idea of "leaving" is conveyed by two verbs: *pṭar*, a play on *paṭṭirē* ("unleavened bread"), and *'bar*, which may be a play on the root of "Hebrew" (*'br*).

55. See Mk 15.6; Mt 27.15; Lk 23.17.

ON THE CRUCIFIXION 6

To the same melody
6+4+4 + 6+4
4+4+4 + 4+4
5+5 + 5+3
R: 5+5 + 5+3

I

Three days were numbered
  for the Messiah,
    just as for Jonah.[1]
Look: it was then preparation day[2]
  when the light
of that people had set,[3]
  and again another,
    the Sabbath day,
symbol of the rest[4]
  which put death to rest.[5]
He who darkens and lightens
  reckoned [as] a day
the duration and time
  when it darkened.

---

1. See Mt 12.40.
2. "Preparation day" (*'rubtā*) is used to describe Friday, the day before the Sabbath, in Mt 27.62; Mk 15.42; Lk 23.54; Jn 19.31, 42.
3. A play on words: *'reb* is related to *'rubtā*.
4. The root *bṭl* generally carries a negative connotation, but in this line we have opted for the translation "rest," given the association with the Sabbath.
5. Or "which brings death to an end."

Refrain: Glory to you, our Lord, for see how
   the pair of luminaries[6] proclaims types of your cross!

2

O the moment which—though brief—
   had greater power[7]
      than years,
for in it the glorious one surrendered
   his spirit[8] to his Father.[9]
In it there was darkness,[10]
   in it there was light,[11]
      in it there was quaking,[12]
in it there was rending,[13]
   in it were all of these things.
Jesus made
   two days out of one,
[just as] Joshua too made
   two out of one.[14]

3

That too was a glorious symbol,
   which Joshua prepared
      for the Lord of his name.[15]
See how [the day] was divided and joined together:
   it was one and two.

---

6. I.e., the sun and moon.
7. Or "weightier."
8. Or "breath."
9. See Lk 23.46.
10. See Mt 27.45, Mk 15.33, Lk 23.44.
11. After the three hours of darkness and before the evening sunset.
12. Of the earth (see Mt 27.51).
13. Of the veil of the temple (cf. Mt 27.51, Mk 15.38, Lk 23.45).
14. See Jos 10.12–13, the story of the sun standing still for Joshua. Because the names "Joshua" and "Jesus" are identical in Syriac, one could read either "Jesus" or "Joshua" in each line. It is unclear which line refers to which.
15. Because of the identical names, Jesus is thus "Lord of [Joshua's] name." Cf. *Nat.* 1.31, *Haer.* 4.18.

By dawning and darkening
    it was one day;[16]
        by the measure of sleep,[17]
it was two days:[18]
    the doubling is simple.
And preparation day was
    one day by means of measurement,
and two by the division
    of its shining.

4

Accept, then, O listener,
    my words about the calculation
        of the three days.[19]
Look: there was preparation day,
    and its great evening,
the Sabbath and its evening,
    and there was also
        another interval
which went dark and [then] shone,
    and was reckoned [as] a day.
The evening of that other day
    —that of the resurrection—
on preparation day
    would become complete.[20]

---

16. In other words, by the measure of sunrise and sunset as markers for the beginning and ending of a day, Joshua's lengthened day was still only one day.

17. Or perhaps, "the year."

18. In other words, in the actual amount of time that elapsed, it was two days.

19. Lit. "the calculation of my words about the three days."

20. Ephrem argues that the full three-day sum was fulfilled by the addition of an extra "night" on Friday afternoon, the three hours of darkness (from midday until the ninth hour). He then deduces that the three hours of darkness would have been followed by three hours of light before sunset at the twelfth hour. At this point, then, two days and one night had elapsed. This was followed by the night and day of the Sabbath, as well as by the night of Sunday, at which time Jesus was raised.

5

Let that moment,
> which went dark and [then] shone,
>> be distinguished by itself.

Look at it by itself
> as if at a day,

for in place of the [missing] hours,
> look, hours entered
>> from that evening,

and what preparation day lacked
> was completed!

Three hours of darkness
> and three of light:

reckon the night of the daytime
> [as] one day.

6

O you symbolic foretelling
> of three more
>> hours![21]

Every four years an entire day
> is intercalated:[22]

it is a great symbol,
> for he revealed beforehand
>> the three hours

that were prepared
> in order to darken at his murder.[23]

---

21. Lit. "you, O preceding symbol of three more hours."

22. Ephrem mentions the practice of *intercalation*, the addition of extra time to the calendar for the purpose of keeping it on track. Although intercalation is a necessity for both lunar and solar calendars, Ephrem is describing the regular intercalation of the solar calendar. Ephrem's solar calendar appears to have been an adapted version of the Julian calendar, likely what scholars call the Syro-Antiochene calendar (see Sacha Stern, *Calendars in Antiquity: Empires, States, and Societies* [Oxford: Oxford University Press, 2012], 255–57). Like our modern calendar (itself a revision of the Julian calendar), Ephrem's solar year featured 365¼ days. Since the ancient day was divided into twelve hours, if a day was intercalated every four years to account for the extra ¼ of a day, that ¼ of a day would equal 3 hours.

23. Contrary to the meter, this line ("in order to darken at his murder") contains five syllables.

ON THE CRUCIFIXION

The Lord of lights
   inscribed his symbols with a light,
and the sun went before
   as his herald.

7

These added [hours]
   do not fill
      something missing:
they are hours that overflow
   from their container.[24]
They are[25] neither a mending,
   nor an ordering;
      what's more, the fact
that three hours confuse
   the year is a problem.[26]
For this [reason] alone
   they are established: to announce
the three hours that grew dark
   at the crucifixion.[27]

8

There are learned ones who say
   that the deficiency of the moon
      was fulfilled in them.[28]
Now to this too let us inquire:
   "Why then did

---

24. Lit. "from the mouth of the measure."

25. Syr. singular.

26. Or, "What's more, the fact that three hours are confused by the year is a conundrum."

27. In other words, the excess hours in the calendar are not to correct *mistakes* or fix problems in the created order. Rather, according to Ephrem, the only reason that there are extra hours in the calendar is to testify to the *extra day* that took place on Good Friday. Elsewhere, in the *Second Discourse to Hypatius,* Ephrem argues that the deficiencies in the calendar point to the deficiencies of the sun and moon as objects of worship. Cf. *PR* I, xl (Syr. 23–25).

28. Ephrem argues against unknown experts who posit that the hours that must be made up by intercalation every four years exist to round out the "deficiency" in the lunar calendar (which falls approximately half a day short of the solar calendar).

the moon lose
 half of a day?"[29]
  For again, this
is just like their confusion
 of the months.[30]
Glory to you, our light,
 whom the luminaries have depicted:
the sun and the moon
 with their symbols.

9

The sun first proclaimed him
 through its three added
  hours.
They are hours which the mind
 alone is able
to explore,
 within the number
  of hours of the year,[31]
which are hidden
 from the eyes—
a type of that day
 when the sun hid its light
to proclaim through visible things
 his hidden things.[32]

10

Look, those hours
 which were darkened are not
  distinguishable to the eye,

---

29. Ephrem here asks why each lunar month only consists of 29½ days.

30. Cf. Ephrem's similar critique in *Hypatius II,* xxxviii (Syr. 20): "the shortage of Light, however, does not make any lessening in the Moon, nor does the increase of Light fill up this defective part. So let this defective part of a day convict the Heretics that they are altogether lacking in truth."

31. In other words, one cannot *see* the extra hours in the year. They are only accessible to the mind.

32. Both the sun hidden by darkness and the added hours attest to a further level of symbolism to which Ephrem alludes here at the end of stanza 9: the hiddenness of God made known in revealed things.

> but the mind
>   can grasp them
> through a water clock:[33]
>   for the symbol
>   is like
> the reality:
>   both are hidden.
> These three [hours] joined,
>   clothed, and fulfilled the three:
> the hidden hours
>   to the invisible ones.[34]
>
> II
>
> But not because I have called it
>   "three" should you hear
>   in the three "six" [total hours].[35]
> For there are three extra [hours] in every
>   year,
> and in that year,
>   there were these [three hours]
>   when it went dark to teach
> that because of this
>   it was established in the beginning.
> The symbol passed on
>   and walked through every place,

---

33. The Syriac literally reads "staircase of water" (*ḥuqā d-mayyā*). There were numerous forms of the device known in Greek as the κλεψύδρα (lit. "water thief") in use in antiquity. Such devices measured time by controlling a steady flow of water either in or out of a large basin. A water clock large enough to measure out the twelve hours of the day could then show the passage of time through indications of the hours inscribed within. See Robert Hannah, *Time in Antiquity,* Sciences of Antiquity (Abingdon: Routledge, 2008), 100–115.

34. Ephrem appears to mean that the three extra hours in the solar year, though invisible to the eye, provide a "hidden" witness to the three hours of darkness at the Crucifixion, which are likewise invisible to those who were not present at that event.

35. In other words, Ephrem is arguing that in the year of the Passion there were not three extra hours symbolizing the hours of darkness *and* the three hours of darkness themselves. Instead, there were only the three hours of darkness that are in every other year signified by the need for intercalation.

and when it found its Lord,
  it suffered with him.

12

O glorious Jesus,
  whom even the moon,
    behold, proclaims,
because half a day in every month
  has lost its measure.
And how much greater
  is the full measure
  of the hours of the year?
Thus they have lost
  their measure of months.
The cross which he rode
  was the yoke of his chariot,
and to it he harnessed
  the sun and the moon.

13

For the luminaries that served
  that Lord
  of all luminaries,
the sun and the moon that were worshiped,
  are the servants
of the worshiped Son—
  the sun with three [hours],
  and the moon with six—
with both symbols
  they were harnessed and bore him.
Jesus inscribed his symbols
  on the sun and the moon
to proclaim through them the symbol
  of his coming.

14

But why then was that extra [part]
  found
    in the measurement of the sun?

ON THE CRUCIFIXION

And why is the measurement of the moon
  lessened and diminished?
The sun is
  the symbol of the gift
  of his divinity,
which from his fullness
  it[36] poured out and gave.
The moon is the symbol of the body:
  the measure is diminished.
The perfect one who put on [the body],
  perfected it.

15

The sun proclaims three:[37]
  three hours of light
    in the image of its Lord.
The moon also proclaims three
  hours of darkness
in the image of Adam.
  And the three which it received,
    the symbol of grace.
See how the ninth hour
  proclaims them both,
the time at which the Son,
  "around the end of the ninth hour,"
committed his spirit to his Father[38]
  with a cry.[39]

16

Through Joshua son of Nun, a day
  was doubled and became longer
    than all [other] days,
in a symbol of the people which he made greater
  than all the peoples.

---

36. I.e., "divinity" (*alāhutā*).
37. This line has seven syllables, against the meter.
38. Against the meter, this line has six syllables.
39. Mt 27.46; Mk 15.34.

Through our Lord Jesus,
>one day became shorter
>>than all [other] days,
in a symbol of the one people[40]
>more despised than all.
There, the luminary was strengthened,
>in a symbol of the strength of the people.
But here the people grew dark,
>like the sun.

17

Our Lord, strengthen [me] to write
>in another way
>>the matter[41] of the moon.
For look: eleven days
>are lacking from its year,[42]
from
>365
>>days,
the reckoning of the
>full solar year.
For what I have said, and what I am saying
>to you, my Lord, [is] for praise,
but for me, propitiation
>through your mercy.

18

Moses mixed and mingled
>the reckoning of the year
>>and the calculation of the moon.
He ordered, constructed, and put together
>the reckoning of the year.

---

40. Against the meter, this line has five syllables.
41. Or "story," "account."
42. Ephrem is referring to a lunar month of 29½ days, and thus a lunar year of 354 days. See also *Hypatius II*, xxxviii (Syr. 19).

ON THE CRUCIFIXION

The year of the house of Noah
   [had] two reckonings:[43]
of two luminaries
   the skillful scribe[44]
     made one reckoning.[45]
Our Lord, may I become a scribe
   of secrets for you.
Translate parables through your
   servant![46]

19

Our Lord, permit me to speak
   of that moment
that was hidden from all!
Let the boldness of [my] desire
   be a cause of love.
And even though, however,
   the glorious hour
     of your resurrection is hidden
—look, [even] your birth
   is a terror to approach![47]
Yet perhaps on the sixth hour
   of that blessed night

---

43. Or "calendars." This probably refers to the muddled chronology of Gn 8, in which two different dates are given on which the earth became dry.

44. Probably a reference to Moses. According to Sokoloff, the phrase also appears in Ps 45.2 (P). See Sokoloff, s.v., *mhirā*.

45. *Hypatius II*, in *PR* II, xxxix (Syr. 21–23). Here, Ephrem again turns to Moses, who, he says, wisely utilized both the reckoning of the Sun (for marking days) and the reckoning of the Moon (for marking months).

46. Ephrem typically characterizes his poetic actions as *singing, playing,* etc. Here, however, he refers to himself as a "scribe," and requests divine assistance to help him "write" (*ktab*) (st. 17) and "translate" (*targem*) (st. 18). These examples call to mind a more "scholastic" image than we often encounter in Ephrem's *madrāšē*.

47. Rouwhorst (*Hymnes pascales*, vol. 1, p. 71) interprets this as a polemical remark against "Arians." To call this remark polemical, however, is something of an overstatement. Ephrem is likely playing on the ambiguity of the word *mulādā*, which can refer both to the "generation" of the Son by the Father and the human "birth" of Jesus from Mary. In our reading, Ephrem seems to be hedging his speculation on the exact time of the Resurrection with a comparison to Jesus's "birth." It too is an awe-inspiring event that should give pause to the speculative.

our Lord and our God[48]
   was raised.

20

My Lord, see my hunger to gather up
   the crumbs of the symbols
      and interpretations![49]
The tongues of the just are outstretched
   to interpret
the symbols of your richness—
   I worship you, my Lord!
      Even from your servant,
let the gift of my words
   ascend to you, my Lord.
"Remember me" too,
   with the thief,[50]
that I may enter your kingdom
   in his shadow.

---

48. Cf. Jn 20.28.
49. Cf. Mt 15.27; *Fid.* 10.
50. Lk 23.42.

ON THE CRUCIFIXION 7

Again on the Crucifixion
To the melody: "The Exalted Assembly"

1

Let April from its flowers adorn[1] a crown for him.
    It spread out grass[2] for the crowds; they ate and were full.
What a marvel—that fullness was unfurled[3] upon fullness!
    Visible April has adorned and honored the hidden April.[4]
Victorious deeds and flowers were intermingled:
    blooming lilies of the field[5]
with the radiant[6] signs of our Lord.

Refrain: In April they slaughtered and ate a lamb; the lamb of
    God lives and gives life.

2

April has begun; he sealed and fulfilled [it].[7]
    With its blossoms it[8] crowned the unworthy people,
when they ate, honored, and exalted a temporal lamb.

---

1. Or "trim," "dress" (*neṣbat*).
2. This word (*'esbā*) appears in the P version of Jn 6.10 (in reference to the feeding of the five thousand).
3. Or "distributed" (*pras*), which might make more sense of the allusion to the feeding of the five thousand. The verb *pras* also sounds like the noun *parsā*, which among other things can refer to an allotted portion of food.
4. The reference to "the hidden April" in this case is somewhat obscure.
5. Cf. Mt 6.28, Lk 12.27.
6. Or "glorious," "victorious."
7. Or "it was sealed and completed."
8. I.e., April.

Instead of bitter [herbs], they wander around to collect thorns,
to mock the true lamb,
   to crown[9] the king in a jest,
and to kill the just one in wickedness.

3

Let Moses offer you a crown of the righteous,
   who also plaited for you the bones of the just that were put back together.[10]
And at the thunder of your voice they sprouted up as blossoms.
   In the month of April, there was April in Sheol,
the countenances of the dead became joyful.
   See how their dried-up bones became resplendent!
See how their snuffed-out beauty shone![11]

4

In the darkness the sun adorned your crown,
   it withdrew itself and plaited it; in three hours it finished it,
to crown the three days of his death.[12]
   [The sun] proclaimed the struggle he had with Death,
for by the cross everyone is overcome by Death.
He lifted it and thereby it conquered him,[13]
   like Goliath, who with his own sword perished.[14]

---

9. Following Beck's correction (adding a *d-* prefix).

10. The role of Moses here is somewhat obscure. Beck speculates that Moses may be presenting the crown of the dead raised at Jesus's death (Mt 27.52–53) as the most significant representative of the saints raised at that time (Beck, *Paschahymnen*, trans., 56). This is supported by the allusion to the "voice" of Jesus raising the dead (Mt 27.52) in line 3.

11. In this stanza, Ephrem once more evokes the events of Mt 27.50–53. Here, Christ's dying cry from the cross is a life-giving "thunder" that brought forth "blossoms" of the dead who came out of their tombs. In the context of the spring festival, the thunderstorms and budding flowers of April shape his portrayal of that event. His lovely image of "April in Sheol" imagines the dead sprouting up from their tombs, bringing life to a place of death.

12. Ephrem here envisions the three hours of darkness on the Friday of the Crucifixion as a "crown" woven by the sun to symbolize the three days of Jesus's death. Cf. *Cruc.* 6.

13. The Syriac (*ṣaqleh w-beh zkā[hy]*) is ambiguous. It could also read, "He lifted it and he conquered it," or "It lifted him and conquered him."

14. 1 Sm 17.51.

5

The sun proclaimed concerning him that he is both hidden and visible,
    for its body put on suffering and its nature was without suffering.[15]
In a symbol of his body, it suffered, but in a symbol of his power, it grew radiant.
    O visible sun which mourned over the invisible,
and luminary that grew gloomy[16] because of the light,
    be comforted! Rise and comfort us,[17]
for he rose from the grave for his church!

6

The sun hid in the heights[18] and the moon in the depths,[19]
    and the just fled in all directions to take refuge.
The sun resembled[20] the watchers, and the moon the buried.
    Since those deceitful ones in between turned away and killed their Lord,
the sun rose, like the watchers who were sent.
    The moon ascended, with the dead who were awakened.[21]
The crucifiers were in between and were suffocated.

7

Let the East with her right hand offer him a crown!
    Let her plait into it the symbols and types of the ark.
From the mountains of Qardu[22] she gathered her blossoms.
    From thence [came] Noah and Shem and even the first of the world.[23]
From thence [came] the illustrious Abram,

---

15. This can also be read in direct reference to Christ: "for his body put on suffering, but his nature was without suffering."

16. The root *kmr* has the connotation of both "sadness" and "darkness."

17. Or "it/he was comforted, and rose, and comforted us."

18. Lit. "the height."

19. Lit. "the deep."

20. Or "agreed with," "corresponded to."

21. Mt 27.52–53.

22. Following Gn 8.4 (P), in which Noah's ark lands upon the "mountains of Qardu."

23. Or "chief," "head," "origin." A reference to Adam.

and the blessed magi, and the star,[24]
and paradise [is] its glorious neighbor.

8

Let the West offer two splendid crowns,
  crowns whose aromas have wafted in all directions.
The West, in which the twin luminaries[25] set,
  there the two apostles are ever buried,
and never-setting rays shine forth.
  See how Simon has overcome the sun,
and the apostle[26] has eclipsed the moon!

9

Let the South offer him a crown from Paran.[27]
  With Hebrew flowers she sprouted and blossomed.
And the law of power, never fulfilled by anyone,[28]
  is our Lord's crown, for he completely fulfilled it.
And having grown old, it is calm and at rest.[29]
  It is read for testimony alone,[30]
and like a weary old man, takes rest.

10

The North in her harshness, her land does not blossom:
  snow and ice, fierce gusts.
In the wind[31] of the north is depicted the paganism of Greece.
  See how she offers a crown of new flowers
to that sun of compassion who has made her bud.
  Look: in her, martyrs' bones[32]
and radiant virgin blossoms have flourished.

---

24. Mt 2.1–2.
25. I.e., the sun and moon, which set in the west.
26. I.e., Paul.
27. A desert in or around Sinai; see Gn 21.22, Nm 10.12, Dt 32.2, Hab 3.3.
28. Lit. "which no one ever fulfilled."
29. Or "quiet," "peaceful." This language is very reminiscent of Ex 31.17 (P), which describes God's rest on the seventh day of Creation in relation to the Sabbath rest.
30. Probably its testimony to Christ.
31. Or "spirit."
32. For other references by Ephrem to the emerging cult of the saints (especially the power of bones), see *Nis.* 33 and *Nis.* 42.

11

The heights and the depths crown you, our Lord.
  See how the six directions[33] offer their crowns,
just as on the sixth day they plaited you a crown of thorns.
  Let them also crown you, and through you, your Father!
That body of Adam which conquered through you,
  great was his shame when he was conquered,
but you have buried his debt in crowns.

12

From all directions, praise be to him who was born in the sixth [millennium]![34]
  The number six is perfect, without deficiency,
and the number 100 is a crown in the right hand.[35]
  With the symbol of crowns our right hand offers poems.[36]
May you save us from the left through its symbol,[37]
  and lead us to the right by its type,
in which the number 100 is plaited.

---

33. I.e., the heights, depths, and the four cardinal directions. Gerard Rouwhorst speculates that this passage implies a polemic against Bardaisanite doctrine of pre-existing *'ityē* (Rouwhorst, *Hymnes pascales*, vol. 2, 79, n. 9).

34. This is certainly a reference to the millennium. Ephrem elsewhere envisions Christ's death on the tree occurring in the "sixth millennium," paralleling Adam's disobedience with a tree on the sixth day. See *Fid.* 6.7.

35. For this image, see also *Eccl.* 24.4–5.

36. Syr. *madrāšē*.

37. Ephrem sometimes uses "the left" to refer to the powers of darkness and evil, probably drawing on the parable of the sheep and the goats (Mt 25.31–46). Cf. *Nis.* 35.1. The saving "symbol" here is presumably that of the crowns, or perhaps that of the number six.

ON THE CRUCIFIXION 8

To the melody: "Blessed are You, Ephratha"
Meter unclear

1

Blessed are you, place[1] which was worthy to have
   the sweat of the Son fall upon you.[2]
With the earth he mixed his sweat, to drive away[3]
   the sweat of Adam, who labored on the earth.[4]
Blessed is the earth he sweetened with his sweat,
   and when sick it was restored when he sweated on it.
Who has ever seen a sick man
   restored by sweat which was not his own?

Refrain: Praises to your sender!

2

Blessed are you, place, for through your prayers
   you made joyful the garden of delights,[5]
in which Adam's will was divided
   against his Creator, so that he stole and ate.

---

   1. Probably an allusion to the Garden of Gethsemane.
   2. Or "that you were worthy that / the sweat of the Son fall upon you."
   3. Beck emends the text to *d-nešrē*. The MS reads *d-našdē* ("that he might cast away/drive off") or *d-nešdē* ("that he might pour out"), but Beck argues that this is written in a secondary hand and should be corrected. Regardless of the hand, the meaning of the *apʿel* ("to cast out") makes sense in the context, so there seems to be insufficient evidence to accept the emendation.
   4. See Gn 3.19.
   5. *Gnat ʿedānē* sounds like *gnat ʿedēn* ("Garden of Eden").

[Jesus] entered into a garden and prayed, to reconcile[6]
   the will which had been divided in a garden.[7]
In his prayers, he said, "Let not my will be done,
   but your will."[8]

3

Blessed too are you, reed of mocking,[9]
   that you were attached to the hand of our king.
It was symbolically that fools gave him a reed,
   for like a judge he has written to remove them.
Woe to Zion and Jerusalem that they provoked him
   to devastate the cities. They cried out and asked [for] a thief.[10]
The king they rejected wrote a decree,
   that they should be devastated without mercy.

4

They handed him that reed as a reproach,
   but he made them a broken reed.[11]
Let no one rely upon that reed,
   whose strength is weak and whose tip is sharp.[12]
David wrote [about] a simple staff[13]
   to shame that people, who reproached him with a reed.
David wrote [about] a "staff of iron"[14] and gave it to him
   to pound his crucifiers.

5

Blessed too are you, O Golgotha.
   Heaven has envied your smallness.
For it was not when our Lord was hidden
   in heaven above [that] reconciliation occurred.

---

6. Lit. "level," "smooth," or "even out."
7. Probably an allusion to the Garden of Eden.
8. Lk 22.42.
9. Mt 27.29; cf. Rouwhorst, *Les hymnes pascales*, vol. 2, ch. 3, 3.2.2.5.
10. I.e., Barabbas.
11. 2 Kgs 18.21.
12. Or "hard" (*qāšā*).
13. Cf. Ps 45.7.
14. Ps 2.7.

Upon you was our debt repaid,
  for from you, the thief opened up and entered Eden.
Heaven could not become our place of refuge.
  It is the slain one who through you saved me!

6

Blessed are you, inscription,[15] for they fashioned you
  and affixed you on him like a portrait of a king.
The king was clothed with the hue of mortals,[16]
  the inscription, his portrait, with the hue of kings.
You were not clothed with his outer image,
  for you were dressed in the likeness of the hidden things
of that crucified king, in order to proclaim,
  through your visible form, the beauty of his hiddenness.[17]

7

You, too, inscription, the just man[18] wrote
  from among the peoples on behalf of all the peoples.
Lines that, though silent, became eloquent
  prophets for the Son from among the peoples.
When the crucifiers rolled up the prophets[19] and set them aside,
  prophecy proclaimed their writings[20]
from among the peoples. And their voices were
  put to shame, and bear witness that the people killed their[21] Lord.

8

Blessed too are you, O thief,
  for from your death, life met you.
They hurled you down to be cast from one evil to another,[22]
  but our Lord took [you] and placed you in Eden.

---

15. The inscription posted on the cross. See Mt 27.37, Mk 15.26, Lk 23.38, Jn 19.19–21; the word *petqā*, however, appears only in the C and S of Lk 23.38.

16. Or "the dead."

17. Syr. *kasyuteh*. This reading follows Beck's correction from the manuscript's "*your* hiddenness" (*kasyutāk*).

18. I.e., Pilate.

19. I.e., they rolled up the scrolls on which the prophets' words were written.

20. An allusion to the prophets' own writings.

21. Lit. "its" (collective singular).

22. Lit. "from evil to evil."

Our tongue cannot tell of you,
   for Judas deceived him and handed him over.
Even Simon denied, and the disciples fled and hid,
   but you proclaimed him!

9

Symbolically was he crucified between thieves,
   one of whom blasphemed and the other confessed—
a symbol that revealed the people of our day:
   see how they mock him while the peoples confess.
With silence he despised the denier[23] in a symbol of them
   that look: those [people] are also despised in the world.
To the believer,[24] he showed honor through his word,
   and see how his companions have increased!

10

His cross they raised and placed on high,
   and went down to stand beneath him.
They depicted a symbol for him who sits upon the throne,
   and makes them a "footstool for his feet."[25]
Golgotha is a mirror of his church,
   which he lifted up and built upon the height of his truth.
Even today, the church
   is established upon the same Golgotha.

11

Blessed are you who bore the same name as Joseph the just,[26]
   you who covered and buried the living departed one.
For you closed [the eyes of] the wakeful[27] sleeper
   whose soul slept, and plundered Sheol.
Woe to Death, since he has overcome its wakefulness[28]—

---

23. I.e., the doubting thief.
24. I.e., the good thief.
25. Is 66.1.
26. Probably an allusion to Joseph of Arimathea.
27. The word *'irā* typically refers to the angelic "watchers" (see, e.g., stanza 12), but in this stanza the reference is clearly to Christ as the "wakeful" or "vigilant" one.
28. Or "his [Christ's] wakefulness has overcome [Sheol]." The verbal root *'war* is often connected to being overcome by sleep.

that wakeful one who slept that he might deceive it.[29]
Our plunderer is plundered! Our captor[30] is captive!
 Come, let us rejoice and praise him!

12

Blessed are you, unique[31] tomb,
 for in you, dawned the only-begotten light.
In you, proud Death was conquered,
 when in you, the living dead one expelled [it].
Blessed is your womb, in which was shut
 that all-swallowing, never-sated mouth.[32]
The watchers crowned your entrance with rays
 for they rejoiced at our resurrection.

13

His tomb and his garden are a symbol of Eden,
 in which Adam died a hidden death.
For [Adam] fled and hid among the trees,[33]
 and entered and was concealed as within a tomb.
The living buried one, who was resurrected in a garden,
 raised up him who fell in a garden.
From the garden's tomb to the garden's wedding feast,
 he made him enter in glory.

14

Where are you, greedy serpent, companion
 of that thief who slew Adam?
The Evil One deceived [him], slew [him], and shut his mouth,[34]
 multiplying corpses for greedy Death.

---

29. Or "rob," "steal."

30. Probably a reference to Death.

31. Or "single" (*iḥidā*). A variant of this word (*iḥidāyā*) is the Syriac rendering of "only-begotten" (Greek μονογενής), which appears in the following line.

32. Probably an allusion to Death.

33. Gn 3.8.

34. The reference is to the Evil One deceiving Adam and keeping him from objecting to Eve's temptation (shutting his mouth), which brought about Adam's death.

Woe to the two of you, for look, you were defeated by [a single] one.[35]
By [a single] one you were hung up[36] and have perished.
Eve is in the garden, and Adam in paradise,
but you are in torment!

15

Blessed too are you, O Bethany,
   whom the mountain of the ark and Mount Sinai
envy, for from them did not ascend
   the Lord of the heights, who ascended from you.[37]
Blessed are your lands, which were blessed by his ascension,
   when you saw his glorious chariot,
the cloud whose height bent down to the lowly one,[38]
   who reigns above and below.

16

Blessed then are you three without rival,
   which are worthy of the Father's third one:[39]
his birth in Bethlehem, his dwelling in Nazareth,
   and his ascension in Bethany.
In these he began, and also finished.
   He was taken up[40] and hid his leaven in the people,
and look: he was hung up[41] and drew all peoples without labor.[42]
   Praises be to his sender!

---

35. Probably an allusion to Jesus.
36. The verb *tlā* is also used in reference to the Crucifixion, implying an inversion of roles for Death and Satan.
37. Ephrem is referring to the account of the Ascension in Lk 24.50–51.
38. See Acts 1.9.
39. Ephrem occasionally uses this enigmatic Syriac word "third" or "threefold" (*tlitāyā*) to refer to Christ. It could possibly be interpreted as "three-day-one" in reference to the Resurrection.
40. See Jn 12.32.
41. The same verb (*ettli*) appears in Gal 3.13 (P), in reference to the Crucifixion.
42. The reading *d-lā 'amel* is Beck's suggestion; the reading is uncertain.

ON THE CRUCIFIXION 9

To the same melody
Meter unclear[1]

I

Blessed are you, too, Simon, who carried
   the living cross after our king:[2]
haughty are the standard-bearers of kings,
   but kings perish, with their standards.
Blessed are your hands, that were lifted up[3]
   and carried the cross that bent down,
and your bearer[4] revived you, bearing you
   to the house of life, and brought you across,
      for it is the vessel[5] of the kingdom.

Refrain: Blessed is he who was crucified in our place!

---

1. In this case, the metrical pattern 8+8 + 9+8 + 5+7 + 7+5+5 + R: 5 seems probable for the *qālā* "Blessed are You, Ephratha," but we have not yet verified that hypothesis with the other two poems bearing that meter.

2. Perhaps the most obvious allusion would seem to be to Simon of Cyrene (see Mk 15.21–22 et par.). In his translation Beck interprets this as a reference to Simon Peter, who "bore the cross" himself at the time of his own crucifixion. Given that the consistent reference of the poem is to the Passion narrative, this reading seems less likely.

3. The passive "were lifted up" seems to suggest that this Simon was himself crucified. This would seem to support an allusion to Peter's crucifixion, unless Ephrem has conflated the two Simons or believed that Simon of Cyrene was crucified.

4. "Your bearer" (*ṭā'unā*) probably refers to the cross that Simon carried, paradoxically carrying him to salvation. Rouwhorst, in his French translation, alters it to "burden." See Rouwhorst, *Hymnes pascales,* vol. 2, 85, n. 2.

5. Or "the Aleph," the letter that symbolized the sign of the cross or stake.

2

Blessed are you also, living wood,
    that you became a hidden lance against Death.
For that lance which smote the Son,[6]
    though it struck him, he slew Death with it.[7]
Truly his lance removed the lance,[8]
    for his forgiveness cut up our document.[9]
See how paradise rejoices,
    that the exiles have returned,
        and the disinherited to their habitation!

3

For through your symbol the waters of Marah[10] became sweet.
    Through you bitter things—look—are made sweet!
For they were not able ...[11]

---

6. Jn 19.34.

7. Or "though it struck him, *it* killed death through him."

8. I.e., the lance of the cherubim guarding Paradise (Gn 3.24). Interestingly, the Syriac text of Gn 3.24 describes the weapon as a *harbā*. Further complicating the issue, the P version of Jn 19.34 identifies this weapon as a *lukaytā* ("spear"). From the evidence of Ephrem's *Commentary on the Diatessaron,* it appears that the Diatessaronic text read *rumḥā*. Murray hypothesizes that the Diatessaron introduced the word *rumḥā* based upon a reading of the Greek ῥομφαία, common to both the LXX of Gn 3.24 and the text of Simeon's prophecy in Lk 2.35 (but not, however, to the Greek of Jn 19.34, which describes the weapon as a λόγχη!) See Robert Murray, "The Lance Which Re-Opened Paradise: A Mysterious Reading in the Early Syriac Fathers," *Orientalia Christiana Periodica* 39, no. 1 [1973]: 224–34, especially 229–30.

9. An echo of the "document of indebtedness" of Col 2.14.

10. See Ex 15.23. In both Hebrew and Syriac, the name "Marah" is related to the word "bitter."

11. Lacuna in manuscript. The remainder of the poem is lost.

TEACHING SONGS ON THE RESURRECTION

Translated by BLAKE HARTUNG

ON THE RESURRECTION 1

The melody indication is missing. The stanzas consist of 4 lines of 8 syllables each, and one of 4 syllables. The first letters of the first six stanzas of the poem form an acrostic spelling the name "Ephrem," and the remaining stanzas begin with the letter *mim*.

1

For us has come a lamb from David's house,
   a priest and pontiff from Abraham.
For us he became a lamb, and for us a priest,[1]
   his body a sacrifice, his blood[2] a sprinkling.
Blessed is his fulfillment![3]

Refrain: Blessed be your raising!

2

That shepherd of all flew down
   and sought Adam, the sheep that strayed.[4]
He bore him[5] upon his shoulders and ascended.
   He became an offering for the master of the flock.
Blessed is his mercy![6]

---

1. Although the first few lines are missing in MS B, they are preserved in the printed Mosul *Fenqitho* (VI.162–64). See *Ephrem the Syrian: Select Poems*, ed. Brock and Kiraz, 79.

2. Following Beck's correction from *d-meneh* to *dmeh*. This correction fits a parallel between the sacrificed body and the sprinkled blood.

3. Or perhaps "his fullness" (used, e.g., to translate the Greek πλήρωμα).

4. Echoing the language (particularly *tʿā*— "to stray") used in the C, S, and P texts of Mt 18.12.

5. This verb (*tʿen*) may reflect a unique variant of Lk 15.5 (the Parable of the Lost Sheep) not found in any of the three extant Syriac versions (P, S: *šqal;* C: *sām*). It may also have been chosen for its similarity to *tʿā* in the previous line.

6. This word tends to refer to the Holy Spirit's "brooding" or "hovering," but here seems to be used in the other sense of "mercy," as found in the P of Phil 2.1.

3

Dew and living rain dripped
 upon Mary, the thirsty ground.[7]
Then like a grain of wheat he fell into Sheol,[8]
 and came up like a sheaf and new bread.
Blessed is his offering!

4

His Knowledge chased out straying[9]
 from humanity, which was lost.
Through him, the Evil One went astray, and through him, he grew alarmed:
 it[10] poured into the Peoples all wisdom.
Blessed is his fountain![11]

5

He brought down power to us from the heights,
 and hope sprouted forth for us from within a womb.
Life shone upon us from the grave,[12]
 and the king sat down for us at the right hand.
Blessed is his glory!

6

From the heights he flows like a river,
 and from Mary like a root.
From the tree[13] he falls like a fruit,
 and went up to heaven like firstfruits.[14]
Blessed is his will!

---

7. Cf. *Nat.* 11.4; 8.8; 26.6.
8. Cf. *CD* 17.7.
9. Or "error." This line has only seven syllables, making it an outlier to the meter.
10. I.e., "knowledge" (*ida'tā*).
11. Or "source" (*mabu'ā*).
12. This line has only seven syllables, making it an outlier to the meter.
13. Lit. "wood" (*qaysā*). This word is typically an allusive reference to the cross, but given the imagery of roots and fruit, I thought it appropriate to render it "tree."
14. Syr. *rišitā*. This word can also mean "origin" or "source."

7

The Word of the Father came from his womb
 and in another womb,[15] it[16] put on a body.
She went out from a womb to a womb,[17]
 and through her, chaste wombs were filled.
Blessed is the one who has dwelled in us!

8

From the heights he came down as the Lord,
 and from within the womb he went out as a created being.[18]
In Sheol, death knelt before him,
 and at his resurrection, life bowed down to him.
Blessed is his triumph!

9

Mary carried him[19] as an infant,[20]
 the priest[21] carried him as an offering,
the cross carried him as one slain,
 heaven carried him as God.
Glory to his Father!

10

From all sides he stretched out and gave
 healings with counsels.[22]
The innocent ran to his healings,
 the discerning to his counsels.
Blessed is his revelation![23]

---

15. I.e., the womb of Mary.
16. The pronoun "it," although the Syriac for "word" (*meltā*) is feminine.
17. This line has only seven syllables, making it an outlier to the meter.
18. Or a "servant" (*'abdā*).
19. The same verb is used here and in the following lines.
20. This line has nine syllables, making it an outlier to the meter.
21. Probably an allusion to Simeon (Lk 2.25). Cf. *Nat.* 25.16.
22. Or "advice," "counsel."
23. P uses this word to translate both ἀποκάλυψις and ἐπιφάνεια ("revelation" and "manifestation").

11

From the mouth of a fish he gave a coin[24]—
  a temporal stamp and perishable[25] currency.[26]
From his own mouth he gave us
  a new stamp—of the new covenant.
Blessed is its giver!

12

From God his divinity,
  and from mortals his humanity.
From Melchizedek his priesthood,[27]
  and from the house of David his kingship.
Blessed is his mixture!

13

He was among guests at the wedding feast,[28]
  and among fasters amidst the temptation.[29]
He was among vigil-keepers[30] in the struggle,[31]
  and was a teacher in the temple.[32]
Blessed is his discipleship!

14

The impure he did not despise,
  and of sinners he was not ashamed.[33]
He rejoiced greatly in the upright,
  and greatly desired the simple.
Blessed is his teaching!

---

24. The word used for the coin taken from the fish in the P of Mt 17.27. This line has nine syllables, making it an outlier to the meter.

25. Lit. "that wasted away."

26. The primary sense of the word *npāqā* is "mine." Secondarily, it has the meaning "cash," "money," or "expenditure."

27. Cf. Ps 110.4, Heb 7.13–17.

28. See Jn 2.1–12. This stanza, like the preceding three, begins with *men*, which I have translated above as "from." In this case, the sense is closer to "among," so the English translation cannot capture the repetition of the Syriac.

29. Mt 4.1–11 et par.

30. Or "watchful," "vigilant."

31. An allusion to the agony of Jesus in the Garden of Gethsemane (Mt 26.36–46 et par.).

32. Lk 2.41–52.

33. Or "afraid."

15

His feet did not fail the sick,[34]
  nor did his words [fail] the simple.[35]
He extended his descent to the lowly,
  and his ascent to the exalted.
Blessed is his sender!

16

His birth is our purification,
  and his baptism our propitiation.
His death is our vivification,
  and his ascension our exaltation.
How much should we praise him!

17

Among the gluttonous he is considered a gourmand,[36]
  but among the knowledgeable, the feeder of all.
Among the drunken he is considered an inebriate,[37]
  but among the wise he is the quencher[38] of all.
Blessed is his sustenance![39]

18

To Caiaphas, his conception was impure,[40]
  but to Gabriel his birth was glorious.
With deniers, his ascent is slandered,
  but for disciples, his ascension is a wonder.
Blessed is his discernment![41]

---

34. Or "his feet were not outmatched by the sick."
35. Or "unskilled," "simple," "stupid."
36. Lit. "eater." This word appears in the accusations against Jesus in Mt 11.19. The implication of the accusation (and of Ephrem's reference here) is that Jesus was an excessive eater and drinker (a glutton and drunkard), which is why I opted for the more interpretive word choices above.
37. Lit. "drinker." This word also appears in Mt 11.19.
38. Or "drink-giver."
39. Or "care," "support," "providence."
40. Stanzas 18 and 19 break from the acrostic pattern (spelling out Ephrem's name followed by a series of stanzas beginning with the letter *mim*). They may therefore represent later additions to the poem.
41. The word can also mean "departure." Ephrem might have intended a sort of double meaning—the ability to discern the truth as well as an allusion to the Ascension.

19

With his Begetter his begetting is true,
  but for the investigators his birth is difficult.
For the exalted, the truth is clear,
  but for the lowly, it is disputation and wandering.
His womb is sealed![42]

20

By the Evil One he was tempted,[43]
  and by that people he was questioned.
By Herod he was tried:[44]
  with silence, he refuted whoever wished to investigate him.
Blessed is his Begetter!

21

In the river they considered him among the baptized,[45]
  and in the sea they accounted him among the sleepers.[46]
As a slain man they hung him on the tree,[47]
  as a corpse, they placed him in the tomb.
Blessed is his humble state![48]

22

To us, who is like you, my Lord?
  The great one who became small, the wakeful one[49] who slept,
the pure one who was baptized, the living one who passed away,
  the king who was despised that he might honor all.
Blessed is your honor!

---

42. Or "silent." In other words, the "womb" of divinity (the nature of the begetting of the Son) is closed to disputation. The "sealed womb" is also likely an allusion to the virgin birth.

43. Mt 4.1–11 et par.

44. Lk 26.6–12.

45. A reference to Jesus's baptism by John in the Jordan River (Mt 3.13–17 et par.).

46. A reference to Jesus falling asleep on the boat in the Sea of Galilee (Mt 8.24 et par.).

47. Lit. "wood."

48. Or "abasement," "humiliation."

49. Or "watcher."

ON THE RESURRECTION 2

To the melody: "The Infants were Slain"[1]

Five lines of 7+7

1

Your law became a chariot,
  conveying me to paradise,[2]
and your cross became a key,
  to open paradise for me.[3]
From the garden of delights[4] I have carried,
  from paradise I have brought and gathered,
a rose and eloquent flowers,
  and look: they are sprinkled in your festival
with melodies for humanity.
  Blessed is he who crowned and was crowned!

2

See the cheerful feast day,
  full of mouths and tongues,[5]
on which[6] chaste women and men have become
  like trumpets and horns,

---

1. Also the melody of *Res.* 3; *Cruc.* 2; *Haer.* 22–24, 48; *Nis.* 17–21; *Nat.* 23–24.

2. Or, reading the verb as *glā*, this could read: "Your law became a chariot, and revealed Paradise to me."

3. An allusion to the Genesis creation narrative (contained in the law) and to the account of the repentant thief on the cross (Lk 23.42–43).

4. Syr. *ganāt 'edānē*, which sounds like "the root of Eden" (*ganāt 'eden*).

5. Lit. "which is entirely mouths and tongues."

6. Alternatively, "through which," which could refer to *kuleh:* "See the cheerful feast day: there are all its mouths and tongues / through which chaste women and men have become like trumpets and horns, / through which …"

on which girls and boys have become
   like lyres and kitharas.
Voices with voices woven,
   and all of them have risen up to reach heaven.
They gave glory to the Lord of glory.
   Blessed are the silent who have thundered forth through him!

3

See how the earth has thundered forth below,
   and above, heaven has thundered forth!
April has mixed voices with voices:
   exalted ones with low ones,
voices of the sanctified church mixed
   with the thunder[7] of divinity,
and amidst the glow of its[8] lamps
   are mixed flashes of lightning.
With the rain, the passion's weeping,
   and with the field, the fast of Pascha.[9]

4

In the same way, on the ark,
   every voice shouted joyfully from every mouth.
Outside were terrible waves,
   but inside were beautiful voices.
Pairs of tongues
   within sang together purely—
a type of this, our festival,
   in which virgin men and women
chant chastely.[10]
   Glory to the Lord of the ark!

5

At this feast, when each has brought
   his victorious deeds[11] as his offerings,

---

7. Syr. plural.
8. I.e., April's.
9. Or "fast of rejoicing" (*ṣawmā d-psāḥā*).
10. Or "in a holy fashion," a play on another word for the chaste in Syriac (*qaddišē*).
11. Lit. "victories" or "triumphs."

> I lamented for myself, my master,[12] for I saw
> > that I stand [here] meagerly.
> My intellect, moistened by your dew,[13]
> > became an April anew.
> Its flowers became my offerings.
> > Look: they are woven into many crowns,
> and adorn the doorway of the ear.
> > Blessed is the cloud[14] that has poured down upon me!

6

> Who has seen blossoms budding forth
> > from books[15] as from mountains,
> from which chaste women fill up
> > spacious wombs of the mind?
> Hear [their] chant, like the sun,
> > scattering blossoms over the assemblies.
> Holy are the flowers.
> > Accept them with your senses,
> as our Lord [accepted] the oil of Mary.[16]
> > Blessed is he who was crowned by his mothers!

7

> Exquisite, eloquent flowers
> > did the children[17] scatter before the king:
> the donkey was crowned with them,
> > the road was full of them.

---

12. The word *rabuli* can also mean "chief shepherd," in keeping with the pastoral wordplay throughout the stanza.

13. I.e., the "dew" of penitential tears. *Re'yān(y)* ("my intellect") also sounds like the imperative verb "pasture me," and closely resembles the nouns "my shepherd," or "my pasture," perhaps evoking the Eucharist.

14. The noun *'enānā* ("cloud") sounds similar to *'ānā* ("flock") and *'ānē* ("hearer").

15. Or "Scriptures."

16. Jn 12.3. The allusion is probably to Mary of Bethany, sister of Martha and Lazarus. Another possible reading is *māšḥā d-Maryam*, "the anointer of Mary," a change from the more familiar and perhaps expected passive *mšiḥā d-Maryam*, "the anointed of Mary." The possibility of two Marys (Mary Magdalene and Mary the mother of Jesus) explains the plural "mothers" at the end.

17. The word for "children" sounds like the word *šabārā*, a kind of flower known as Syrian rue.

Praises did they scatter[18] like flowers,
>   and melodies like lilies.
>   Now, too, in [this] feast,
>   the assembly of children scatters for you, my Lord,
> Hallelujahs like blossoms.
>   Blessed is he who was praised by the young!

8

See how our hearing like a [mother's] lap
>   is filled with infants' songs.
> The deep places of our ears are filled too, my Lord,
>   with the melodies of chaste women.
> Let each one gather up all flowers
>   and with them mingle
> the blossoms sprung up in his land,
>   that we may plait a great crown for him
> at this great feast.
>   Blessed is he who called us to plait it!

9

Let the bishop[19] plait his interpretations
>   into it as his blossoms,
> the priests[20] their victorious deeds,
>   the deacons[21] their readings,
> the youths their praises,
>   the children their psalms,
> the chaste women their songs,[22]
>   the leaders their actions,
> and the common people their customs.
>   Blessed is he who has multiplied our victories!

10

Let us summon and call the victorious
>   martyrs, apostles, and prophets,

---

18. Or imperative: "Scatter praises like flowers, and melodies like lilies!"
19. Lit. "chief shepherd."
20. Lit. "elders."
21. Lit. "ministers" or "servants."
22. Syr. *madrāšē*.

whose blossoms are like them:
> victorious are their flowers,
and rich are their roses,[23]
> the sweet fragrance of their lilies
they gather from the garden of delights,
> and bring lovely flowers
to crown our beautiful feast.
> Glory to you from [all] the blessed!

11

The crowns of kings are impoverished
> before the richness of your crown,
in which purity is plaited,
> in which faith shines,
in which humility gleams,
> in which holiness is woven,
in which great love glimmers.
> See how perfect is the beauty of your crown,
great King of the blossoms!
> Blessed is he who gave it to us to plait!

12

Our King, receive our offering,
> and give us salvation in its stead!
Bring peace to the lands which were ruined,
> build up the churches which were burned,
so that when there is great peace [again],
> we may plait for you a great crown,
as blossoms and those who plait them
> come in from all sides,
that the Lord of peace might be crowned.
> Blessed is he who has acted and can act!

---

23. There are two possible readings here: either "their flux [rendered here as 'seeds']" (*redyayhōn*), or (accepting Beck's emendation) "their roses" (*wardayhōn*).

ON THE RESURRECTION 3

To the same melody

1

April [is] the blameless month,
 for it was sent by the blameless one.[1]
In Egypt, it became radiant and blameless;
 it delivered and brought forth the king's bride.
It sprinkled the land with its showers before her;
 it scattered and filled it with its flowers.
Lamps of lightning shone,
 thunder clapped;[2]
the mountains skipped before her.[3]
 Blessed is the lofty one who escorted[4] the contemptible!

2

In the wilderness was a pure wedding feast,
 and on Mount Sinai was the bridal chamber.
The holy one descended, betrothed, and wed
 the daughter of Abraham, his beloved.
Suddenly, a great scandal:
 the bride committed adultery in her bridal chamber!
The betrother[5] went up to the bridegroom,
 and a foreigner[6] entered the bridal chamber.

---

1. Or "victorious," "justified."
2. Lit. "there was a sound that was thundering."
3. Cf. Ps 114.4.
4. As in procession to a wedding feast. Alternatively, "adorned" or "lifted up" (*ziḥ*).
5. Perhaps a reference to Moses.
6. If the reading *giyorā* ("stranger," "foreigner") is correct, it would, especially in light of the deep textual connections between this poem and *Cruc.* 1, refer to the

She hated the king, but loved the calf.
> Blessed is the pure one who wrote to dismiss her![7]

3

In the wilderness she served a lie,
> and in the wilderness was her pit.

For the pure one did not bring her into the land of the Peoples,[8]
> lest he be mocked by her.

But in her place, he magnified her daughter
> and gave her the adornments of her mother.

He warned her against her uncleanness,
> and promised that if she was chaste,

the king's Son would be her betrothed.
> Blessed is he who betrothed the church of the Peoples!

4

Cheerful April was sent
> to the daughter just as to her mother

to crown the daughter of Sarah,
> and they set out to meet the Son of the king.[9]

A great procession went before the bridegroom,[10]
> that the bride might rejoice in her betrothed:

the lame leapt like stags,[11]
> the blind shone like lamps.

There were acclamations with palm branches.[12]
> Blessed is he who chastened the unfaithful one![13]

---

golden calf as the "foreign" object of the Israelites' affections, as described in the following line. The reading *gāyorā* ("adulterer") is also possible and would be defensible, given the description of "adultery" in the bridal chamber.

7. Lit. "wrote and dismissed her." Reminiscent of the instructions for writing a certificate of divorce (Dt 24.1).

8. I.e., Canaan.

9. Or "and it [April] went out to meet the Son of the king."

10. What follows is an allusion to the account of Jesus's triumphal entry into Jerusalem (Mt 21.1–11 et par.). This and the following two stanzas are very similar to *Cruc.* 1.1–3.

11. This word (*'aylā*) also appears in P Ps 114.4.

12. The word (*sawkē*) used in P Mt 21.8.

13. Feminine (the reference is to the "daughter of Sarah").

5

The daughter of Sarah saw the king's Son;
  she observed that he was chaste and grew sad.
She saw that he was pure, and was grieved,
  for she was accustomed to adulterers.[14]
She accused him lest she be accused,
  and concocted[15] pretexts,
that he would divorce her just like the other.[16]
  For when she raged,[17] she did not know
that her bridegroom was chaste.
  Blessed is he who endured her impurity!

6

But April the just month
  stripped away[18] her adornments.
In it she donned, and in it she stripped:
  it[19] tore apart the temple veil,[20]
that pure garment over her,
  with which were concealed the adornments of the holy place.
It[21] stripped away her festivals,
  and from her took her greatest feast,
upon which all feasts are hung.[22]
  Blessed is he who left her forever!

7

The king's Son, when he saw her iniquity,
  came and betrothed the church of the Peoples,

---

14. These two lines are deeply reminiscent of *Cruc.* 1.3.

15. This word can be vocalized in two different ways: *gārat* is 3fs *p'al* perf. from *g-w-r*, "she committed adultery"; and *gerat* is 3fs *p'al* perf. from *g-r-r*, "she accused."

16. I.e., her mother, the Israelites. Or "so that by another he repudiates her."

17. Or "became insane" (*pqar*). The root also carries the connotation of promiscuous or irreverent activity.

18. Two verbs in Syriac: "strip off" (*šlaḥ*) and "take away" (*šqal*).

19. This could refer to either April or God (the former is more likely in this context).

20. Lit. "the curtain of the entrance." See Mt 27.51 et par. The verb *ṣrā* ("tore," "ripped") is that used in Mt 27.51.

21. Again, this could refer to either April or God.

22. I.e., Passover. Cf. Mt 22.40 et par.

for he tested her love and her truth,
 united her to himself, and was joined together with her.
That there may never be separation,[23]
 see her dwelling in the king's palace
arrayed in the king's adornments!
The month of April serves her,
adorning and putting on blossoms.
 Glory to you, Lord of April!

8

 In April, flowers tear[24] their calyxes,
 and their roses come forth,[25]
leaving them bare,
 and they become garlands[26] for others.
Like April is April's feast,
 in which the high priest tore his garments,[27]
and priesthood fled from him,
 leaving him naked,
and it was exposed[28] before our Savior.
 Blessed is the just one who claimed what is his!

---

23. Or perhaps in this context "divorce." Another alternative would be to read *puršānā* as "distinction."

24. Ephrem repeats again the verb *ṣrā*, used in Mt 27.51 to describe the tearing of the Temple veil.

25. There are two possible readings here: either "and their flux" (*w-redyayhon*), or "and their roses come forth" (*w-napqin wa-rdayhon*).

26. Syr. singular.

27. In this stanza, Ephrem demonstrates his keen eye for identifying common biblical vocabulary. The Syriac versions of Mt 26.65 and Mk 14.63 (Jesus's trial before the council) record that the high priest tore (*ṣri*) his garments in response to Jesus's perceived blasphemy. Ephrem's allusion to that account preserves the verb, but does not use any known biblical variant to describe the high priest's garment. Instead, he describes the high priest as tearing "his bosom" (*'ubaw[y]*), the same word translated as "calyxes" above. Ephrem presents a carefully constructed parallel between blossoming flowers (which "break open" their buds and are later plucked to be plaited into festal crowns) and the reaction of the high priest and subsequent transferal of the priesthood to Jesus. Ephrem's use of traditional springtime imagery provides him with a metaphorical framework to unite the Paschal celebration of the Church (represented by garlands of flowers) and the account of Jesus's Passion.

28. I.e., the priesthood.

9

In April, when the Spirit saw
    that high priest, Caiaphas,
she tore the priesthood from him,
    and he was stripped of the ministry.[29]
She tore also that curtain,
    went forth, and brought out everything.[30]
For the sanctuary that is served
    no longer saw a priest serving,
so it departed to where it is served.
    Blessed is he who adorned his ministry!

10

In April, the thick cloak,
    darkness, is torn apart completely:
lightning bolts strike[31] in the darkness,
    their flashes splitting it.[32]
[In] the feast that took place in April,
    tombs split open through a voice,
Death, killer of all, heard
    the voice that is the life-giver of all,
and yielded up its treasures.[33]
    Glory to you, Son of the life-giver of all!

---

29. Lit. "priesthood" (*kāhnūtā*) but a word different from the one in the preceding line.

30. Ephrem continues the theme of "tearing," drawing upon the reappearance of the same verbal root (*srā*) in Mt 27.51 to describe the tearing (*eṭari*) of the Temple veil and the breaking of rocks (*eṭari*) in the earthquake following Jesus's death. Through this common vocabulary and imagery, Ephrem presents the tearing of the Temple curtain and the high priest's garment as symbolic representations of the passing away of these institutions in favor of Christ and the Church.

31. Lit. "fly" (*prahīn*).

32. I.e., the darkness.

33. Once more, Ephrem employs the traditional imagery of spring to draw parallels with the Passion narrative. Like the high priest and the Temple in the previous stanzas, which "tore" (*srā*) their garments, and like the flower calyx, the outer covering that tears (*srā*) to reveal the blossom within, so the lightning of spring thunderstorms tears open the darkness, its "cloak." Ephrem then parallels the flashing lightning of the thunderstorm (which "splits" [*srā*] the darkness) to the dying cry of Jesus, which "split" the tombs and brought the dead (Death's "treasures") to life (Mt 27.52).

11

In [April], on the day that symbolic lamb
   (which came to an end) broke open Egypt,
it had shown its power through its killing,
   that a dead thing had broken off life.[34]
On the day of his slaughter, the firstborn also
   broke open Sheol just like Egypt:
the dead went forth proclaiming the power
   of that lamb, who by his slaughter
brought forth [the dead] from Sheol's womb.
   Glory to you, deliverer[35] of your[36] own!

12

April lightens the heavy
   burden on created things.
It lifts the load from mountains,
   and the mantle from springs.
For with its warmth it melts snow
   and frosty[37] streams.
Its peace[38] cools springs,
   it treads out paths through the valleys
for merchants after profits.[39]
   Glory, my Lord, to your providence!

---

34. That is, the dead lamb broke off the life of the firstborn sons of the Egyptians through its power. An alternative reading would be "that a dead thing was rescuing (*pāreq hwā*) unto life," which would anticipate the motif of the deliverer in the last line of the stanza.

35. This could also be read as an adverb modifying *apeq*: "Glory to you, delivering his own."

36. Syr. "his."

37. Lit. "the ice of streams."

38. Or "its cultivated land."

39. Syr. plural. In other words, the warmth and calm of April (characterized by melting of snow and an abundance of water) make economic activity viable once more, after the interlude of winter.

13

Terrible frost strikes all,
>and intense heat torments all.

Mingling its delight in the air,
>sweet April has conquered.

It clothes the naked trees,
>for its symbol is that of the Father of the fatherless.

The earth's nakedness teaches chastity,
>like its Lord, who taught chastity and clothed

Eve's nakedness in Eden.
>Blessed is he who taught chastity to our nakedness!

14

April, the victorious month,
>by which are surrounded all days,

and by which are encompassed all months,[40]
>on its right and on its left,

half of the months on its one side,
>and half also on its other side.

The rich month of October[41]
>stands opposite,[42] afar off,

and brings an offering.[43]
>Blessed is the power, the arranger of all!

---

40. In relation to the Julian or the modern Gregorian calendar, Nisan (April) is clearly not the middle of the year, as this image presents it. Although, however, the Syro-Antiochene or Syro-Macedonian calendar utilized in much of the Near East adopted the solar calendar with its 365 1/4-day year, it retained the earlier structure of the lunar calendar, beginning the year in October (known in Syriac as Tešri Qdim). This would place Nisan (April) six months later, with "half the months on its one side, and half also on its other side."

41. The two months of Tešri in the Syro-Antiochene solar calendar are equivalent to October and November, the months of harvest. Presumably, Ephrem refers here to Tešri Qdim (October).

42. This phrase can have a negative connotation ("standing/rising against"), but here it seems more to imply simply that autumn balances out spring, especially since October honors April, metaphorically making an offering to it. See also *Eccl.* 51.5.

43. The word *qurbānā* is also the standard Syriac term for the Eucharist.

15

The prophet cried out: "O barren woman,
    he has enlarged your womb,[44] that it[45] might suffice for your children."[46]
While Jerusalem killed the uncircumcised,
    the church gives life to the circumcised.
See how he[47] persuades the bodily
    to be born spiritually:
they rejoice in fleshly birth
    and boast in infants' milk,
they look for an inheritance of land.[48]
    Blessed is he who has promised a blessing to the Peoples!

16

The small womb of the daughter of Zion
    has refuted itself, since it is temporal.
It was sufficient for the small People
    to celebrate the feast within:[49]
in Jerusalem alone he commanded
    the People to offer their sacrifices.[50]
How can all Peoples
    from all ends [of the earth] come there
to offer up their sacrifices?
    Blessed is he who has broken his body in every place!

---

44. Syr. plural.
45. Syr. plural.
46. A very loose citation of P Isaiah 54.1.
47. I.e., the prophet Isaiah.
48. Or "an earthly inheritance" (*yurtānā d-arʿā*).
49. I.e., Jerusalem.
50. For the biblical command not to sacrifice the Passover "except in the place he will choose as a dwelling for his name," see Dt 16.5–6. For the Christian use of this passage as a means to invalidate the continued celebration of Passover, see Christine Shepardson, "Paschal Politics: Deploying the Temple's Destruction against Fourth-Century Judaizers," *Vigiliae Christianae* 62 (2008): 233–60, especially 250–58.

17

The rock Daniel saw
 filled out of itself the entire earth,[51]
the cloud Elijah saw
 spread out and became a type[52]
for the gospel which stretched itself
 and spread over all Peoples.
It sprinkles its rich showers
 and rains, which can
quench the thirst of the Peoples.
 Blessed is he who is served in every place!

51. See Dn 2.35.
52. See 1 Kgs 18.44.

ON THE RESURRECTION 4

To the melody: "This is the Fast of the Firstborn"[1]
$$6+5+5 + 5+5+6$$
$$+ \ 4+4 + 5+5 + 5+7 \text{ (or } 7+5)$$
$$+ \ 6+6+4 + R: 6+6+4^2$$

I

Extend[3] to us, blessed Lord,
   a little of your richness
      in the all-enriching month:
in April, your gift
   has been spread out over all:
      in it, enriched and adorned are
mountains with grasses,
   furrows with seeds,
seas[4] with goods,
   dry land with possessions,
the heights[5] with glimmering lights,
   and valleys with blossoms.
April, adornment of the earth,
   and April's feast,
the adornment of the holy church.

---

1. This melody is shared by *Ieiun.* 1, *Res.* 4, and *Res.* 5. The melody title comes from the first line of *Ieiun.* 1. Beck renders the hymn in seven-line stanzas, but is unable to discern the meter. This metrical pattern is our own reconstruction.

2. The refrain is missing from this poem in the MS.

3. The verb here carries the connotations of "offer" (in connection with the gift) and the image of flowers "putting forth" their blossoms.

4. Syr. singular.

5. Syr. singular.

2
Eloquent April
  counsels me to be bold,[6]
    ask, and speak, my Lord.
For if the closed mouths
  of the creeping killer[7]
    are opened by April—
the accursed serpent
  opened his mouth
when he deceived and killed all—
  in your mercy, my Lord, open
the mouth of your servant, and make him[8]
  a lyre of truth.
Let it[9] play a wholesome sound,
  full of blessed truth
    for all its[10] hearers!

3
If even the air is altogether eloquent
  with all sounds[11]
    during April's thunder,[12]
then how much more
  will the church of words[13] resound
    on the day of your eloquent Pascha,
that like a kithara,
  all of it might sing
at your great feast,
  the companion and yokefellow

---

6. *Mlilā*, translated here as "eloquent," might also be translated as "endowed with reason" or "rational."

7. Syr. singular.

8. Or "it" in reference to the "mouth."

9. Or "him" in reference to the "servant."

10. Or "it" with reference to the "lyre" or the "mouth."

11. Or "voices," "melodies" (*qālin*).

12. Syr. plural.

13. This image is hard to capture in English translation. The "wordy" or "eloquent" (*mlilā*) air of April shares the same root as the "wordy" or "eloquent" (*mellē*) church.

of that feast in which
> the watchers resounded at Bethlehem.

In April, let the church plait
> the crown of glory that the watchers
>> plaited in December![14]

4

See too, how April weaves
> the earth, clothing it
>> in a garment of all colors.

Creation is robed
> in a cloak of flowers,
>> and a mantle of blossoms.

Adam's mother[15]
> at the feast of April,

Wears a cloak
> not woven with hands.

She exults[16] that her Lord came down
> and raised up her son.[17]

Two festivals for the earth
> together with two feast days
>> for her Lord and son.[18]

5

The earth is like a womb
> and bosom for all the living,
>> and a shroud for the dead.

Woe to the earth, by which
> all who are naked clothe themselves,
>> for no one can cover her.

---

14. Syr. *Konun*. Ephrem presents the feasts of Nativity and Pascha as "companions." The feast of Nativity fell on December 25 in the Julian calendar, which is January 7 in the Gregorian calendar.

15. Probably to be understood as the personification of the earth. Cf. *Par.* 9.1.

16. Or "bursts into song" (*etpasaḥ*).

17. I.e., humanity, and by extension, Christ in his humanity.

18. In a continuation of the theme developed in the previous stanzas, the months of December and April ("feasts of the earth") are paired with the two Christian festivals of Nativity and Pascha.

April is ashamed[19]
 at [the earth's] nakedness,
and like the exposed Noah,
 covers her shame.[20]
With a cloak, the two brothers covered[21]
 the father of all.
But with cloaks of flowers,
 April alone covered
  the earth, mother of all.

6

The weak-winged [bee],[22] too,
 in the month of flowers,
  has come forth, laboring fruitfully.
Look at it,
 feebler[23] than all,
  and labor fruitfully in its likeness!
It is clothed in symbols,
 laden with types:
out of each flower[24]
 it gathers up benefits.
Its treasure,[25] too, is hidden and neglected,
 but when it is opened up,[26]
[it is] a wonder to see how
 [the bee] labored, constructed,
  and filled it. Blessed be its Creator!

---

19. Or "was respectful."

20. Or "nakedness." See Gn 9.21–23.

21. The verb used in Gn 9.23.

22. Syr. *gepā mḥilā*. Beck suggests this refers to *bees*, which is a sensible deduction.

23. The root *ḥlš* can refer to "strip," "undress," in other Aramaic dialects. This may be a rare instance that attests to its use also in Syriac. The context may at least support the double meaning in addition to "weak"— "exposed most of all."

24. Lit. "all flowers."

25. Probably an allusion to the beehive, filled with honey.

26. The usual sense division falls here. But this may be an instance of the thought continuing against the typical pattern.

7

When sweetness is spread about,
  the mouth gathers it up,
    for it is purer[27] than anything.
It is a mirror for the church,
  which has gathered the sweetness
    of the Holy Spirit from the scriptures.[28]
In the wilderness, the synagogue
  gathered up manna.[29]
It collected it greedily,
  though its mind was impure.
Instead of fine manna,
  come gather up pure love!
Manna stank[30] when the night had passed;
  love, if the night passes,
    becomes even sweeter.

8

April has broken
  the chill of winter,
    its bitter sting.
A symbol of love
  is April, for its warmth
    conquers the icy cold.
See how feet leap for joy
  when it binds up winter;
see how hands are released
  when it enchains idleness;
see how fruitfulness comes forth
  when it adorns the earth.
Let the soul look and be envious
  and instead of the earth,
    adorn itself!

---

27. Or "more satisfying," "more wholesome."
28. Cf. *Nat.* 28.9.
29. See Ex 16.
30. This verb (*sri*) appears in Ex 16.20.

9

April has become great,
   in the likeness of the One who released all,
      for it has released merchants.
For the prisoners of winter,
   when April reigned,
      it released to go forth and rejoice,
in the likeness of its Lord,
   who in April released
those bound in Sheol,
   and they tore open their tombs.[31]
Let freedom release itself,
   for it has fettered itself.
Who shall release one
who is placed in great fetters by his will?

10

In you, gentle April,
   the thunder overhead
      has soothed[32] our hearing.[33]
In April also
   the Lord of thunder
      moderated[34] his strength with his mercy.
He descended and released
   through Mary's womb.
In April, again,
   he grew strong, broke open
Sheol's womb, and rose, moreover, in April.
He softened his voice and persuaded
   those who heard and despaired
      at his resurrection.

---

31. See Mt 27.52–53.

32. Or "softened," "assuaged." I am reading this verb as the *aphel* form of the root *rkk*. Another possibility would be to read it as "extend," "lengthen," from the root *'rk*.

33. Or "our obedience" (*mašma'tā*).

34. Same root as the verb translated "soothed" above.

ON THE RESURRECTION

11

This is glorious April,
  opening all treasures
    and bringing forth all riches[35]
...
  ...
    ...
...
  ...
...
  ...
...
  ...

In it too,[36] the treasure of the depths
  below has given the body of
    the One who gives life to all.

12

A censer of spices
  was sweet[37] April,
    and shed abroad all aromas.
God had come down
  to walk on the earth:
    April saw him, and glowed;
Like the high priest,
  it offered him
a censer of spices,
  an aroma of perfumes.
It prophesied, for see how the high priest
  came down to us from the heights![38]
His sacrifice is the love of truth,
  his censer mercy,
    and his hyssop the cleansing of sins.

---

35. The majority of the following strophes of the folio are not legible.
36. Reading uncertain.
37. Wordplay between "spices" (*besmē*) and "sweet" (*bsimā*).
38. Syr. singular.

13

It is in April that our Lord
  came down from the heights,
    and Mary bore him.
It is in April, again,
  that he was raised and went up,
    and again, Mary saw him.[39]
She sensed him
  when he came down …

…
  …
…[40]

  the heights and the depths.[41]
You again, April, for you saw
  the conception, conclusion, and resurrection
    of your Lord.

14

The renowned one[42] put on
  compassion, was moved, and came down
    from the heights[43] in April.
He was crowned in April
  with a multitude of triumphs,
    and came up too, from the abyss.
The dead plaited you a crown
  when they came to life,
the disciples plaited you a crown
  when they were comforted,
the watchers plaited you a crown
  when they marveled at your agony.

---

39. Probably an allusion to a resurrection appearance of Jesus to his mother Mary, or to Mary Magdalene's encounter with the risen Jesus (Jn 20.11–18).

40. Lacuna.

41. Syr. singular.

42. Syr. *bḥirā*. The verbal root *bḥr* is used, among other things, for testing or refining of metal in a crucible, and thus Christ would be the "tried," "tested," "approved," or "chosen one."

43. Syr. singular.

ON THE RESURRECTION

In place of that crown of thorns,
  all creatures have plaited you
    a crown of glory.

15

Like a steward[44] of symbols,
  April was running
    after our Lord when he arrived,
for Moses had entrusted[45]
  hidden symbols
    to April in Egypt.
April was bringing forth
  its symbols …[46]
…[47]
  …
…
  … both of them.
You, April, when you saw
  the pair of radiant Paschas,[48]
    of Moses and our Lord!

---

44. *Rabitā*, "steward," is correct, given the meter, but is also suggestive of *rbitā*—"sea" or "ocean."
45. As a ruler would to a steward (Syr. *aggel*).
46. Lacuna.
47. The MS is fragmentary until the end of the line, which reads "both of them" or "two of them" (*trayhon*).
48. Wordplay here between *pashē* and *pasihē*.

ON THE RESURRECTION 5

To the same melody

I

In this abundant month,
   your gift has abounded
      over all, ungrudgingly.[1]
My Lord, your bounties
   over all gave success[2]
      to the drops of April.
See how they are scattered
   as far as the brambles;[3]
see how you have bent down
   in the compassion of your gift:
even if tares have sprung up, adorned themselves,[4]
   and held back thanks through silence,
my Lord, withhold not your mercy
   from the one who thirsts to bring forth
      blossoms of praise through song.

---

1. The phrase *d-lā ḥsām* is equivalent to the Greek ἄφθονος ("abundantly," "generously"). In other words, nothing else can come close to rivaling or emulating his gift. It also may be carrying the sense of "differentiation," or "distinction," although lexically this is more of a stretch. In this case, though, the idea would be that God's gift is equal-opportunity; it makes no distinction. This would fit with the theme of God showing his compassion even to deniers (st. 1) and the wicked (st. 3).

2. The verb *zaki* could also mean "overcame" or "cleared of blame."

3. The word *ya'rā* ("brambles") does not appear in the P version of the Parable of the Sower (Mt 13; Mk 4), which Ephrem is likely evoking here. There, the seed falls among "thorns" (*kubē*).

4. Or "were adorned."

ON THE RESURRECTION

2

The empty ponds
fruitful April
has filled up for drinking.
In it, fill, my Lord,
from the abundance of your grace,
the thirsty ponds[5] of our thinking.
For everyone is in need
of your gift.
And unless [your gift][6] stretches out
to heal your creatures,
then they are sick ...[7]
...
...
...
...
...

[3] ...
...
...
...
...
...[8]

For the sun
has never ceased[9]
that has dawned on the wicked[10]
that through the visible dawn,
we might perceive the invisible dawn,
by his love, which has extended[11] over the wicked.

---

5. Syr. singular.
6. The participle "stretch out" is feminine.
7. The text of the folio is illegible at this point.
8. End of lacuna.
9. Or "it never lacks the sun."
10. Cf. Mt 5.45.
11. Reading uncertain (Beck suggests *pras*).

By the steadfast sun,
> he has shown that he will never withdraw[12]
>> his compassion from the unjust.

4

After winter's bleakness,
> mute and silent,
>> hear[13] April thunder!

Truly it is the sound of everything
> that is calm.

It has calmed the sea[14]
> through the sounds[15] of oars and sailors,

it has calmed the wilderness
> through the sounds of cattle,[16]

and the air,
> through the sounds of birds.[17]

In April it calmed[18]
> the bleakness[19] of Sheol, through the sensation
that the living sound had entered[20]
>> . . .
>>> . . .

---

12. I am interpreting this as *pa'el* ("empty," "withdraw"), though it could also be *pe'al* ("suffice," "be enough").

13. *Hā* is added by Beck.

14. *Yamā* added by Beck.

15. Sing. throughout. Note that this noun (*qālā*) can be translated as "sound" and "voice."

16. Lit. "possessions," but can have the meaning of "beasts of burden" or "cattle."

17. Syr. singular. Ephrem gives a similar listing of created things in *Eccl.* 51.4.

18. Or "The chaos of Sheol was *pacified* through perceiving ..."

19. Or "desolation," "chaos."

20. The poem ends here in the MS, though the meter suggests two more.

TEACHING SONGS ON THE UNLEAVENED BREAD

Translated by J. EDWARD WALTERS

ON THE UNLEAVENED BREAD 1

On the unleavened bread, to the melody,
"The One who is Patient in Spirit"[1]

5+5 + 5+5 + 5+5

1
The instructor of all came
  in his love to the stubborn ones.
They remained in stubbornness
  while they were watchful over him.
They persecuted, without discernment,
  the treasure of discernments.

Refrain: Praise to the one who sent you!

2
I marvel at your loving mercies,
  which you have poured out upon the wicked:[2]
for you impoverished your glory
  so that you might enrich our poverty,[3]
in order that, through our treasures,
  we might become companions to those above.

3
He was perfected in his goodness,
  for he gave reward and taught

---

1. This is an acrostic poem from ܐ to ܠ.
2. Cf. Mt 5.45.
3. 2 Cor 8.9.

the sick one whom he healed. He healed him,
   and then [the sick one] learned.[4]
He received a reward because he learned,
   for when he was healed, he learned.

4

He perfected humanity
   through everything he endured:
for he was struck, yet he kept
   teaching, suffering, and consenting.
He was seized like a sheep
   so that he might ensure his promises.

5

The one pronouncing judgments
   was judged and interrogated
instead of the one who deceived.
   For, instead of the wicked ones,
the just one was interrogated.
   Praise be to the one who sent him!

6

The good one who entered was judged,
   through his love, instead of the evil ones.
And this is the amazing thing:
   he was found guilty instead of them!
With their own hands, they crucified him
   because of their own wickedness.

7

He gave himself for them so that
   they might live through his death.
And like the lamb in Egypt that gave life
   through the symbol of its master,
he was slaughtered. He redeemed,
   through his love, those who killed him.

---

4. Perhaps an allusion to Lk 5.17–26.

8

Because Adam sinned
   and went astray in paradise,
in the place of pleasures, the just one
   was beaten instead of him
in the judgment hall,
   in the place of torments.

9

Look: the good one came
   to perfect the righteous ones
who have carried his symbols.
   That is, through his completion
in his body, he perfected
   his siblings as members [of his body].

10

Even as Adam killed
   life within his body,
there was within his body
   a type that perfects all.
Behold, the just ones are perfected
   and sinners obtain mercy!

11

The conqueror came down to be defeated.
   It was not by Satan,
for he conquered and strangled him.[5]
   He was conquered by the crucifiers.
He conquered in his righteousness
   and was conquered by his own goodness.

12

He conquered the strong one
   and was conquered by the weak ones.
They crucified the one who gave himself.
   He was conquered in order to conquer.

---

5. I.e., Satan.

He conquered his temptations
>and he was conquered through his mercy.

13

He conquered Satan in a desolate place
>when he was provoking him,

and he was conquered by Satan in an inhabited place
>when he crucified him.

He killed him as he was being killed,
>so that even in his defeat, he might conquer [Satan].

14

The wisdom that perfected everything—
>which stirred up infants,

questioned the ignorant,
>and debated with scribes—

gave intelligence to all
>and sowed the truth in all.

15

The wisdom of God[6] came down
>to the house of fools.

She gave wisdom through her teaching
>and illuminated through her interpretation.

As a reward for her help,
>they struck her cheeks.

16

The good one came down
>to the wicked in his goodness.

He repaid that which he did not owe,
>and he was repaid what he had not borrowed.

They defrauded him doubly
>when they cheated him and repaid him.

17

The good one bore and made [others] bear:
>a wonder in both regards!

---

6. 1 Cor 1.21.

For while he made us bear the truth,
>   he bore up the iniquity from us.
The needy bore his riches,
>   and they made him bear their sins.

18

The good one loved the crucifiers
>   through their children,
whom he held and blessed.[7]
>   He signified that all of them would become one.
But when he was kissed,
>   they bit him with the mouth of a thief.

19

The error of that people thus
>   dwells in expectation
and waits for sacrifices.
>   It is a wicked thing after
that lamb of God
>   to offer sacrifices again.

---

7. Mk 10.16.

ON THE UNLEAVENED BREAD 2

To the same melody[1]

1
He is the one who knows,
 he who began to hide his knowledge within himself,
and he asked those who were in error:
 "Whose son is the Messiah?"[2]
So that he might make known his divinity,
 he was asking about himself.

Refrain: Blessed is he who was sacrificed for us!

2
The true lamb knew
 that the priests were unclean,
and that the priests[3] were defiled,
 and they were not sufficient for him.
He became, for his own body,
 the priest and high priest.

3
The priests of that people
 slaughtered the high priest,
for our priest became the sacrifice.
 Through his sacrifice, he brought sacrifices to an end.

---

1. Continues the acrostic of poem 1 from ܂ to ܫ.
2. Mt 22.42.
3. Ephrem employs two different words for "priest" (*kumrā* and *kāhnā*) in the following stanzas and does not seem to distinguish between them.

On every side,
>he extended his help.

4

The priests who had been
>better than the animals
had slaughtered and had offered
>sacrifices of the animals.
The priest was being sanctified
>by an unsanctified lamb.

5

There is no lamb that is greater
>than the exalted lamb,
because the priests were earthly
>and the lamb is heavenly.
He himself became
>the sacrifice and the sacrificer.

6

For the blemished priests
>were not worthy to sacrifice
the unblemished lamb.
>He became a peace offering,
and he reconciled what is above and what is below
>through his all-reconciling blood.[4]

7

He broke the bread with his hands
>as a symbol of the sacrifice of his body.
He mixed the cup with his hands
>as a symbol of the sacrifice of his blood.
He sacrificed and offered himself,
>the priest of our atonement.

8

He clothed the priesthood
>of Melchizedek with his type,

---

4. Cf. Col 1.20.

who did not perform sacrifices.
　　He gave the bread and the wine,[5]
but he dismissed the priesthood,
　　weary from libations.

9

His servants dishonored the king
　　from the house of David.
They turned away and regarded him as insane.[6]
　　When they estranged him, they demonstrated
that they had turned away and gone astray,
　　for they dishonored their king.

10

The kingdom of the house of David
　　eagerly awaited the son of David.
It saw him and rejoiced.
　　Zion received the good news.
It saw the beauty that gladdens all,
　　but became gloomy.[7]

11

The people called him—
　　the Lord of prophecy—a prophet.
Their honor is shame;
　　they turned and regarded him as insane.
Their honor is foolish,
　　and their blasphemy is assured.

12

If he were only a prophet,
　　he would be a companion of the prophets,
searching for another
　　who would be greater than he.

---

5. Gn 14.18.
6. Mk 3.21.
7. For a similar formulation of Zion's "sadness" at the arrival of Jesus, see *CD* 18.1, *Cruc.* 1.2, *Res.* 3.5, *Eccl.* 38.21.

He is the Lord of the prophets;
    his servants cry out concerning him.[8]

13

Hope came to the people.
    The people cut off their hope
and sent it to the house of the peoples,
    and they became hopeless.
The peoples hastened to clothe themselves
    with the hope that they had stripped off.

14

This is the hope that the prophets
    waited to see.
Who is not astonished
    that the madmen, upon seeing him,
hastened to insult him, [asking]
    why he had come in their days?

15

For this is the reason
    that he had come in their days:
that if they received him, they might live,
    and that if they rejected him,
they would know how insane they were
    to reject their light.

16

It is difficult for the unjust one
    to know that he is unjust
because he is unaware of his wickedness
    as long as he does not suffer injustice.
He will learn, through his difficulty,
    the taste of his wickedness.

The End [*of the first two teaching songs*]

---

8. Cf. Mt 3.11, Mk 1.7, and Lk 3.16.

ON THE UNLEAVENED BREAD 3

5+4 + 5+4
Again on the unleavened bread, to the melody,
"Gather Together to Celebrate in the Month of April" [1]

1
Behold! The paschal lamb
   was slain in Egypt,
and the true lamb
   was slaughtered in Zion.

Refrain: Praise be to the Son, the Lord of symbols,
who, through his crucifixion, fulfilled all symbols!

2
Let us consider
   both lambs, my brothers and sisters,
let us see whether
   they are similar or different.

3
Let us weigh and compare
   their achievements,
of that symbolic lamb
   and the true lamb.

4
Let us see the symbol
   as a shadow,

---

1. For another English translation and analysis of this poem, see Sebastian P. Brock, "The Poetic Artistry of St. Ephrem," *Parole de l'Orient* 6–7 (1975–76): 21–28.

let us see the truth
   as the fulfillment.

5
Hear about the common symbols
   of that Pascha
and rejoice[2] at the double
   victory of our Pascha.

6
There was from Egypt,
   through the paschal lamb,
an exodus for the people
   and not an entry.

7
And there was from Error,
   through the true lamb,
an exodus for the peoples
   and not an entry.

8
And [there was] from Sheol,
   through the living lamb,
an exodus for the dead
   like [the exodus] from Egypt.[3]

9
Through Egypt a pair of
   symbols was depicted:
for Sheol and for Error,
   [Egypt] was a mirror.

10
Through the paschal lamb
   the greed of Egypt
learned to give back,
   which was against its habit.

---

2. Reading *ḥad* as *ḥdaw* here, as an imperative in parallel with the previous line.
3. An allusion to the raising of the righteous dead at Jesus's death (Mt 27.52–53).

11

Through the living lamb
 the hunger of Sheol
vomited and gave back,
 which was against its nature.

12

Through the true lamb
 the voracious Error
spewed, heaved, and disgorged
 the peoples who received life.

13

Through that paschal lamb,
 Pharaoh sent out
the people whom, like Death,
 he had detained.

14

Through the living lamb,
 Death sent out
the righteous who came forth
 from their graves.

15

Through that true lamb,
 Satan gave back
the peoples whom,
 like Pharaoh, he had detained.

16

Through Pharaoh a pair
 of types was depicted:
there was an example
 of Death and of Satan.

17

Egypt was burst open
 by the paschal lamb,
and before the Hebrews,
 a road extended.

18
Through the true lamb,
  the true road
returned Satan,
  who blocked roads.

19
That living lamb trampled
  for the entombed
a road from the grave
  with a loud cry.[4]

---

4. Mk 15.37.

ON THE UNLEAVENED BREAD 4

To the same melody

1

Hear about the revealed type
 that was in Egypt,
hear about the one who is
 revealed and hidden in Zion.

Refrain: Praise to the Son who through his crucifixion has perfected all the types that his servants have drawn!

2

Our Lord humiliated
 Sheol and Error;
Death and Satan
 he defeated simultaneously.

3

For in Sheol, our Lord
 broke apart Error
in order to teach the power
 that is concealed through what is visible.

4

Just as he broke apart
 Sheol openly,
so also did he break apart
 Error secretly.

5
Just as he defeated
 Death openly,
so also Satan
 was defeated secretly.

6
Many saw the graves
 that were split,
but they did not see
 that Satan was defeated.

7
Through what is near,
 he gave a demonstration
of the power that was
 hidden and distant.

8
For it was when Death
 was being defeated at last,
on a Friday[1] it was that he killed
 the one that causes all life.

9
When the peoples repented,
 Satan was ashamed,
and it was on a Friday that he strangled
 the conqueror of all.

10
Egypt was terrified
 by the paschal lamb;
the slain lamb
 killed her firstborn.

---

1. Lit. "day of preparation" (*rūbtā*); see Mt 27.62; Mk 15.42; Lk 23.54; Jn 19.14, 31, 42.

11

Error was terrified
  because she saw
the true lamb,
  which exposed its deceits.

12

Sheol also heard him
  and her heart burst
at that living voice
  that resuscitated her dead ones.

13

The paschal lamb
  only defeated Egypt;
the true lamb
  defeated Error and Sheol.

14

Through visible Sheol,
  he broke apart Error
so that they blamed each other
  that both of them were defeated.

15

Through that paschal lamb,[2]
  Pharaoh lamented;
he mourned over his firstborn,
  the first of his children.

16

Through that true lamb,
  the evil one lamented
that Adam, the first of the sinners,
  was made righteous.

---

2. This phrase could also be translated, "Through the lamb of rejoicing." It is likely that Ephrem here intends this *double entendre* to emphasize Pharaoh's lament.

17
Through that living lamb,
  Death lamented
that Abel was raised,
  his original firstborn.

18
He broke Satan
  through Death openly
so that they were crying out, one over another,
  that the one had defeated them.

19
Behold, the mighty deeds
  are plain in the typological lamb,
and the glorious deeds
  are double in the true lamb!

20
The people must have
  been ashamed,
for many mediators who stood
  in their midst did not persuade them.

21
For their paschal symbols,
  which are engraved and stamped
on our paschal lamb,
  did not persuade them.

22
The teachers were also ashamed
  that they alienated the Son,
for behold, the law
  bears images of him.

23
Behold, the prophets
  bear, like suns,
examples of the Messiah
  who rules over all.

24
Creatures and scriptures
  bear together
symbols of his humanity
  and his divinity.

25
Indeed the people were ashamed!
  For their covenants
made a mirror
  for our covenants.

26
But glory be to you,
  Lord of our Pascha,
because the Pascha in Egypt
  declared your symbol.

27
Again to you be praise,
  Lord of the prophets,
for all of the prophets
  declared your types.

28
To you be thanks,
  Lord of natures,
because all of nature
  worships you completely.

ON THE UNLEAVENED BREAD 5

To the same melody

1

The lamb of God
  led, by his blood,
the peoples from Error
  as [he led the people] from Egypt.

Refrain: Praise to the Son who redeemed us by his blood just as his symbol redeemed the children of Jacob!

2

Many lambs
  have been slain,
yet it is only by one
  that Egypt was defeated.

3

Lambs have been offered
  on feast days,
yet it is only by one
  that Error was defeated.

4

Samuel offered up
  a suckling lamb,[1]
by which the mighty warriors and force
  of the Philistines were defeated.

---

1. 1 Sm 7.9.

5
By the lamb,
   the son of David:
the mighty evil one,
   the invisible Goliath, was humbled.

6
The priests took the veil
   from the holy place,
and they cast
   pure purple upon him.[2]

7
Just as they slandered him
   by the head-tax:[3]
"he is forbidding
   anyone from paying,"[4]

8
so also did they slander him
   with the garment
so that the purples upon him
   cry out concerning him.

---

2. This is a reference to the "veil over the altar" that was supposed to be a purple cloth according to Nm 4.13. See also *Cruc.* 4.3. This was likely the result of the fact that the Old Syriac (S) text of Mt 28.28 states that the soldiers mocked Jesus by clothing him in a purple cloak. Later versions of the Syriac NT, including the Peshitta, omit this word; see G. A. Kiraz, ed., *Comparative Edition of the Syriac Gospels: Aligning the Sinaiticus, Curetonianus, Peshitta, and Harklean Versions, Vol. 1: Matthew*, 3rd ed. (Piscataway, NJ: Gorgias Press, 2004), 434. Cf. Beck, *Paschahymnen* (Translation), 9, note 4; Rouwhorst, *Les hymnes pascales, II*, 16, note 2. This tradition can also be found in (pseudo) Ephrem's *Commentary on the Diatessaron* §17. For a broader summary of the traditions related to the veil of the Temple, see Daniel M. Gurtner, "The Veil of the Temple in History and Legend," *Journal of the Evangelical Theological Society* 49, no. 1 (2006): 97–114.

3. Mt 22.17; Mk 12.14; Lk 20.22.

4. Lk 23.2.

9

For they were afraid
   that he might not die,
so they cast purple upon him
   in order to kill him.[5]

10

The kings of the earth
   had given purple garments
to the Maccabees[6]
   and to Simon, the high priest.[7]

11

They took some of [the purple cloth]
   and cast it upon the son of the king,
and prophesied about him,
   as Caiaphas [had prophesied].[8]

12

They cast kingship
   upon the son of David;
though unwitting,
   they had made him king.

13

Wanting to snatch
   from him what was his,
they had added
   another kingdom.

14

For he is the king of kings
   and the weaver of crowns;
the whole kingdom
   gathered before him.

---

5. Cf. *Cruc.* 4.4.
6. 1 Mc 10.62.
7. 1 Mc 14.43.
8. Jn 11.51.

15

In this feast the blood
  of the paschal lamb
is sprinkled
  upon all the doors.

16

In this feast the blood
  of the true lamb
is mixed
  among the disciples.

17

In this feast
  the temporal lamb
gave to that people
  temporary salvation.

18

In this feast,
  Error fled
through that true lamb
  who taught the truth.

19

That symbolic lamb
  renewed him,
for the fulfillment came
  and completed the symbols.

20

The truth of the true lamb[9]
  is limitless.
Who is greater than he?
  For by him he shall be succeeded.

---

9. Ephrem may be employing some wordplay here with *'emar* ("to speak") and *'emrā'* ("lamb"). The phrase "the true lamb" could also be translated "the one who speaks the truth."

ON THE UNLEAVENED BREAD

21

For what lamb
  will be able to dismiss
the lamb of God,
  who has dismissed the symbols?

22

The fulfillment
  came and put on
the symbols that the Holy Spirit
  had woven for him.

23

The symbol was in Egypt;
  the truth is in the Church;
the final fulfillment
  is in the kingdom.

ON THE UNLEAVENED BREAD 6

To the same melody

1

Between lamb and lamb
   stood the disciples;
they ate the paschal lamb
   and the true lamb.

Refrain: To you, my Lord, be praise,
King Christ, for through your blood your holy church was delivered!

2

The apostles stood in the middle
   between symbol and truth;
they saw that the symbol was cut off,
   and it joined to the truth.

3

They are blessed, for in them
   there was the end
of the symbol, and so too there was
   the beginning of the truth.

4

Our Lord ate the Pascha
   with his disciples;
by the bread that he broke,
   he abolished the unleavened bread.[1]

---

1. Cf. *Cruc.* 4.2.

5

His bread, which gives life to all,
  gave life to the peoples,
instead of that unleavened bread,
  for its eaters died.

6

The Church gave us
  the living bread
instead of that unleavened bread
  that Egypt gave.

7

Mary gave us
  the bread of rest
instead of the bread of fatigue
  that Eve gave.[2]

8

Abel was a lamb
  and he offered a lamb;[3]
who has seen a lamb
  offer another lamb?[4]

9

The lamb of God
  ate a lamb;
who has seen a lamb
  eat another lamb?

10

The true lamb
  ate the paschal lamb;
the symbol hastened
  to enter the belly of truth.[5]

---

2. Gn 3.17.
3. Gn 4.4–8.
4. Cf. *Cruc.* 2.9.
5. Cf. *Cruc.* 3.11.

11

For all the types
   in the holy of holies
were abiding and anticipating
   the fulfiller of all.

12

The symbols saw
   the true lamb,
broke through the curtain,[6]
   and came out to meet him.

13

All of them[7] were planted
   and proved true about his fullness,
for they all proclaimed
   about his fullness everywhere.

14

For in him, the symbols
   and types were fulfilled,
just as he concluded:
   "Behold, everything is finished!"[8]

[*Azym.* 7–11 are missing, except for two incomplete teaching songs that Beck designates as 8 and 9.][9]

---

6. Mt 27.51.
7. I.e., the symbols.
8. Jn 19.30.
9. For more on the manuscripts, see Beck, *Paschahymnen* (Text), i–iii; Cassingena-Trévedy, *Hymnes pascales,* 8–11; and Rouwhorst, *Les hymnes pascales,* I, 23–26.

[ON THE UNLEAVENED BREAD 8?]

[To the same melody]

1

...
precious.
They repaid
the debt in full.

2

In this feast,
the sea became
the just debt collector
for the defrauded people.

3

For the sea avenged
the vengeance of Joseph:[1]
it drowned the Egyptians
who exacted what was owed to him.[2]

4

In the month of flowers,[3]
the sea became
a trap and a refuge,
for it saved and killed.

---

1. There is a clever wordplay in this line with *tbaʿ* ("to avenge") and *ṭbaʿ* ("to drown").

2. This could also be translated, "the Egyptians, who reneged on their deal with him," referring to the land in Goshen promised to Joseph (Gn 47.6), which had (presumably) been taken by the Pharaoh who "did not know Joseph" and began oppressing the Israelites (Ex 1.8–14).

3. That is, in April, when flowers begin to bloom. For the title "month of flowers," see also *Res.* 4.6.

5

In this feast,
 the flock emerged
from the depths of the sea,
 and the wolves drowned.

6

In this feast,
 the wolves attacked
that shepherd of all,
 who had become a sheep.

7

In that feast,
 Moses sang
a new song of praise
 about the power of the sea.[4]

8

Between sea and dry land,
 Moses sang [about]
those drowned in the sea,
 those saved on dry land.

9

Moses, who was illumined,[5]
 was exalted through the blood;[6]
that one who became God[7]
 succeeded with a staff.[8]

10

Moses, the glory of the
 descendants of the people,
was radiant
 with the symbols of the son.

---

4. Ex 15.1–18.
5. Ex 34.29.
6. Ex 7.20–25.
7. Ex 4.16.
8. Ibid.

11

The maker,
  like a fellow-servant with Moses,
was enslaved
  by the signs of lordship.

12

The sea, like a slave
  to Moses the slave,
was enslaved by
  the staff of the king's son.

13

The creation was subdued
  by its fellow slaves:
by the sign of divinity,
  she was obedient to them.

14

So also humanity:
  to the one who possesses
the authority of kingship,
  humanity is also obedient.

15

Thus, nature also
  teaches us
that power precedes
  the sign of kingship.

16

In the month of flowers,
  the Jordan River
parted its waves
  before the banner of its Lord.[9]

---

9. Ephrem now shifts to the parting of the Jordan and the defeat of the city of Jericho when the people entered the promised land; Jos 3.14–17; 6.1–25.

17
In the season of flowers,
voices cried out,
and the walls [of Jericho]
fell before Joshua.[10]

10. Given the parallelism with the previous strophe and the fact that the Syriac names for Joshua and Jesus are the same, the Syriac audience would catch the *double entendre* that the walls of Jericho fell in the physical presence of Joshua, but through the symbolic presence of Jesus.

[ON THE UNLEAVENED BREAD 9?]

To the same melody

1

In the month of flowers,
  the sounds of Miriam's tambourine
rang out in the
  presence of the people.[1]

Refrain: Thanks be to the firstborn who, through the crucifixion, turned all the peoples toward the one who sent him!

2

The sea was roaring
  against the Egyptians;
the tambourine[2] made
  the children of Jacob rejoice.

3

[Text is too lacunous to translate.][3]

---

1. Ex 15.20–21.

2. This word could also be translated as "the parting" (i.e., of the sea).

3. The following two strophes were restored by Brock on the basis of Mosul Fenqitho (FM V, pp. 127–28; the Syriac text is reproduced in Sebastian Brock, "The Transmission of Ephrem's Madrashe in the Syriac Liturgical Tradition," *Studia Patristica* 33 [1997]: 490–505; see 504). See also Rouwhorst, *Les hymnes pascales II*, 21, note 2.

[4]
In this feast,
   the children rejoiced
for they were delivered from the river,
   the drowner of the wicked.

[5]
In this feast,
   children and parents
rejoiced together,
   because there was no Pharaoh.

6
In April, Hebrew women
   were carrying
their children openly
   on the seashore.

7
Terror passed away
   from the children,
when they saw that
   their drowners had drowned.

8
The children had been hidden
   in the inner chamber,
just as Moses was hidden
   when he was an infant.[4]

9
In April, confined
   blossoms bloomed
and children came out
   of the inner chambers.

---

4. Ex 2.2.

ON THE UNLEAVENED BREAD

10

In this feast,
   little ones and flowers
rejoiced together
   in their beautiful Lord.

11

The calyxes of the lilies
   carried flowers,
and the wombs of the women
   carried children.

12

The slaves in Egypt,
   afraid to cry,
were downcast,
   the voices along with the bodies.

13

In April, the eloquent one
   begets voices
so that they were not afraid,
   even the children.

14–15

[Text is too lacunous to translate.]

16

...
   fear in the wilderness;
the baby chicks chirped,
   because the eagles have perished.

17

The child, who loves
   to play outside,
was thrown down
   and hidden away from the killers.

18

Through that paschal lamb,
 the children came out;
like captive lambs,
 they leaped in freedom.

19

That captive lamb
 that Moses captured[5]
saved the captive lambs
 that had been captured.

20

For even Moses,
 a captive infant,
became the deliverer
 of the captive infants.

21

Through the lamb and Moses,
 two captives,
the flock, with its children,
 went toward the destination.

22

A pair of captives
 depicted the symbol
of that captive lamb
 that saved the peoples.[6]

23

Out of captivity
 they led the paschal lamb;
out of captivity
 they led the true lamb.

---

5. A reference to the Passover lamb (Ex 12.6), which Ephrem presents as instrumental in the deliverance of other "captive lambs" of the Israelites.
6. I.e., Jesus.

24

That typological lamb
  was without blemish,[7]
and that true lamb
  was without stain.[8]

25

The sprinkling [of the blood] of that pure one
  sanctified the people;
the sprinkling [of the blood]
  of that innocent one cleansed [the peoples].[9]

---

7. Ex 12.5.

8. 1 Pt 1.19.

9. This final phrase is supplied by Beck's conjecture because it is missing in the manuscript.

ON THE UNLEAVENED BREAD 12

[To the same melody]¹ ...

1

In this feast
   was repaid
the inner debt
   by the Lord who is within.²

2

In this feast
   our Lord plundered
the treasures which were filled
   with the symbols of his death.

3

In this feast our Lord
   thrust out the symbols
that had grown weary
   in his proclamation.

---

1. The opening lines are missing, as evidenced by the lack of a heading and refrain in the manuscripts. The manuscript catalog for the Deir al-Surian monastery mentions that MS Deir al-Surian 38 contains this poem in its entirety, including the missing refrain; S. Brock and L. Van Rompay, *Catalogue of the Syriac Manuscripts in Deir Al-Surian, Wadi al-Natrun (Egypt)* (Leuven: Peeters, 2014), 274.

2. The phrase "the Lord who is within" here may refer to the consumed body of Christ (i.e., the Eucharist). It is also possible to translate both instances of *gāwa* ("inner"/ "within") as "common" with the resulting alternate translation: "the common debt by the common Lord." It is possible that the missing stanzas from the beginning of this teaching song would provide more context for what Ephrem intends in this stanza.

4

In this feast
  the true lamb
liberated the paschal lamb,
  which had run its course.

5

Our Lord ate the Pascha
  feast and broke his body;
the eater became
  the one being eaten.

6

This feast is
  the invisible furnace
that revealed
  the bronze of Iscariot.

7

This is the feast that
  cast it out and threw it away
from the true ones
  as a fraud.

8

In this feast
  was purchased
the Lord of everything
  for nothing.

9

In this feast
  the thief sold[3]
the liberator of all
  like a slave.

---

3. Jn 12.6.

10

In this feast
 the fraud kissed[4]
the true mouth
 that taught the truth.

11

In this feast
 he was struck on the cheek,[5]
he who brought forth
 water from a jawbone.[6]

12

In this feast,
 he stood in the judgment hall—
the firstborn, the justifier of all—
 and he was silent so that he could be condemned.

---

4. I.e., Judas (Mt 26.47–50).
5. Jn 18.22. Cf. *Cruc.* 4.1.
6. Jgs 15.19.

ON THE UNLEAVENED BREAD 13

To the same melody

1

Come, my brothers and sisters,
  let us celebrate in the month of April
the feast of the victories
  of the true lamb!

Refrain: Let our congregation give thanks to the paschal lamb who slaughtered the ravenous wolves in April!

2

He was bound in the house of Annas,[1]
  yet hidden within him
was the power that unbound
  within the furnace.[2]

3

He was silent in the judgment hall,
  yet hidden within him
were the mouths of the sages
  that overcome all.

---

1. Jn 18.13.
2. Dn 3.8–30. The imagery here invokes the story of Daniel's friends who were sent into the furnace with their hands bound, but whom Nebuchadnezzar observed walking around "unbound" within the furnace (Dn 3.25).

4

He silenced within himself
    the thunder of his voice,
which had terrified
    the people at Mount Sinai.[3]

5

They bound and led him,
    yet silent within him
was the power
    that bound all created things.

6

Judas kissed him,
    yet silent within him
was the imposition of silence[4]
    he gave to the demon that cried out.[5]

7

Herod questioned him and scorned him,
    yet he was silent,
even though all tongues
    were loosed by him.

8

He was mounted upon the tree,
    even though secretly
he was riding[6] the chariot
    of the Cherubim.[7]

---

3. Ex 20.18.
4. Literally: "shutting of the mouth."
5. Lk 4.41.
6. The phrases "he was mounted" and "he was riding" are the same word in Syriac.
7. See the vision of the chariot in Ezekiel 1. Cf. *Cruc.* 5.1.

9

They gave him bitter gall,[8]
 yet hidden within him
was the sweetness by which
 bitter things became sweet.[9]

10

He thirsted and asked for water,
 yet hidden within him
was that source of water[10]
 that gave life to all.

11

Pilate washed
 and cleansed his hands[11]
that the people, who defiled their hands,
 might be condemned.[12]

12

The clay [formed] from his spit
 gave sight to a blind man[13]
so that the people may be accused,
 lest[14] he be dishonored.

13

The Lord of all
 received the spit,
upon whose splendor
 the Seraph cannot gaze.

---

8. Lk 23.11 et par.
9. Ex 15.23–25.
10. Reading ܚܝܐ for ܩܝܐ.
11. Mt 27.24.
12. Cf. *Cruc.* 4.7.
13. Jn 9.6.
14. Reading *dlmn* here as *dalmāʾ*. The root for "dishonored" (*ṣʿr*) occurs in the Peshitta of the Gospel of John in the story immediately preceding the story of Jesus healing the blind man with spit, that is, the story in which Jesus responds to the accusation that he has a demon, saying, "You dishonor me."

14
The Cherubim and Seraphim,
  while he was disgraced,
hid their faces
  for they feared to look.

15
While they scoffed at him,
  Michael trembled;
shocked, amazed, and astonished
  also was Gabriel.

16
Because there was
  no veil for creation,
to cover its face
  as with a garment,

17
darkness unfurled so that,
  like Shem and Japheth,[15]
it would not see the shame
  of its chaste Lord.[16]

18
When he was crying out,
  the wind[17]
greatly magnified his cry
  against the temple.

19
When she[18] heard that he lowered
  his head and cried out,[19]
she tore the curtain
  as in an earthquake.[20]

---

15. Gn 9.23.
16. Cf. *Cruc.* 4.14.
17. Or "spirit."
18. Referring back to the spirit/wind of the previous strophe.
19. Jn 19.30.
20. Cf. *CD* §4–6.

20

Creation wrapped itself
  in a mourning cloak
and shrouded itself with darkness
  because of the Son of her Lord.

21

The glorious presence[21] of the temple,
  as if it were her garment,
tore the curtain
  because of her beloved.

22

Creation asked
  for a mourning cloak,
unfurled it over everything,
  and bowed her head

23

in order to shame the daughter of Zion,
  whose head was uncovered
and whose hands were stained
  by the blood of the possessor of all.[22]

24

The heavens that rejoiced
  when he was baptized
became gloomy and dark
  while he suffered.

25

He hid his glory;
  therefore it was possible for
shame to approach
  the all-glorious one.

---

21. The Syriac word here is related to the Hebrew word and concept of the "presence" of God: *shekinah*.

22. Cf. *Cruc.* 1.9–10.

26

The Red Sea dried up suddenly
 when it saw him;
how did the spit
 even come near his face?

27

He stood within the court,
 yet hidden within him
was that great judge
 who is to come.

28

He was given a crown of thorns
 among the crucifiers,
he who will come in glory
 with the angels.

29

He was given a crown of thorns,
 yet hidden within him
was the power to construct
 and destroy all.

30

He was placed in a tomb,
 yet silent within him
was the voice
 that splits hard rocks.[23]

31

He was embalmed and buried,
 yet hidden within him
was the power that had given life
 to the bones in the valley.[24]

---

23. Mt 27.51.
24. Ezek 37.1–14.

32

He was bound as a corpse,
  yet he possessed the voice
that called Lazarus,[25]
  who was [also] bound.

---

25. Jn 11.43.

ON THE UNLEAVENED BREAD 14

Again to the same melody

1

During a meal, a woman
  kissed his feet,[1]
even though he
  is the Lord of virtue.

Refrain: Praise to the Messiah who came to die
so that through his death the children of Adam
might live!

2

The sinful woman approached
  the one who pardons all,
whose mouth was the hyssop
  that washes away sins.[2]

3

The blameworthy one blamed him,
  "He does not know,"[3]
yet hidden within him
  was all knowledge.

---

1. Lk 7.38.

2. The hyssop here is likely a reference to Ex 22.12, where hyssop is mentioned in the Passover narrative. Cf. the mention of hyssop in reference to Christ's priestly function in *Res.* 4.12. See also Jn 19.29 and Ps 51.7 (LXX 50.7).

3. I.e., Simon the Pharisee (Lk 7.39).

4

Mary[4] anointed him,
  yet a Cherub
is not even permitted
  to approach his head.

5

John also leaned
  upon his breast,[5]
so that he might exalt
  the lowly before the lofty.

6

He thus demonstrated
  that Adam was beloved
while he was pure
  and holy, like John.

7

He thus demonstrated
  that also beloved
are the virgins
  who are sanctified like John.

8

For through the one who was loved,
  he gave a pledge
that he would love
  all the sanctified ones.

9

Iscariot scolded
  the blessed woman;[6]
under the pretense of poor,
  the thief pronounced judgment.

---

4. Jn 12.3.
5. Jn 13.24–25.
6. Jn 12.4–6.

10

Our Lord heard [this]
   yet refrained from exposing him,
even though he is the furnace
   who will reveal [the impurities] to all.

11

The mystery that he hid
   from the disciples
he revealed
   to John as a friend.[7]

12

Virginity drew near
   the holy one;
he demonstrated that the sharer
   of his secret[8] is holiness.

13

He dipped the bread
   and gave it to thievery,[9]
which made itself known,
   even though [Jesus] did not compel it.[10]

14

For he waited patiently,
   that pleasant one,
for that scoundrel
   to accuse himself.

15

He dipped the bread
   and gave to him hidden death;
it became bread from which
   the medicine of life had been washed.[11]

---

7. Jn 13.23–26.
8. Lit. "daughter of his symbol."
9. Jn 13.26.
10. Jn 13.21–30.
11. For another reflection on this episode, see *Cruc.* 3.14–15.

16
The one who gives life
   to all blessed that food,
and it became the medicine of life
   in front of its eaters.

17
Thus it is the bread
   from which the blessings had been washed
that the cursed one took,
   that second serpent.

18
He took the bread
   and departed from the disciples;
that is: he separated himself,
   even though no one drove him away.

19
Our Lord did not isolate him
   so that no one could blaspheme,
for necessity compelled him
   unwillingly.

20
When he was uninvited,
   our Lord drew him out;
but when he departed and left,
   he did not drive him away,

21
for it was good that the chooser
   had chosen him,
for it was bad
   that he rejected himself.

22
But when the hidden wolf
 departed and went out
from among the
 flock of the twelve,[12]

23
the true lamb stood up
 and broke his body
for the sheep who had eaten
 the paschal lamb.

24
There he completed
 the type that had hastened
from the midst
 of Egypt until then.

---

12. Cf. *Cruc.* 3.16.

ON THE UNLEAVENED BREAD 15

To the same melody

1

God, who descended
  upon Mount Sinai,
is the one through whose own power
  the mountain bore him.

Refrain: Praise be to the Son who through
his blood saved us as his symbol saved the children
of Jacob!

2

The mountain melted
  away before him;[1]
the power of its creator
  sustained it.

3

For he is the creator
  through whose own power
the created things
  are able to serve him.

4

It is through his power
  that the heavens lift up his glory;
that is: he bears them,
  and they bear him.

---

1. Ps 97.5.

5

He gave power
  also to the Cherubim;
the chariot bore him
  who gave it strength.

6

He also dwelt in the sanctuary
  because his loving mercies desired
that he should be present there
  for whoever seeks after him.

7

For, in order that whoever seeks him
  might not wander,
he dwelt in the temple,
  even though he is in everything.

8

The cloud in which he dwelt
  received from him
the power through which it was able
  to become his bridal chamber.

9

The apostles, fishermen,
  with his pigments
were able to paint
  a picture of his symbols.

10

The prophets, artists,
  depicted him[2]
because he taught them
  whom he resembles.

---

2. There is a wordplay in the opening phrases of stanza 9 (*ṣayādē*) and stanza 10 (*ṣayārē*).

11

With his pigments,
    they were able to depict his beauty;
they saw him,
    like his Father in every way.

12

Through his own power,
    kings had retained
their positions of kingship
    until he came.

13

Through his atonement,
    priests were able
to atone for sins through
    the symbol of his sacrifices.

14

Through his power,
    the sea lifted him up,
for it was not able
    to bear his weight.[3]

15

The created thing is no match
    for the power of the creator;
but if it were sufficient for him,
    it would be equal to him.

16

Everything is insufficient
    for that Lord of all;
and if it could suffice for him,
    it would be like him.

---

3. Mt 14.22–33 et par.

17

The created thing is weak
  before the creator;
it is through his own power
  that it obeys him.

18

Before him
  Mount Sinai melted.
How the tree bore him
  is a wonder!

19

The mountain of rock
  could not bear him;
how did a donkey
  of flesh carry him?[4]

20

The sun, the enlightener of all,
  looked at him and darkened;[5]
so how did that people
  who darkened gaze at him?

21

The fever saw him
  and fled and escaped;[6]
so how did Zion
  attack him?

22

The fig tree saw him
  and withered immediately;[7]
so did the hand
  that struck him not wither?

---

4. Mt 21.6.
5. Mk 15.33.
6. Mk 1.31.
7. Mk 11.12–14.

23

Demons and pigs
  fell into the sea;[8]
how did Caiaphas and his comrades
  crucify him?

24

The mighty Legion
  howled before him;[9]
how could the evil servant
  strike him?[10]

25

The hand that had withered
  was restored by a word[11]
so that the hand that struck him
  might stand accused.

26

He gave the haul of fish
  to Simon as a lofty one;
he asked and ate
  from it as a lowly one.[12]

27

He brought Lazarus
  to life as God,
yet he asked about
  his grave as a human.[13]

---

8. Mk 5.13.
9. Mk 5.6–9.
10. Jn 18.22.
11. Mk 3.1–5.
12. Jn 21.1–13.
13. Jn 11.34.

28

He drove out the demons
  as the one who has mercy on all,
yet he asked about the child
  as one who has to learn all.[14]

29

He revealed hidden things
  to the disciples;
he asked and learned things
  about revealed things.

30

He chose Judas
  as one who does not know,
yet he gave him "woe"
  as one who knows everything.[15]

31

Mary anointed
  his head with oil;
the gift that was from him,
  she returned to him.

---

14. Mk 9.21.
15. Mt 26.24.

ON THE UNLEAVENED BREAD 16

To the same melody

1

The firstborn willed [it]
  and closed the feeble tomb,
for whatever he wills
  is not in vain.

Refrain: Praise to the Son, everyone, he who, because of our debt, subdued his great power to the tree!

2

Concerning everything that he wills:
  it is not possible
to prevent his will
  from whatever he wills.

3

For he willed it,
  and everything came into being;
for because he willed it,
  created things came to be.

4

He willed it, and he closed
  the womb of Sheol,
and because he willed it,
  he closed the womb of Mary.[1]

---

1. Cf. *Nat.* 4.190 and *Nat.* 10.6–10.

5

Because he willed it,
  greedy Death devoured him;
it devoured him, and spat him back out
  because he willed it.[2]

6

He hid his life;
  therefore,
dead Death was able
  to devour the living one.

7

The scent of his life
  drifted[3] into Sheol;
it vomited and threw him out
  because it could not endure him.

8

He willed it, and his captors
  took him captive;
he hid his power within himself,
  so they took him captive.

9

For when he uttered
  a breath of his power,
all of his captors
  fell and bowed down.[4]

---

2. For the image of the "gluttonous" figure of Death unknowingly swallowing up Jesus, only to vomit him out, cf. Ephrem's *Homily on our Lord* 3.3–4.

3. As Brock notes, the Mosul Fenqitho preserves several stanzas of this *madrasha*, including the variant reading *pāḥ* ("wafted") in place of *praḥ* ("flew"). FM V, p. 454, cited in Brock, "The Transmission of Ephrem's Madrashe in the Syriac Liturgical Tradition," 501.

4. Jn 18.5–6.

10

And when they threw him down
  from the mountaintop,[5]
he did not will that he should be harmed,
  so he was not harmed.

11

When they threw him down,
  he flew[6] and showed them
how bodies will be
  carried away in the end.[7]

12

He made the air
  like his chariot,
and his body
  like a driver.

13

For the air will be
  like a chariot:
it will fly the righteous
  up to meet its Lord.

14

A chariot came down
  for Elijah;
it ascended and descended
  without a driver.[8]

---

5. Lk 4.29.

6. Ephrem apparently believed that Jesus flew through the air after being thrown from a cliff by the people of Nazareth, in contrast to the standard accounts of the episode in the four gospels. Although the exact text of this passage in the Syriac Diatessaron is unknown, scholars have attributed Ephrem's "flying Jesus" to the gospel harmony. See T. Baarda, "'The Flying Jesus': Luke 4:29–30 in the Syriac Diatessaron," *Vigiliae Christianae* 40 (1986): 313–41. Cf. *CD* §27.

7. Cf. *CD* §6.

8. 2 Kgs 2.11.

15

Horses endowed with speech
  were harnessed to it;
they were also
  guides for it.

16

This is also the case
  with the chariot of the Cherubim
whose guide is
  silent [and] invisible.

17

The silent will
  of that silent[9] one
guides the chariot
  along with created things.

18

For still and silent
  is that creator of all;
through his silent will,
  he guides everything.

19

Thunder is born
  from within his stillness,
and mighty lightning
  from within his silence.

20

Though he is silent and still,
  he stirs up created things;
with one quiet nod,
  the fullness of creation.

---

9. Ephrem employs two different roots for words meaning "silent/silence/stillness" in these strophes. *Silence* is a characteristic Ephremic descriptor of the divine nature (see *Fid.* 4.1,6, 11.7–9, 37.18), as well as of the proper human attitude toward that nature. He regularly urges his subordinationist opponents to be silent regarding the relationship of the Father and Son (see *Fid.* 1.18–19, 2.4, 3.4,9, 4.17–18, 5.13, et al.).

21

It is he that willed it
  and made whatever he willed;
it is he, again, who makes
  whatever he wills.

22

It is he that struck the earth
  with the rod of his mouth;
with the breath of his lips,
  he kills the wicked.[10]

23

The wicked Iscariot
  kissed him,
for he willed that the breath of his mouth
  not kill him.

24

It is a wonder that the chaff
  could kiss the fire;
the fire withheld her power
  and did not harm it.

25

She showed gentleness
  toward him;
he made for himself
  a noose.

26

His hands, which took
  the price of his Lord,
also strung him up
  with a noose.

---

10. Is 11.4.

27

As to the mouth that kissed
  the fiery coal,[11]
its lips were as cold
  as a hanged man.

28

Because greed[12]
  was strong within him,
his belly burst open
  from avarice.[13]

29

The noose suspended
  him in the air[14]
because he betrayed the Messiah
  who flies in the air.[15]

30

He was suspended
  between earth and heaven
because he betrayed
  the earthly and heavenly one.

31

He betrayed the Son,
  who is heavenly,
but he killed the body,
  which is earthly.

32

Heaven rejoiced at this,
  for he handed over her Lord;
the earth rejoiced at this,
  for he killed its king.

---

11. Is 6.7.
12. Lit. "greatness of the belly."
13. Acts 1.18.
14. Mt 27.5.
15. See note 6 above on "the flying Jesus" of Lk 4.29.

33

Through his own power,
  the tree bore him;
the tree that bore fire
  did not burn.

34

From that which was his own,
  the givers gave to him;
from his treasure house,
  the takers took.

35

With the myrrh[16] that he created,
  Joseph[17] anointed him;
with what belonged to him,
  the buriers also buried him.

---

16. Jn 19.39.
17. I.e., Joseph of Arimathea.

ON THE UNLEAVENED BREAD 17

To the same melody

1
April, which renews
    all roots
was not able to renew
    that ancient people.

Refrain: Blessed is he who rejected the people and their unleavened bread because their hands are stained with the precious blood!

2
For when they were leaving,
    the people carried
the leaven of paganism
    along with the unleavened bread.

3
For Moses did not allow
    them in Egypt
to knead leaven with[1]
    the unleavened bread.[2]

4
In this manner he taught [the people],
    lest they hide
the leaven of the Egyptians
    within their thought.

---

1. Reading *'āq* here as *'ām*, in parallel with the previous stanza.
2. Ex 12.15.

5
The unleavened bread is a symbol
    of the living bread;
the ancient ones ate
    the new symbol.

6
Moses revealed the symbol
    of the renewer of all;
he gave it to the gluttons
    who craved flesh.

7
The flesh from the earth
    weighed them down,
and their mind
    stooped to avarice.

8
The earthly ones ate
    the heavenly manna,[3]
and they became dust in the earth
    through their sins.[4]

9
The spiritual bread
    lightened and flew,
and the peoples flew up
    to dwell in paradise.

10
Through that one who enters,
    everyone entered it;
for through Adam, the one who departs,
    everyone departed.

---

3. Ex 16.
4. Cf. Nm 16.32–33.

11

Since the body is there—
  the second Adam[5]—
the hungry eagles[6] were gathered
  together before him.

12

Through the spiritual bread
  everyone will become
an eagle that will arrive
  at paradise.

13

Whoever has eaten
  the living bread of the Son
will also fly to meet him
  in the clouds.

14

The nature of the unleavened bread
  is also heavy;
a sign that the people
  are unable to fly.

15

Elijah ate from
  the pitcher and the jug:[7]
a small symbol
  that he would fly in the air.

16

It was not a daughter of Jacob
  that gave the symbol;
Elijah ate it in the presence
  of a daughter of the Gentiles.[8]

---

5. 1 Cor 15.47.
6. An allusion to Jesus's saying "Where the corpse is, there the eagles will gather" (Mt 24.28; Lk 17.37).
7. 1 Kgs 17.14–16.
8. I.e., the widow of Zarephath (1 Kgs 17.7–16).

17
If the symbol of his bread
    thus caused flight,
how much more will it cause
    the peoples to fly to Eden?

ON THE UNLEAVENED BREAD 18

To the same melody

1

During the Pascha,
  the peoples ate the leavened bread;
through the ancient food,
  their mind was renewed.

Refrain: Give thanks to the Son who gave
us his body instead of that unleavened bread
that he had given to the people!

2

Is it not fitting
  that his food renew a person?
It is his heart
  that is fitting to renew.

3

For behold, in April,
  a bull eats
a fresh pasture,
  while it is goring.

4

And the people, by eating
  that unleavened bread,
pierced the Son
  with a spear in April.[1]

---

1. Jn 19.34.

5

Again, the wild ass
> grows fat on wild pasture;
the people likewise kicked
> and grew fat.[2]

6

So if that new food
> is advantageous,
then the beast
> is better than that people.

7

She is also better than the one
> who was reviled by her,
for also unlike her,
> he knew his Lord.

8

The serpent also sheds its skin
> and is renewed;
inasmuch as it sheds the outside,
> so also it ages on the inside.

9

See the people renew
> their outward appearance,
but in their heart
> dwells deadly venom.

10

For it resembles
> that ancient serpent,
who deceives and offers
> to us the fruit of death.

---

2. Cf. Dt 32.15.

11

For behold, he offers to us
 from their unleavened bread
so that it would be in us
 a deadly poison.[3]

12

O people who went stale,
 who with the unleavened bread,
see, they make the young ones go stale,
 as though with leaven.

13

O unleavened bread
 that gradually
draws out its eaters
 from the unbelievers!

14

In the new unleavened bread
 they hide and offer
the ancient leaven
 of infidelity.

15

It is the symbol of the Son
 that Moses had hidden
within that unleavened bread
 as the medicine of life.

16

[Jesus] washed the medicine of life
 from the unleavened bread;
he gave it to Judas
 as the poison of death.[4]

---

3. The Syriac phrase *sām mawtā* ("deadly poison") here is contrasted with *sām ḥayyē* ("medicine of life") in stanzas 15 and 16.

4. Cf. *Azym.* 14.15–17.

17
Thus the deadly poison
　of Iscariot
is what one receives
　from that unleavened bread.

ON THE UNLEAVENED BREAD 19

Again to the same melody

1

The true lamb stood up
  and broke his body
for the innocent ones
  who had eaten the paschal lamb.

Refrain: Praise to the Messiah who, through his body, abolished the unleavened bread of the people in the presence of the people!

2

He slaughtered and ate the Pascha,
  and he broke his body;
he removed the shadow
  and gave the truth.

3

The eater was dispersed[1]
  within the unleavened bread;
his body became for us
  the true unleavened bread.

4

There was limited
  the symbol that had run
from the days of Moses
  until then.

---

1. Reading *ptira* here as a passive participle of *ptr*, in the sense of "to be separated, cut."

5

But the evil people
   who desire our death
enticingly offer us
   death by food.

6

Enticing was the tree
   that Eve saw;[2]
likewise, enticing
   is the unleavened bread.

7

From that desire[3]
   death was revealed;
in the pleasant unleavened bread
   death is hidden.

8

Although the dead lion
   was impure,
its bitterness
   gave sweetness.[4]

9

In the bitter lion
   was pleasant honey;
in the sweet unleavened bread,
   there is bitter death.

10

The watchers were tempted
   by that unleavened bread
that Sarah had baked[5]
   because of its symbol.

---

2. Gn 3.6.
3. I.e., of Eve.
4. Jgs 14.9.
5. Gn 18.6.

11

Reject, my brothers and sisters,
>   the unleavened bread
> in which the symbol
>   of Iscariot dwells.

12

Flee all the more, brothers and sisters,
>   from the unleavened bread
> because stench dwells
>   within its purity.

13

For that word, rotten,
>   which Moses wrote,[6]
> dwelt in the purity
>   of that unleavened bread.

14

Garlic with onions[7]
>   the people desired;
> their unleavened bread stinks,
>   along with their food.

15

From unclean ravens
>   Elijah received
> breads[8] that he knew
>   were pure.

16

My brothers and sisters, do not take
>   that unleavened bread
> from the people whose hands
>   are stained with blood,

---

6. Ex 16.20.
7. Nm 11.5.
8. 1 Kgs 17.6.

17
lest there stick
  to that unleavened bread
some of the filth
  that fills their hands.

18
Although the meat is pure,
  no one eats
what has been sacrificed
  because it is defiled.

19
Thus how impure
  is that unleavened bread,
since the hands that killed the Son
  kneaded it?

20
The hand that is stained
  by the blood of animals—
it is an abomination for us
  to take food from it.

21
Who then shall receive
  from that hand,
which is thoroughly stained
  with the blood of the prophets?

22
My brothers and sisters, let us not eat
  with the medicine of life
the unleavened bread of the people
  as the poison of death.

23
For the blood of the Messiah
  is mixed and dwells in
the unleavened bread of the people
  and in our Eucharist.

24

Whoever received it[9] in the Eucharist
    received the medicine of life;
whoever ate it with the people
    received the poison of death.

25

As for the blood for which
    they cried out that it be upon them,[10]
it is mixed in their festivals
    and their Sabbaths.

26

And whoever adheres
    to their festivals
to him also comes
    the splattering of blood.

27

The people that does not eat
    from a pig
is a pig that is
    bathed in much blood.

28

Flee and keep away from it,
    for look, it is shaking,
lest you be defiled
    by the splattering of blood.

---

9. "it" = "the blood" in the previous stanza.
10. Mt 27.25.

ON THE UNLEAVENED BREAD 20

To the same melody

1
Come, my brothers and sisters,
  let us hear about the hidden Son
who revealed his body
  and hid his power.

Refrain: Praise to the Messiah into whom,
during this feast, the unfaithful people
drove nails!

2
While [his] hands were restrained,
  he broke open the graves;
for his freeing power
  is his will.

3
They did not bind his power
  along with his hands;
his hands were bound,
  but his power was unbound.

4
For his body was nailed
  entirely to the tree,
but his power was completely
  and utterly free.

5

It is not by hands that his power
  should be defeated;
it is by the will that the conqueror of all
  brings into effect.

6

Even when the hands
  of our Lord were free,
it was not with his hands that he bore the dead one,
  and he came forth.

7

It is his hidden power
  that entered and bore
that bound dead one
  who flew and came out.

8

Even Moses, who was victorious
  through the stretching forth of his hands,[1]
forged the symbol of that one who gave the victory
  and prevailed through his hands.

9

For if this power
  were of arms,
how did they conquer
  from that distance?

10

Indeed, a hidden power
  was victorious through arms,
for it abides in arms
  so that it might depict symbols.

11

Thus the prophet was victorious
  through symbols of the Son;

---

1. Ex 17.8–13.

how much more would the firstborn
accomplish without hands!

12
The will of the Son
   is his treasure;
he distributed his wealth
   wherever he willed.

13
For his word is
   the storehouse of treasures;
wherever he opens it,
   he enriches created things.

14
His gift is the fountain
   of good things,
and if he opens it,
   creation rejoices.

15
His will is
   the great key
by which the treasures[2]
   of mercies are opened.

16
His goodness
   is merciful,
carrying medicines
   like a nurse.

17
Justice
   is prudent,
carrying terrors
   like minds.

---

2. Following Beck's corrected reading here. The manuscript reads *'aqlīdē* ("keys").

18
The hand of his goodness
  is gentle to all;
it binds all wounds
  like a mother.

19
The hand of his justice
  is fierce for all;
it cuts all wounds
  like a doctor.

20
His justice
  had retracted her hand
when he came to be
  among humanity.

21
No one has ever lamented
  because of his justice
except for Satan,
  as the adversary.

ON THE UNLEAVENED BREAD 21

To the same melody

1

As to the Pascha that was commanded
  to take place in purity,
look, the one who eats from it
  is a prostitute.

Refrain: Praise be to the one who redeems
the peoples through his blood in place of the
symbol that redeemed that one people!

2

The feast that was commanded
  to take place in Zion;[1]
behold, it takes place everywhere
  like nothing at all.[2]

3

For Moses
  did not permit the people
to celebrate their feast
  wherever they happened to be.

---

1. Ephrem probably has in mind Dt 16.5–6.
2. As mentioned in the introduction, Ephrem argues throughout this poem that the continued observance of Passover by Jews outside of Jerusalem is in violation of biblical commands. In this discussion, Ephrem participates in a broader early Christian line of argument. See Shepardson, "Paschal Politics," 250–58.

4
For Moses bound the feast
   to the sacrifice,
and the sacrifice he bound
   to the Holy of Holies.

5
Now, as to the feast
   taking place anywhere—
it does not allow a sacrifice
   that has been bound to it.

6
Again, as to the sacrifice
   taking place anywhere—
it cannot happen,
   since he bound it to the holy altar.[3]

7
The feast never took place
   without the sacrifice;
the sacrifice never ascended
   without the holy place.

8
Thus, if [Moses], while in his land,
   did not allow
one to celebrate the feast
   outside of Zion,

9
then how is it that
   among the peoples today,
one celebrates the feast
   wherever they want?

---

3. Dt 12.2–12.

10

In Babylon, Daniel did not
    celebrate the feast;
he dared not celebrate it
    like the unbelievers.

11

Daniel knew that a feast
    that takes place
where it is not allowed
    is an impure feast.

12

For in April,
    the month of feasts,
Daniel fasted
    for three weeks.[4]

13

He did not, as he said,
    eat meat during his fast;
thus, he did not eat
    the paschal lamb.

14

Moses rejoiced in the year
    they celebrated the consecration
of the temporary tabernacle,
    with sacrifices and libations.

15

It was necessary for Moses
    to sacrifice in the wilderness
in order to teach what the law
    of sacrifices is about.

---

4. Dn 10.3.

16

He did not sacrifice, and he did sacrifice,
  in order to teach doubly
that no one should sacrifice
  wherever he wants.

17

For as to the people who did not sacrifice
  in the wilderness—
behold, the prophet crying out
  that they did not sacrifice:

18

"Were there any
  sacrifices or offerings
that you offered me
  for forty years?"[5]

19

And if anyone again affirms
  a word of truth,
he is bound to another
  that Moses spoke:

20

"Let no one behave
  in that land
as one does here
  in the wilderness";[6]

21

"at the place where
  your Lord will dwell,
there he will allow you
  to offer sacrifice."[7]

---

5. Am 5.25.
6. Dt 12.8.
7. Dt 12.11.

22

In Jerusalem alone
  was it permitted by him
to perform the feast
  and the sacrifices.

23

Therefore our Lord gave
  a parable about the fig tree,[8]
because it deprived
  the earth of sacrifices.

24

For instead of the sacrifices
  of all animals
that were being sacrificed
  in Jerusalem alone,

25

behold, throughout the whole land,
  the living body
is offered today,
  a living sacrifice.

The end of the twenty-one teaching songs concerning the unleavened bread by the Holy St. Ephrem

---

8. Lk 13.6–9.

INDICES

GENERAL INDEX

In light of the variable, contextualized capitalization of nouns in the translated texts, all the nouns below are capitalized in order to achieve consistency within the index.

Aaron, 93
Abel, 15n55, 29, 128, 143n32, 239, 247
Abraham, 127, 132, 155, 189, 200
Acrostic, 31–32, 58, 87, 189, 193, 223n1, 228n1
Adam, 23–24, 52–54, 64–66, 68, 71, 80n7, 89n10, 90, 140, 144nn36–37, 151,158, 169, 175n23, 177–78, 182–83, 189, 211, 225, 238, 268–69, 287–88
Adultery, 105n18, 118–119, 122, 200–202
Amalek, Amalekites, 75, 85
Angels, 62n6, 103–4, 138, 148, 266. *See also* Watchers
Anger, 56, 58, 83, 99, 110, 136, 138, 143–44, 146
Animals, 63–64, 94, 101, 121, 135n41, 145, 220, 229, 291, 297, 307
Apostles, 153, 176, 198, 246, 274
April, 13, 16–20, 22, 38, 110, 117, 130n4, 147n53, 173–74, 196, 200–206, 209–20, 232, 249n3, 254–55, 261, 286, 290, 305
Arioch, 108
Ark, 6, 22, 175, 183, 196
Arm (body part), 108, 123
Arms (weapons), 54, 72, 78, 81, 94, 300
Arrow, 6, 55
Ascension, 183, 193
Assembly, 81, 85, 173, 198

Babel, 76, 92–94, 99, 105–7, 305
Babylon. *See* Babel

Banquet. *See* Feast
Baptism, 60n43, 79n2, 133n22, 147, 193–94, 265
Barabbas, 121–22, 179
Bardaisan, Bardaisanites, 4n2, 156, 177n33
Bartimaeus, 24, 89
Beasts. *See* Animals
Beauty, 23, 62, 74, 76, 102–3, 106, 174, 180, 196, 199, 230, 250, 275
Begetter. *See* Begetting
Begetting, 182, 194, 255
Begotten. *See* Begetting
Belly, 71–72, 78, 81n13, 96, 106, 247, 284
Bitterness, 103, 113, 126, 155, 159–60, 174, 185, 213, 263, 295
Blasphemy, 100, 203n27, 230
Blindness, 14, 59n38, 83n19, 86, 88–89, 110, 117, 143, 201, 263
Blood, 19, 29, 40, 60, 65n2, 68, 120, 126, 143, 148, 159n53, 189, 229, 241, 244, 246, 250, 257, 265, 273, 286, 296–98, 303
Body, 23, 26, 68, 102, 111, 123, 127, 132, 133, 148–49, 169, 175, 177, 189, 191, 207, 215, 225, 228–29, 259, 272, 281, 284, 294, 299, 307
Books, 156–58, 197
Bread, 18n64, 40, 56n24, 58n32, 73n15, 77, 80n9, 104n13, 113, 126–27, 133–35, 160, 190, 229–30, 246–47, 270–71, 286–97

GENERAL INDEX

Bread, Unleavened. *See* Bread
Breath, 64, 73n19, 75n28, 91n3, 101n23, 111n11, 120, 162n8, 280, 283
Bridal Chamber, 80, 200–201, 274
Bridegroom, 15n55, 117–19, 200–202. *See also* Christ
Brightness, 24, 53, 79, 91, 98, 102–3, 151

Caesar, 29, 119, 121, 143, 154n32
Caiaphas, 193, 204, 243, 277
Cain, 62, 143
Calf, 26, 41, 110–11, 118, 123, 124n57, 132, 201
Camp, 70, 73, 80n6, 111
Captivity, 63, 105–6, 113n20, 142, 182, 256, 280
Cedar, 93–94
Chaldean, 99–100, 145
Chariot, 150, 168, 183, 195, 262, 274, 281–82
Chastity, 9, 19, 22, 27n81, 66, 118–19, 152, 191, 195–96, 197–98, 201–2, 206, 264. *See also* Virginity
Cherubim, 150, 185n8, 262, 264, 269, 274, 282
Children, 19, 70n3, 73, 143n34, 197–98, 227, 238, 241, 253–56, 268. *See also* Infant
Christ, 14, 16, 27–29, 30, 86n41, 87n3, 128–29, 121, 175n15, 183n39, 216n42, 228, 239, 246, 258, 268, 284, 294, 297, 299. *See also* Firstborn, Lamb, Son
Church, 7, 17–22, 27, 31n99, 33, 38n120, 51, 74, 80, 103n8, 134, 148, 175, 181, 196, 199, 201–2, 203n27, 205n30, 207, 209, 210–11, 213, 245–47
Circumcision, 152–53, 207
Clothing, 14n45, 18, 61, 66, 68, 72–76, 88, 212, 229, 231, 242n2, 243
Color, 24n77, 110n6, 112–13, 211
Commandments, 57n30, 127, 153
Concord. *See* Unity
Corpse. *See* Death
Covenant, 5, 9, 86, 132, 192, 240
Craving, 26, 72, 110–11, 113, 287

Creation, 54n16, 132–33, 147, 176n29, 195n3, 211, 251, 264–65, 282
Creator, 30, 118n8, 178, 212, 273, 275–76
Cross, 69, 121, 126n12, 142n27,150–52, 154n26, 162, 168, 174, 180n15, 181, 184, 190n13, 195
Crown, 9, 29, 39n122, 60, 73, 79, 101, 107, 135, 140, 152n14, 173–77, 182, 195, 197, 198–99, 201, 203n27, 211, 216–17, 243, 266
Crucifiers, 35, 41, 85, 150, 158, 175, 179–80, 225, 227, 266. *See also* Jews, Judaism
Crucifixion, 12, 30–31, 120n24, 130n4, 144n39, 151, 152n13, 154, 165, 167n34, 174n12, 183n36, 184nn2–3, 232, 236, 253
Cup, 99–100, 133, 136n45, 156n45, 229
Curtain (of the Temple), 142, 145, 202n20, 204, 248, 264

Daniel, 14, 18, 25, 56, 63–64, 92–97, 101–7, 208, 261n2, 305
Darkness, 30–32, 92n7, 120–21, 135, 146, 148, 151, 161–70, 174–75, 177n37, 204, 264–65, 276
Daughter of Zion, 117–24, 207, 265
David, 117, 141, 157, 179, 189, 192, 230, 242–43
Death, 6, 12, 27n81, 28–31, 33, 38–40, 56, 83n21, 111, 120n18, 124, 126n10, 128, 141–42, 148, 152n17, 156, 161, 174, 177n34, 180–85, 191, 193–94, 204, 224, 233–37, 239, 258, 267–68, 270, 280, 288n6, 291–92, 295, 297–98
Debt, 58n31, 60, 71, 107, 120n19, 142–44, 151n8, 177, 180, 185, 249, 258, 279
Deeds (actions), 18, 51, 84–86, 105n22, 118, 121, 129, 173, 196, 198, 239
Defeat. *See* Victory
Delectables. *See* Food
Demon, 60n40, 262, 263n14
Desire, 40, 70, 103–4, 110n4, 121, 123–24, 171, 192, 274, 295–96
Dew, 94, 190, 197
Diatessaron, 148n57, 185n8, 281n6

GENERAL INDEX

Disciples, 131, 135–37, 181, 192–93, 216, 244, 246, 270–71
Disease, 26, 111
Disgrace, 66, 90, 99, 147, 154n30, 158, 264
Divinity, 22, 169, 192, 194, 196, 228, 240, 251
Division, 81–82, 123, 133, 135n38, 143, 152–53, 162–63, 178–79
Dogs, 68
Dove, 67, 93
Dream, 107
Drink, 99, 111, 113, 155, 159, 193, 219. *See also* Wine

Eagle, 92, 255, 288
Ear, 61, 112, 137, 197
Earth, 20, 22, 30, 63n12, 113n20, 132, 140, 143n32, 144, 146, 162n12, 171n43, 178, 196, 207–9, 211–13, 215, 243, 283–84, 287
Eating, 28–29, 103, 111, 113, 126–27, 160, 247, 297–98, 305. *See also* Food
Eden, 23, 144, 178n5, 179n7, 180, 182, 195n4, 206, 289
Edessa, 7, 11, 19, 34n109, 35–36, 38n120
Egypt, 6n13, 12, 44, 76n42, 83, 93, 113n20, 117, 125, 131, 155, 200, 205, 217, 224, 232–34, 236–38, 240–41, 245, 247, 249, 253, 255, 272, 286
Egyptians, 109, 205n34, 249, 253, 286
Elder, 103–4, 122, 198n20
Elijah, 18, 77, 91, 96, 108, 208, 281, 288, 296
Elohim, 44, 62
Enemy, 23, 54n16, 75n34, 85n36
Envy, 57, 84, 94, 179, 183
Error, 58n31, 80n9, 97, 106–8, 118n8, 130n4, 156, 159, 190n9, 227, 228, 233–34, 236, 238, 241, 244, 254, 301
Esther, 26, 74–75
Eucharist, 56n24, 134n31, 197n13, 206n43, 258n2, 297–98
Eve, 23, 45, 65–69, 72, 127, 158, 183, 247, 295

Evil, 40, 43n126, 44, 53, 59, 66–68, 73, 75n29, 81, 90, 108n38, 177n37, 180, 224, 277
Evil One, 13–14, 23, 182, 190, 194, 238, 242
Eye, 24, 53–55, 58–59, 89, 123n48, 166–67. *See also* Vision

Face, 89, 103, 127, 146, 158, 264, 266
Fairness, 76, 86n42, 92n6, 98, 101–2. *See also* Beauty
Faith, 24, 131, 153, 199, 201, 299
Fast, 11–18, 22–27, 51–62, 68–82, 87, 91–96, 100–104, 107–13, 122, 192, 196, 220, 305
Father, 57n30, 68, 162, 169, 171n47, 177, 183, 191, 206, 212, 275, 282n9. *See also* God
Fear, 96, 101, 105, 127, 141, 143, 255, 264
Feast, 7n15, 9, 14n46, 16–22, 33, 37, 40, 74, 79, 83, 100, 103, 110, 117n4, 120n24, 131, 160, 182, 192, 195–96, 198–200, 202–4, 207, 209–11, 241, 244, 249–50, 254–55, 258–61, 299, 303–5
Fight, 55, 73, 80, 88
Finger, 100–101
Fire, 76, 81, 94–98, 283, 285
Firstborn, 13n40, 14n46, 16n60, 23, 44, 52, 56, 58, 61, 71, 73, 76, 84, 85, 117, 128, 134, 205, 209, 237–39, 253, 260, 279, 300. *See also* Christ, Lamb, Son
Flavor, 112–13
Flesh, 27, 56n24, 58n32, 68, 92, 94, 136n46, 137, 207, 276, 287
Flower, 18, 113n23, 135, 173–74, 176, 195–200, 203–4, 209n3, 211–12, 249, 251–52, 255
Food, 23, 25, 40, 53–54, 56, 58, 60, 68, 71, 73, 77, 80, 92–94, 96, 104, 126, 173n3, 271, 290–91, 295–97. *See also* Eating
Fool, 14, 82, 84, 118n5, 120, 124, 159, 179, 226, 230
Fraud, 58–59, 96, 107, 119, 156, 226, 249, 259–60

Free Will, 89
Freedom, 71, 81, 139, 214, 256
Fruit, 23, 52, 57, 65–67, 97n36, 113n23, 128, 190, 212–13, 219, 291
Furnace, 76, 94–98, 101, 106n26, 259, 261, 270

Gabriel, 103, 193, 264
Garment, 66n5, 75–76, 87, 140–41, 152–53, 202–4, 211, 242, 243, 265
Gem, 79, 112n14
Gethsemane, Garden of, 137n56, 178n1, 192n31
Glutton, 26, 94, 96, 107, 111, 113, 193, 280, 287
Goats, 108, 135, 177n37
God, 6, 14, 15n55, 23–24, 26, 28, 29, 31n99, 33, 39, 44, 52–54, 66n5, 68n20, 77n46, 83, 86n41, 89n10, 91, 93n13, 96, 97n31, 98, 100n17, 102, 105n17, 106n26, 109, 111, 117, 118n8, 123, 128, 134, 142n24, 144n37, 155n35, 166n32, 172–73, 176n29, 191–92, 202, , 215, 218n1, 226–27, 241, 245, 247, 250, 265n21, 273, 277. *See also* Father
Gold, 26, 76, 89, 98, 123n49, 201n6
Golgotha, 85n33, 121, 159, 179, 181
Goliath, 174, 242
Grace, 58, 89, 169, 219
Grave. *See* Tomb
Greed, 26, 43n126, 53, 71, 76, 80, 92, 94–96, 100–103, 110, 111, 175, 182, 213, 233, 280, 284
Gregory of Nazianzus, 3

Habit, 72, 103n6, 111, 123n49, 233
Haman, 75, 83n21
Hananiah, 107
Hand, 6, 13, 42, 63, 84, 85, 86, 101, 108n38, 122–23, 143, 159n53, 175, 177, 179, 190, 276–77, 297, 302
Health, 26, 111
Heart, 30, 56, 60, 65, 91, 92–93, 102–3, 126n10, 238, 290–91

Heaven, 6, 22, 32, 59n37, 100, 104, 108, 110, 112–13, 140, 144, 147, 179–80, 190–91, 196, 229, 265, 273, 284, 287
Heaviness, 25, 52, 64n19, 79, 92, 102, 205, 288. *See also* Weight
Height, 20, 25, 63, 69, 78n56, 104n14, 109n3, 110, 123, 159, 175, 177, 181, 183, 190–91, 209, 215–16
Herod, 119–20, 131, 194, 262
Herodias, 120
Hidden Things, 23, 152, 166, 180, 278
Holy Spirit, 44, 107, 189n6, 213, 245
Honey, 103, 109, 112, 212n25, 295
Horn, 111, 145, 195
Hours, 30–32, 162–74. *See also* Time, Year
Humanity, 68–69, 118n8, 121, 128n20, 147, 190, 192, 195, 211n17, 224, 240, 251, 302
Humility, 72, 118, 153n30, 194, 199, 242
Hunger, 67, 92n7, 102, 113, 154, 172, 234, 288

Idol, 60, 62, 96–97, 99, 101, 105–6, 152
Idolatry, 104–6, 110–11, 152n13
Ignorance, 67, 226
Image, 19, 21, 25, 27–29, 53n13, 54n18, 72n9, 76n38, 77n48, 79n2, 82, 89, 95n25, 97, 112, 119, 121, 123, 128, 148, 169, 180, 209n3, 239
Infant, 103, 125, 191, 195, 198, 207, 226, 254, 256. *See also* Children
Invisibility, 85, 123–24, 135–36, 167, 175, 219, 242, 259, 282
Ire. *See* Anger
Isaac, 15n55, 29, 127n19, 128n20
Isaiah, 61, 207n47
Iscariot. *See* Judas

Jacob, biblical patriarch, 109, 241, 253, 273, 288
Jacob, of Nisibis, 5
Jacob, of Sarug, 9
Jerusalem, 15n55, 39, 106n23, 117n3, 143n29, 145n40, 153n19, 157n49, 179, 201n10, 207, 303n2, 307

GENERAL INDEX

Jesus, 12, 15, 17, 25, 27–30, 33, 38–40, 42, 89, 117–20, 122n45, 124n54, 126n10, 133n22, 135–37, 140n9, 142, 144–45, 153n18, 154n25, 156n44, 159n53, 162–63, 168, 170–71, 174, 179, 183n35, 192n31, 193–94, 197n16, 201n10, 203–4, 216n39, 230n7, 233n3, 242n2, 252n10, 256n6, 263n14, 270, 280–81, 284, 288, 292

Jethro, 28, 125

Jews, Judaism, 15, 19, 30, 33–39, 41, 44, 59, 70, 75n34, 83–84, 110, 112, 124n54, 131, 142n27, 143n32, 144, 146, 151–53 152n13, 157–58, 161, 169–70, 173, 179–81, 183, 194, 198, 207, 227–28, 230–31, 233–34, 237, 239–41, 244, 249, 253, 257, 263, 276, 286, 288, 290–92, 294–99, 303, 306. *See also* Crucifiers, People

John, apostle, 135n35, 269–70
John, baptizer, 120, 194n45
John Chrysostom, 10n29, 36–37
Jonah, 18, 26, 30, 76–77, 161
Joseph, of Arimathea, 181, 285
Joseph, biblical patriarch, 119, 249
Joshua, son of Nun, 162–63, 169, 252
Joy, 22, 56–57, 70, 102–3, 113, 174, 178, 196, 213
Jubal, 62
Judas, 132n20, 133n21, 135–36, 181, 259–60, 262, 269, 278, 283, 292–93, 296
Judgment, 6, 42, 76–77, 100, 104–5, 108n38, 119, 135, 142–43, 224–25, 260–61, 269
Julian, emperor, 6
Justice, 65, 86n42, 137, 301–2

Key, 87–88, 107, 195, 301
King, 51, 74–77, 87, 93, 95–97, 99, 105–6, 108, 120n18, 134, 140–42, 145, 148, 154, 157, 174, 179–80, 184, 190, 192, 194, 197, 199, 201, 230, 243, 246, 251, 275, 284
Kingdom, 92, 99, 105, 107, 109–10, 113, 141–42, 172, 184, 230, 243, 245

Knowledge, 30, 32, 66n3, 67, 69n25, 107, 190, 193, 228, 268

Lamb, 15, 19, 27–29, 44, 83–84, 125–31, 134–36, 150, 159–60, 173–74, 189, 205, 224, 227–29, 232–35, 237–39, 241–42, 244–48, 256–57, 259, 261, 272, 294, 305. *See also* Christ

Lamp, 19, 22, 80, 120, 130n2, 146, 196, 200–201

Land, 20, 95, 113n20, 117, 153, 157, 160, 176, 183, 198–201, 205n38, 207, 209, 250, 251n9, 304, 306–7

Law, 39, 65, 84, 137, 141, 152, 176, 195, 239, 305

Lazarus, 197n16, 267, 277
Legion, 100, 110, 138, 277
Lent, 4, 11–12, 17
Liar, 76n38, 96
Life, 3, 5, 7, 11, 16, 25, 27, 52, 54, 68, 69n24, 70, 72n8, 74–75, 79n3, 91, 111n11, 113n20, 126, 148–49, 173–74, 180, 184, 190–91, 204–5, 207, 215–16, 224–25, 234, 237, 247, 263, 266, 270–71, 277, 280, 292, 297–98

Light (wave-particle), 24–25, 30–32, 53n9, 64, 66, 80, 86, 97, 110n5, 112, 117n2, 121, 135, 147, 150–51, 161–66, 169, 175, 182, 231

Lightness (weight), 24–25, 92, 102
Lion, 101, 108n36, 295
Liquid, 82
Lord, 14n47, 20, 22, 31–32, 56, 58–59, 77, 83, 86, 89–90, 104n17, 106n23, 117, 126, 131–33, 140, 144–45, 147, 150, 152, 154, 156, 159, 162, 165, 168–73, 175–77, 179–80, 183, 191, 194, 196–99, 203, 205–6, 209–11, 214, 216–19, 230–32, 236, 240, 246, 251, 255, 258–59, 263–65, 268, 270–71, 275, 281, 283–84, 291, 300, 306–7

Love, 69, 82, 94, 99n11, 108–9, 118, 120, 122–24, 133, 135–36, 148, 171, 199, 201, 203, 213, 215, 219, 223–24, 227, 255, 265, 269

GENERAL INDEX

Lowliness, 69, 75, 78n56, 101, 183, 193–94, 269, 277
Lyre, 62, 69, 196, 210

Maccabees, 243
Madrāšē (teaching songs), 3–4, 6–19, 21, 33, 45, 51n1, 70n1, 79n1, 106n24, 110n6, 113, 156n41, 171n46, 177n36, 198n22, 280n3
Mani, Manichaeans, 34n109, 36n116, 156
Manifest Things, 55n21, 82, 101, 103, 133, 191. *See also* Revealed Things
Manna, 26, 112–13, 213, 287
Marcion, Marcionites, 34n109, 118n8, 124n54, 156
Marriage, 104
Martyrs, 85n34, 176, 198
Mary, 69n24, 133, 148, 171n47, 190, 191, 197, 216, 247, 278–79
Measure, 77–78, 163, 165, 167–69
Medes, 64n18, 99
Media, 99, 105
Medicine, 26, 56, 110n6, 111, 126, 270–71, 292, 297–98, 301
Melchizedek, 192, 229
Merchandise, 71
Merchant, 87, 104, 122, 205, 214
Mercy, 14–15, 58n31, 68–69, 81, 107n34, 151, 158, 170, 179, 189, 210, 214–15, 218, 225–26, 278
Messiah. *See* Christ
Michael, 264
Milk, 82, 103, 109, 207
Mind, 53–55, 57–58, 69, 76n41, 86, 92–93, 166–67, 197, 213, 287, 290
Miriam, 253
Mirror, 25, 27, 56, 82, 86, 132, 181, 213, 233, 240
Mishael, 106
Mixture, 57, 101, 159, 192
Mole, 113
Moon, 130, 147, 162n6, 165–66, 168–71, 175–76
Moses, 14, 18, 25–26, 28, 39–40, 77, 85–86, 91, 93, 102, 108–13, 119, 125–26, 132, 170–71, 174, 200n5, 217, 250–51, 254, 256, 286–87, 292, 294, 296, 300, 303–6
Mother, 57n30, 68, 99, 108n39, 118–20, 122–23, 136, 197–98, 201–2, 211–12, 216n39, 302
Mountain, 20, 25–26, 53–54, 63n13, 70, 78n56, 85n32, 96, 110–11, 132, 175, 183, 197, 200, 205, 209, 273, 276, 281
Mouth, 9, 22, 56, 58, 60, 63–64, 68, 75, 77, 82–84, 92, 96, 111–13, 118, 121, 133, 145, 158, 165n24, 182, 192, 195–96, 210, 213, 227, 260, 261–62, 268, 283–84

Naboth, 26n79, 68
Nakedness, 24, 66, 90, 203, 206, 211–12
Name, 12, 37–38, 42, 44, 63, 68n22, 75n34, 87n1, 96, 100n16, 101, 104–7, 121, 129, 137n54, 156n45, 162, 181, 185n10, 189, 193n40, 207n50, 252n10
Nature, 8, 13, 19, 32, 41, 57, 77, 94, 123, 132, 175, 194n42, 234, 240, 251, 282n9, 288
Nazareth, 183, 281n6
Nineveh, 26, 76–77
Nisan. *See* April
Nisibis, 3, 5–7, 11, 19, 35–36, 38n120
Noah, 6, 22, 171, 175, 212

Oil, 80, 112, 197, 278
Olive, 93
One-eyed, 59, 83–86, 89
Onions, 113, 296
Orthodoxy, 10, 37, 72

Palm, 60, 79, 99, 101, 201
Parable, 100n14, 118n5, 128, 132, 171, 177n37, 189n5, 218n3, 307
Paradise, 64, 67, 176, 183, 185, 195, 225, 287–88
Parent, 73, 254
Pascha, 4, 11, 16–19, 21–22, 27, 37, 38–39, 41, 76n42, 83, 103n8, 117n4, 119n13, 126n10, 131, 134, 196, 203n27,

GENERAL INDEX

210–11, 217, 232–34, 237–40, 244, 246–47, 256, 259, 261, 272, 290, 294, 303, 305
Passion, 12, 16–18, 20–22, 27–30, 32–33, 38–39, 61, 81, 117–18, 124n54, 130–31, 144n38, 147, 167n35, 184n2, 196, 203n27, 206n33
Passover, 15, 21n69, 27–29, 37, 39–41, 68n19, 76n42, 110n7, 120n24, 202n22, 207n50, 256n5, 268n2
Path, 59, 77–78, 124n54, 205
Penitent, 18, 57, 77, 88, 107, 197n13
People, 40, 44, 63, 83, 110, 112, 122, 143–44, 152–53, 157–58, 169–70, 180–83, 207, 230–34, 239–40, 250, 251n9, 253, 257, 262–63, 286–91, 296–98, 306. *See also* Daughter of Zion; Jews, Judaism
Peoples, 33, 53–4, 82, 120–21, 131, 146–47, 152–54, 169, 180–81, 183, 190, 201–2, 207–8, 231, 233–34, 237, 241, 247, 253, 256–57, 287, 289–90, 303–4
Persia, 5–7, 64n18, 105
Pharaoh, 25, 109–10, 234, 238, 249n2, 254
Pharaoh's Daughter, 25, 109
Pharisees, 36n115, 57n30, 159, 268n3
Pilate, 39, 119–20, 142–43, 180n18, 263
Place, 85, 97, 106, 123, 131–37, 140–46, 153, 167, 174n11, 178–81, 184, 198, 202, 207–8, 225–26, 242, 304–6
Pleasure, 72, 109, 225
Poison, 37n116, 40, 56, 292–93, 297
Poverty, 88, 223
Power, 6, 23, 25, 44, 52, 77, 81, 94, 105, 157, 162, 175–77, 190, 205–6, 236–37, 250–51, 261–62, 266, 273–76, 279–80, 283, 285, 299–300
Praise. *See* Worship
Prayer, 18, 24, 51, 55–58, 60, 74, 80, 101, 108, 110, 122, 178–79
Priest, 18, 29, 93, 105, 133–34, 137n56, 140n9, 142, 145–46, 189, 191, 198, 203–4, 215, 228–30, 242–43, 275
Priesthood, 142, 145–46, 192, 203–4, 229–30

Prophet, 40, 85, 96, 145, 180, 198, 207, 230–31, 239–40, 274, 297, 300, 306
Prudence. *See* Wisdom
Purity, 39–40, 118, 123, 131, 199, 202, 296, 303

Rain, 6, 22, 108n40, 190, 196
Resurrection, 12, 16–17, 30–31, 33, 149, 163, 171, 182–83, 191, 214, 216
Revealed Things, 32, 111, 112, 135–36, 164, 166n32, 181, 195n2, 236, 259, 270, 278, 287, 295, 299. *See also* Manifest Things
Rewarder, 113
Richness. *See* Wealth
Riddle, 100n14, 107
Righteousness, 14, 92, 122, 147, 174, 225, 233–34, 238, 281
Roar, 101, 108, 253
Robe of Glory, 66, 74n20, 142
Rome, Roman, 5–6, 20n66, 21, 32–33, 141n15, 152n13, 153n19

Sabbath, 30–31, 161, 163, 176n29, 298
Sackcloth, 18, 61, 72–73, 75, 88
Sacrifice, 28–29, 125–26, 128, 129n27, 134, 151n10, 189, 207, 215, 227–30, 275, 297, 304–7
Sage, 91, 107n32, 261
Samson, 144–45
Samuel, 241
Sarah, 117, 201–2, 295
Satan, 27n81, 54n17, 100, 107, 183n36, 225–26, 234–37, 239, 302
Scent, 74, 80, 101, 113, 280
Scripture, 4, 10n30, 25, 27, 31–32, 56, 63n12, 71–72, 83–84, 87, 93n13, 100n17, 112n15, 197n15, 213, 240
Sea, 20, 60, 63n11, 194, 217n44, 249–51, 253, 266, 275, 277
Seed, 20, 95, 107n27, 112n14, 199n23, 209, 218n3
Seraphim, 127, 132, 263–64
Serpent, 23, 45, 65, 67, 72, 158, 182, 210, 271, 291

GENERAL INDEX

Servant, 86, 106n23, 129, 137n56, 168, 171–72, 191n18, 198n21, 210, 230–31, 236, 251, 277

Seth, 62n6, 63

Shame, 24, 39, 54, 57, 61n2, 66n5, 75, 82, 97, 98–100, 107, 119, 121–22, 150, 152, 177, 179–80, 192, 212, 230, 237, 239–40, 264–65

Shapur, king, 6

Sheep, 28, 108, 125, 127, 135–36, 177n37, 189, 224, 250, 272

Sheol, 137, 147, 174, 181, 190–91, 205, 214, 220, 233–34, 236, 238, 279–80

Shepherd, 15n55, 28, 125–28, 137, 147, 174, 189, 197–98, 250

Sickness, 111, 113, 178, 183, 219, 224

Sight, 6, 23–24, 52, 55, 86, 96–97, 124, 263

Silence, 7, 19, 75, 77, 83, 101, 136, 180–81, 194, 196, 218, 220, 260–62, 266, 282

Silver, 61

Simon, 138, 176, 181, 184, 243, 268, 277

Sin, 23, 53n9, 56, 58n31, 63–64, 98, 105–7, 110, 159n51

Sinai, 18, 25–26, 70, 111, 176, 183, 200, 262, 273, 276

Slave, 107n31, 139, 142, 144, 148, 157, 251, 255, 259

Snake. *See* Serpent

Solomon, 59, 131

Son, 5, 29–30, 80, 89, 124, 132, 135, 144, 168–69, 171n47, 178, 180, 185, 194n42, 201–2, 204, 211, 228, 230, 232, 236, 239, 241–43, 250–51, 265, 273, 279, 282n9, 284, 288, 290, 292, 297, 299–301. *See also* Christ, Firstborn, Lamb

Sorrow, 103

Soul, 23, 26, 62n7, 102, 111, 149, 155, 181, 213

Spirit, 72, 81, 91, 93, 100n17, 103, 110, 162, 169, 176n31, 204, 223, 264n17

Stillness, 93, 282

Stomach, 72

Stranger (Marcionite God), 118n8, 124

Strength, 65, 77, 80, 82, 101, 118, 121, 137, 145, 155, 159, 170, 179, 214, 225, 239, 241–42, 274, 277, 282. *See also* Weakness

Sun, 32, 121, 130, 137n57, 146–47, 151, 162–71, 174–76, 197, 219–20, 239, 276

Sweetness, 81, 105, 111–13, 151, 159, 178, 185, 199, 206, 213, 215, 263, 295

Sword, 111, 122, 137, 138, 174

Symbol, 15–17, 27–35, 38–41, 43–45, 82, 85–86, 93, 94n15, 95, 105–7, 125–28, 130–31, 133–34, 137, 140, 144–51, 153, 156, 159–62, 164–70, 172, 175, 177, 179, 181–82, 184–85, 204–6, 212–13, 217, 224–25, 229, 232–33, 239–41, 244–48, 250, 252n10, 256, 258, 270n8, 273–75, 287–89, 292, 294–96, 300, 303

Synagogue, 37, 128n23, 213

Table, 25, 92, 94, 109, 113, 134

Taste, 103, 109n4, 111–12, 156, 159, 231

Tears, 55n21, 66, 73, 88, 113n20, 197n13

Temple, 30, 40n24, 106n23, 122, 131, 143n29, 145–46, 162n13, 192, 202–4, 242n2, 264–65, 274

Thirst, 103, 113, 190, 208, 218–19, 263

Thunder, 19, 22, 174, 196, 200, 204n33, 210, 214, 220, 262, 282

Time, 31–33, 107, 130–31, 134, 161, 163n18, 167, 169. *See also* Hours, Year

Tomb, 147–49, 159, 174n11, 175, 182, 190, 194, 204, 214, 234–35, 237, 266, 277, 279, 299

Treasure, 14, 71, 87–88, 91, 107, 109, 118, 122, 152, 154, 204, 212, 215, 223, 258, 285, 301

Tree, 64–67, 83, 158, 177n34, 182, 190, 194, 262, 276, 279, 285, 295, 299, 307

Truth, 28, 58–59, 83, 86, 96–98, 101, 106–7, 124, 131, 140, 149, 157, 159–60, 181, 194, 203, 210, 215, 226–27, 233, 244–47, 260, 294, 306

Tubal-Cain, 62

GENERAL INDEX 319

Types, 22, 27, 38–39, 83, 126, 137n52, 151, 159, 162, 166, 175, 177, 196, 208, 212, 225, 229, 234, 236, 240, 248, 272

Uncircumcised. *See* Circumcision
Unity, 81–82, 133

Vegetables, 18, 92–95, 104, 107. *See also* Food
Veil, 30, 140n9, 142, 146, 162, 202–4, 242, 264
Victory, 23, 54n16, 72–73, 75, 85n36, 93, 95, 99, 103n6, 119, 174, 176, 181, 183, 218n2, 225–26, 236–39, 241, 251n9, 261, 300
Vigil, 18–19, 51, 55n21, 60, 66n3, 74, 80, 181n27, 192
Vine, 26n79, 93–94, 155
Virginity, 22, 27n81, 118n5, 135, 176, 194n42, 196, 269–70. *See also* Chastity
Vision, 24, 53n10, 63, 107, 136n50, 262n7. *See also* Eye
Voice, 22, 58, 61, 68, 86–87, 119, 142, 174, 180, 196, 204, 210n11, 214, 220n15, 238, 252, 255, 262, 266–67
Vomit, 54n13, 147, 156, 234

Watchers, 54n15, 102, 132, 147, 148, 175, 181n27, 182, 194n49, 211, 216, 295. *See also* Angels
Water, 18n64, 93, 110, 126, 133, 143, 167, 185, 205n39, 260, 263
Weakness, 23, 52, 66n3, 71, 72, 77, 78, 80, 81, 82, 123, 132, 133, 179, 212, 225, 276. *See also* Strength

Wealth, 20, 71, 88, 104, 109, 172, 199, 209, 215, 227, 301
Weaning, 73, 92, 103
Wedding, 79, 87, 182, 192, 200
Weight, 24–25, 52, 64, 92–93, 102, 162n7, 232, 275, 287. *See also* Heaviness
Wholeness. *See* Unity
Will, 81, 89, 214, 299–300. *See also* Freedom
Wine, 18, 53, 92–94, 103, 155, 230. *See also* Drink
Wisdom, 52, 88, 91, 100, 108n36–37, 190, 193, 226, 301
Womb, 133–34, 182, 190, 191, 194, 197, 205, 207, 211, 214, 255, 279. *See also* Virginity
Women, 9–10, 19, 22, 195–98, 207, 255, 268–69
Wood, 121, 126, 150–51, 185, 190n13, 194n47
Worship, 18–19, 22, 29, 37, 41, 58, 104–6, 110n9, 111, 118n9, 119n11, 124, 128, 135, 140, 150, 154, 165n27, 168, 170, 172, 177–78, 182–83, 193, 198, 218, 223–24, 232, 236, 240–41, 246, 250, 268, 273, 279, 294, 299, 303
Wrath. *See* Anger

Year, 19, 21, 31–32, 103, 162–68, 170–71, 206n40, 305–6. *See also* Hours, Time
Youths, 19, 69, 76, 92–94, 98n2, 99, 102–4, 106n26, 122, 198

Zion, 40, 93, 107, 158, 179, 230, 232, 236, 276, 303, 304

INDEX OF HOLY SCRIPTURE

Old Testament

Genesis
2.7: 89
2.17: 66
2.25: 66
3.6: 295
3.7: 24, 66, 158
3.8: 182
3.15: 72
3.17: 247
3.19: 178
3.21: 66
3.24: 185
4.4: 128, 247
4.21–22: 62
6.1–4: 62
8.4: 175
9.21–23: 212, 264
14.18: 230
18.6: 295
18.8: 132
21.22: 176
22.1–19: 53
22.10: 127
22.12–13: 128
47.6: 249

Exodus
1.8–14: 249
2.2: 254
2.10: 109
3.1: 125
4.2: 125
4.16: 250
7.20–25: 250
12.5: 257
12.6: 125, 130, 256
12.8: 113, 126
12.10: 126
12.11: 127
12.13: 76
12.15: 286
12.46: 126
12.51: 70
15.1–18: 250
15.20–21: 253
15.23: 185, 263
16: 287
16.20: 213, 296
16.31: 112
17.8–13: 85
20.18: 262
24.9: 122
25.30: 134
30.8: 130
31.17: 176
32.11: 108
32.19: 110
32.27–29: 111
34.29: 110
34.29–31: 102

Leviticus
33.5: 130

Numbers
4.13: 242
4.15: 141
9.11: 127
9.12: 126
11.5: 113, 296
11.7–8: 112
16.32–33: 287

Deuteronomy
12.2–12: 304
12.8: 306
12.11: 306
16.5–6: 303
24.1: 202
32.15: 291
32.32: 155

Joshua
3.14–17: 251
6.1–25: 251
10.12–13: 162–63, 169

Judges
14.9: 296
15.19: 260

1 Samuel
7.9: 241
17.51: 174

2 Samuel
6.14: 141
24.18–25: 53

1 Kings
3.16: 59

INDEX OF HOLY SCRIPTURE

17.1: 108
17.6: 296
17.14–16: 288
18.19: 96
21.12–13: 68

2 Kings
2.11: 281
18.21: 179
25.8–10: 106

1 Chronicles
21.18–30: 53

Esther
4.1: 75
4.16: 74–75
5.3–8: 75
7.2–4: 75
7.7–8: 75
8.7: 83
9.14: 83

1 Maccabees
10.62: 243
14.43: 243

Psalms
2.7: 179
22.18: 152
45.2: 171
45.7: 179
51.7: 268
54.1: 207
75.8: 99
80.9: 93, 155
80.10: 93
80.11: 93
97.5: 273

110.4: 192
114.4: 200–201

Proverbs
17.22: 103
21.13: 61

Wisdom
16.20

Isaiah
6.2: 127
6.9: 61, 284
11.4: 283
12.2: 53
51.6: 131
51.17: 99
54.1: 207
58.1: 61
58.5–6: 62
61.1: 126
66.1: 181

Ezekiel
1.13–14: 150
37.1–14: 266

Daniel
1.1–7: 104
1.1–20: 102
1.6–7: 106
1.7: 96
1.12: 107
2.12–13: 107–8
2.14: 108
2.17–19: 108
2.27: 99
2.31: 107
2.46: 105

3.8–30: 261
3.11: 106
3.19: 95
3.21: 76
3.22: 98
3.23: 106
3.25: 97–98
3.28: 106
4.7: 99
4.12: 86
5.5: 100–101
5.6: 99
5.11: 99
5.30–31: 99
6.10: 104
7.2: 63
7.5: 64, 145
7.10: 63
7.19: 64
8.20: 105
9.20–23: 103
10.3: 103–4, 305

Joel
2.12–13: 56

Amos
5.25

Jonah
3.4: 77
3.7–8: 77

Zechariah
9.9: 117

Malachi
4.2: 147

New Testament

Matthew
2.1–2: 176
3.11: 231
3.13–17: 194

4.1–11: 51, 194
4.3: 80
4.4: 56
5.17: 84

5.41: 78
5.45: 219, 223
6.16: 56
6.28: 173

INDEX OF HOLY SCRIPTURE

Matthew (cont.)
8.24: 194
11.19: 193
12.20: 161
12.25: 82
12.26: 107
13.10–17: 59
13.13: 83
14.22–23: 275
15.1–20: 60
15.5: 57
15.27: 172
17.27: 192
18.12: 189
21.1–11: 201
21.6: 276
21.8: 201
22.17: 242
22.40: 202
22.42: 228
23.25–27: 60
23.34–37: 122
24.15–17: 63
24.28: 288
25: 135
25.1–13: 80
25.5–6: 118
25.31–46: 177
25.33: 108
25.45: 52
26.23: 159
26.24: 278
26.25: 136
26.36–46: 192
26.47–50: 260
26.52: 146
26.53: 138
26.60: 131
26.65: 203
27.5: 284
27.15–17: 120, 160
27.20: 122
27.24: 120, 143, 263
27.25: 120, 144, 298
27.29–30: 39, 157, 179
27.34: 155, 159
27.38: 153
27.45: 162
27.46: 169
27.48: 39, 156
27.50: 142
27.51: 142, 145–46, 162, 202–4, 248, 266
27.52–53: 147, 174–75, 204, 214, 233
27.60: 147
27.62: 161, 237
28.28: 242

Mark
1.7: 231
1.31: 276
3.1–5: 277
3.21: 230
4.1–11: 192
5.6–9: 277
5.9: 100
5.13: 277
6.19–24: 120
7.4: 60
9.21: 278
10.16: 227
10.46–52: 24, 89
11.12–14: 276
12.14: 242
12.40: 122
14.63: 203
15.6: 160
15.19: 39, 157
15.21–22: 184
15.23: 159
15.29–32: 154
15.33: 162, 276
15.34: 169
15.37: 235
15.38: 162
15.42: 161, 237

Luke
2.25: 191
2.35: 185
2.41–52: 192
3.16: 231
4.18: 126
4.29: 281, 284
4.41: 262
5.17–26: 224
7.38–39: 268
8.30: 100
10.3: 136
12.27: 173
13.6–9: 307
15.5: 189
17.37: 288
20.22: 242
20.46–47: 122
22.27: 86
22.36: 137
22.42: 179
23.2: 242
23.11: 263
23.17: 160
23.36: 159
23.38: 180
23.40–43: 154, 172, 195
23.44: 162
23.45: 142, 162
23.54: 237
24.50–51: 183
26.6–12: 194

John
2.1–12: 192
3.14: 120
3.19: 120
6.10: 173
8.28: 120
9.6: 89, 263
11.34: 277
11.43: 267
12.3: 197, 269
12.4–6: 269
12.6: 259
12.32: 120, 183
13.1: 131
13.4–5: 132
13.21–30: 270
13.23–30: 135–36

13.24–25: 269
14.2–4: 59, 78
18.5–6: 280
18.10–11: 137
18.13: 261
18.22: 139, 260, 278
19.1: 144
19.6: 126
19.7: 141
19.14: 237
19.15: 154
19.23: 152–53
19.29: 268
19.30: 248, 264
19.31: 161, 237
19.34: 185, 290
19.39: 159, 285
19.42: 237
20.11–18: 216
20.28: 172
21.1–13: 277

Acts
1.9: 183
1.18: 284

Romans
11.11–31: 155

1 Corinthians
1.21: 226
10.5: 70
11.24: 132
15.47: 288

2 Corinthians
8.9: 223

Ephesians
6.13: 75
6.15: 72

Philippians
2.1: 189
2.6–7: 86

Colossians
1.20: 229
2.14: 60, 185

Hebrews
7.13–17: 192

James
5.16–18: 108

1 Peter
1.19: 257

RECENT VOLUMES IN THE FATHERS
OF THE CHURCH SERIES

CASSIODORUS, ST. GREGORY THE GREAT, AND
ANONYMOUS GREEK SCHOLIA, *Writings on the Apocalypse,*
translated by Francis X. Gumerlock, Mark DelCogliano,
and T. C. Schmidt, Volume 144 (2022)

*MORALIA ET ASCETICA ARMENIACA: THE OFT-REPEATED
DISCOURSES,* translated by Abraham Terian, Volume 143 (2021)

ORIGEN, *Homilies on Isaiah,* translated by
Elizabeth Ann Dively Lauro, Volume 142 (2021)

ORIGEN, *Homilies on the Psalms: Codex Monacensis Graecus 314,*
translated by Joseph W. Trigg, Volume 141 (2020)

ST. AMBROSE, *Treatises on Noah and David,* translated by
Brian P. Dunkle, SJ, Volume 140 (2020)

RUFINUS OF AQUILEIA, *Inquiry about the Monks in Egypt,* translated
by Andrew Cain, Volume 139 (2019)

ST. CYRIL OF ALEXANDRIA, *Glaphyra on the Pentateuch, Volume 2: Exodus
through Deuteronomy,* translated by Nicholas P. Lunn, Volume 138 (2019)

ST. CYRIL OF ALEXANDRIA, *Glaphyra on the Pentateuch, Volume 1:
Genesis,* translated by Nicholas P. Lunn, with introduction by
Gregory K. Hillis, Volume 137 (2018)

ST. MAXIMOS THE CONFESSOR, *On Difficulties in
Sacred Scripture: The Responses to Thalassios,* translated by
Fr. Maximos Constas, Volume 136 (2018)

WORKS BY ST. EPHREM IN THE FATHERS
OF THE CHURCH SERIES

ST. EPHREM THE SYRIAN, *Selected Prose Works,* translated
by Edward G. Mathews, Jr., and Joseph P. Amar, edited by Kathleen McVey,
Fathers of the Church 91 (1994)

ST. EPHREM THE SYRIAN, *The Hymns on Faith,* translated by
Jeffrey T. Wickes, Fathers of the Church 130 (2015)

ST. EPHREM THE SYRIAN, *Songs for the Fast and Pascha,*
translated by Joshua Falconer, Blake Hartung, and J. Edward Walters,
Fathers of the Church 145 (2022)